FORGING
THE AMERICAN
CURRICULUM

FORGING
THE AMERICAN
CURRICULUM

Essays in
Curriculum
History and
Theory

HERBERT M.
KLIEBARD

NEW YORK ·
LONDON

Published in 1992 by

Routledge
An imprint of Routledge, Chapman and Hall, Inc.
29 West 35 Street
New York, NY 10001

Published in Great Britain in 1992 by

Routledge
11 New Fetter Lane
London EC4P4EE

Library of Congress cataloging in publication data

Kliebard, Herbert M.
    Forging the American curriculum : essays in curriculum history and
theory / Herbert M. Kliebard.
        p.   cm.
    Includes bibliographical references and index.
    ISBN 0-415-90468-4   ISBN 0-415-90469-2 (pb)
    1. Educational—United States—Curricula.   2. Education—United
States—Curricula—History.   I. Title.
LB1570.K584   1992
375'.00973—dc20   91-39049
                                                                            CIP

British Library Cataloging in publication data also available

To Diane and Ken

Contents

Acknowledgments

I was assisted in the preparation of this volume by many people, and, given the fact that these essays were written over a long period of time, to try to name them all would be hazardous since I am very likely to omit some. Suffice to say that bouncing ideas off colleagues and students alike has proven invaluable to me. Thank you. I must specifically acknowledge, however, the very able assistance of Ting-Hong Wong who undertook the unenviable task of checking the references in the various essays. His dedication as well as ingenuity in accomplishing that task is very much appreciated.

I am also grateful to the following for granting permission to republish certain essays: The National Society for the Study of Education for "The Decline of Humanistic Studies in the American School Curriculum" and "The Liberal Arts Curriculum and Its Enemies: The Effort to Redefine General Education"; *The Journal of Curriculum Theorizing* for "Dewey and the Herbartians: The Genesis of a Theory of Curriculum"; *Curriculum Inquiry* for "The Rise of Scientific Curriculum-Making and Its Aftermath"; *Peabody Journal of Education* for "Success and Failure in Educational Reform: Are There Historical 'Lessons'?"; the Association for Supervision and Curriculum Development for *Bureaucracy and Curriculum Theory*; Jossey-Bass Publishers for "What Is the Question in Teacher Education?" (originally published as "The Question in Teacher Education";) the *American Journal of Education* (formerly *School Review*) for "The Tyler Rationale"; the *American Educational Research Journal* for "Vocational Education as Symbolic Action: Connecting Schooling with the Workplace"; and *Theory into Practice* for "Curriculum Theory as Metaphor." The essay, "Keeping Out of Nature's Way: The Rise and Fall of Child-Study as the Basis for Curriculum, 1880–1905" is published here for the first time.

Herbert M. Kliebard

Introduction

When I was a graduate student there was no such thing as curriculum history as an identified area of scholarship. Of course, elements of what we now think of as curriculum history were commonly incorporated into the general history of education, but no one was identified as a curriculum historian, and I do not think anybody aspired to be one. Somehow, along the way, I acquired that label, and all the essays included in this volume are, I suppose, essays in curriculum history. The fact that they are also about curriculum theory reflects my abiding effort to use historical analysis as a way of disentangling what we could possibly mean by a curriculum theory. For purposes of convenience, six of the essays are grouped under the subheading Curriculum History and six under the subheading Curriculum Theory. The balance in the first instance tilts toward curriculum history per se, and more directly toward curriculum theory in the second set. In fact, however, all the essays are part of a continuing endeavor on my part to explore both curriculum history and curriculum theory, not really separately, but at one and the same time. The publication of this volume has afforded me the opportunity of reflecting briefly on what that enterprise of curriculum history has become over the course of the last quarter century or so.

One major stream in the writing of the history of education has been devoted to access to schooling. In fact, much of the history of American education has been written in terms of ever-expanding educational opportunity with more and more groups, variously defined, availing themselves of the chance to go to school. But what we mean by education, as Raymond Williams once observed,[1] is in a constant state of flux, and so an over-concentration simply on who goes to school presents us with an incomplete picture of what school attendance implies. If we think of what schools have to offer as a commodity, then we would certainly want to know to whom it is available, but we also need to know as precisely as possible what that commodity is. Without some knowledge of what is taught, it is well-nigh impossible to interpret what the effects of schooling are in any society. There is no question, then, that history of curriculum is part of the history of education broadly conceived, but, more particularly, it is that part of history of education that focuses most directly on what it is that gets distributed to those who attend educational institutions and, if possible, with what effect.

This is no easy task. Not only is the curriculum constantly fluctuating over time in response to various social and economic demands; it is not even at any given moment a coherent or explicit reflection of what a given society wants its children and youth to know. Even the formal and documented expressions of what the curriculum should consist of are anything but consistent and are often even self-contradictory. At one and the same time, for example, American schools are now urged to be the repositories and purveyors of standard academic fare and instruments for addressing a wide range of social problems. Higher mathematics stands alongside programs for the prevention of child abuse, and various foreign languages vie for their place in the curriculum with sex education and courses designed to combat drug abuse. In this sense, the curriculum represents a nebulous cross-section of what various interest groups in a given society prize rather than a unified and unambiguously articulated expression of the values of that culture.

Beyond the formal statements of what the curriculum at any given time is or should be, there is also the curriculum that actually goes forward in schools and classrooms. It is widely assumed that prestigious national committees, school boards, and edicts emanating from state departments of education influence the curriculum in some way, but it would be a mistake to assume a direct congruence between those formal expressions of the curriculum and what is sometimes called the curriculum-in-use. Nevertheless, even these formal declarations of what the curriculum ought to be, whether they are converted directly into practice or not, can become important artifacts from which the values of a given society may be assembled. If nothing else, formal expressions of what the curriculum should be give us some idea of what given groups in a society value. To be sure, they are often expressions of social elites and the pronouncements of select professional cadres, but to ignore or dismiss them would be to miss one source of where the power to forge the curriculum in a given society lies. One sort of mistake a curriculum historian can make is to assume that explicit assertions about the program of studies become the curriculum that school children actually experience. Without question, those expressions are filtered through and sometimes even transformed by local politics, institutional cultures, interpretations by individual teachers, and the vagaries of classroom interaction. But the other kind of mistake would be to dismiss those expressions of curriculum ideology as irrelevant to actual schooling or to historical examination. For one thing, what goes on in schools can hardly remain unaffected by national debates and deliberate professional influences. For another, these expressions emanating from political, business, and professional sources are themselves indicators of how certain elements in a society seek to define the world in which they live as well as what they want a society's children to know.

Easier access to concrete and widely disseminated declarations of what the curriculum is or should be is undoubtedly one reason why curriculum historians have, for the most part, concentrated their efforts on interpreting the meaning and effect of those explicit statements. National curriculum movements such as the child-study movement or scientific curriculum-making, the pronouncements of national leaders in curriculum such as a George Counts or a Hollis Caswell, and the work of national committees devoted in large measure to curriculum reform, such as the Committee of Ten, have become the standard fare of curriculum history. Only in relatively recent years have individual case studies of curriculum and, to some extent, studies of the evolution of particular school subjects begun to add an important new dimension to curriculum history. It has even become fashionable here and there to deprecate the former type of curriculum history in favor of the latter.

Despite the obvious imbalance, there is no reason why these two forms of curriculum history should not be seen as complementary rather than antagonistic or why one form should be perceived as innately superior to the other. In part, the potency of curriculum history in terms of broad national movements lies in its ability to identify and reflect who the respective interest groups are in a given society as well as how and under what circumstances their ideologies translate themselves into expressions of what the schools teach. It also can hold these ideologies up to critical examination. In a field like curriculum, where ideologies are often submerged or ambiguous, this can serve a useful purpose. The power of the case studies lies in examining the curriculum, insofar as possible,

as the lived experience of various social groups. It also opens up
the possibility of generating new conceptual frameworks for understanding the reasons why the curriculum in fact took the twists
and turns that it did over any period of time.[2]

In both these forms of curriculum history, the curriculum should
be seen neither as a straightforward reflection of social trends nor
as the product simply of ideas about schooling proclaimed by individuals or groups. It seems clear that whatever the curriculum
becomes, it is not, strictly speaking, dictated either by social trends
or by prevailing ideologies about the nature and purpose of
schooling. Neither a massive social change, such as the Industrial
Revolution, nor a powerful idea, such as scientific curriculum-
making, alone makes for curriculum change. Rather, a curriculum
is the ambiguous outcome of a complex interplay between certain
social conditions and prevailing conceptions of how schools are
supposed to function. Although it should be acknowledged that
those conceptions of schooling do not arise *ab initio* and are themselves affected by social, political, economic and intellectual forces,
they are not preordained. A persistent theme in this volume, the
promise of a curriculum controlled by science, for example, was
neither a unitary concept nor an inevitable consequence of prevailing social and intellectual forces. Not only did a scientific curriculum take different forms (compare "Keeping Out of Nature's
Way" and "The Rise of Scientific Curriculum-Making and Its
Aftermath"); it competed against other conceptions of what the
curriculum ought to be within the same social and intellectual setting.

One more point needs to be made in this regard. Any curriculum
policy will inevitably be only imperfectly realized, and it is often
crucial to assess any such policy in terms of actual practice; but
the tangible outcome of a curriculum policy is not the only way
to gauge its significance. It may also be important to consider any
policy's symbolic meaning. As I tried to argue in "Vocational Education as Symbolic Action," the most significant effect of a given
educational policy may lie in its status as symbolic action rather
than its instrumental value as the realization of announced intentions. A proclaimed curriculum is a potent way to validate certain
forms of knowledge and belief and, whether or not it is implemented in any substantial way, it can be extraordinarily revealing
about the values a given society or some segment thereof cherishes.
As such, it confers status on those whose beliefs are so legitimated
and, in that way, bestows power on certain social bodies as op-

posed to others. The curriculum thus becomes one of those arenas in which various interest groups struggle for dominance and control. In large measure, curriculum history seeks to record and interpret that struggle.

Notes

1. Raymond Williams, *The Long Revolution* (London: Chatto & Windus, 1961), p. 215.
2. See, for example, David F. Labaree, *The Making of An American High School: The Credentials Market and the Central High School of Philadelphia, 1838–1939* (New Haven: Yale University Press, 1988). Labaree's interpretation is based largely on the idea that the market value of the high school credential influenced the course of curricular change.

Part I

Essays in Curriculum History

1

The Decline of Humanistic Studies in the American School Curriculum

"Humanism", John Dewey once remarked, "is a portmanteau word."[1] It packs together a variety of meanings, some drawn from its origins in fifteenth- and sixteenth-century Italy, some from its association with literature, particularly classical literature, some from its alleged opposition to religion, and, in more recent times, from its anti-romantic and anti-naturalistic temper. On its education side, it has come to be associated with a set of subjects, a segment of the school curriculum, believed to have the power to stir the imagination, enhance the appreciation of beauty, and disclose motives that actuate human behavior. From its early association with the study of Latin and Greek, humanism has gradually been expanded to the study of language generally as a distinctive possession of human beings, and with the arts—music, painting, sculpture, poetry—as the highest forms of expression by which human beings convey their experience and their aspirations. These, it turns out, are the very subjects that have suffered the steepest decline in the American school curriculum during the course of the twentieth century, a decline which, if continued, will at best make artistic expression and appreciation the province of a handful of sensitive souls whose mission it will be to preserve the higher culture and to protect it from degradation by the mob. In fact, the most persistent problem that humanism has had to face in the twentieth century is its inability to reconcile its central doctrine with the realities of mass public education. In some sense, that problem is a legacy dating back to the origins of humanism itself.

First appeared in *The Humanities in Precollegiate Education*, edited by Benjamin Ladner, Eighty-third Yearbook of the National Society for the Study of Education, Part II (Chicago: University of Chicago Press, 1984), pp. 7–30.

It is commonplace to refer to the Renaissance as a period characterized by a rebirth of learning. Actually, however, it would be difficult to argue that that period saw the spread of education to a significant segment of the European world. Instead, when compared to the scholasticism that preceded it, there emerged from the Renaissance not the spread of learning, but a redefinition of what it meant to be learned. The Renaissance was not only a time where learning was revered; it was a period when educational theory flourished and where education itself was being reconstructed. Many of the great works of that period are treatises making the case for one or another combination of studies, including their order and sequence. Desiderius Erasmus's *De Ratione Studii*, François Rabelais's *Gargantua* and *Pantagruel*, Joannes Ludovicus Vives's *De Tradendis Disciplinis*, and various works issuing from the school founded by Vittorino da Feltre are pedagogical tracts and, more directly, arguments for a particular curriculum. It is hard to imagine another period in which the scholars of the time dedicated themselves so assiduously to the central curriculum question, what should we teach?

From the way the leading scholars of the Renaissance framed their answer to that question we have derived our basic conceptions of what constitutes a humanistic education. As Émile Durkheim has pointed out, however, there were actually two, not unrelated but nevertheless distinctive, streams of thought in educational theory that emerged from that great body of pedagogical scholarship.[2] In the first, as represented mainly by Rabelais, the curriculum was conceived of as a vast and actually unending feast, a banquet so vast that it could only be consumed by giants. Nothing is omitted, not the casting of artillery, physical strength and manual dexterity, skill in every musical instrument, the work of apothecaries, geometry, Greek, Latin, Chaldean, Hebrew, Arabic, the dialogues of Plato, agriculture, metals, and precious stones. In short, Rabelais's curriculum is hardly a selection from what was known in the Western world; it is practically a comprehensive catalog of everything known. His selection of authors places Virgil alongside obscure writers of the fifteenth century and lumps together Plato and Pausanias. The special association of humanism with literary style and linguistic elegance is not basically derived from Rabelais.

It is difficult if not impossible to distill from his curriculum catalog any body of studies that could be deemed more valuable than any other. The sciences of the day along with the practical arts enjoyed equal status with literary and linguistic studies. Durkheim interprets Rabelais's contribution to educational theory as turning the direction in educational thinking from the purely formal to a curriculum that was designed to feed the mind. As Durkheim put it, in Rabelais we find a "curriculum whose object will be not to train the mind in formal intellectual acrobatics, but rather to nourish it, to enrich it, and to give it some substance."[3] A human being's intellectual appetite was seen by Rabelais as insatiable, and essentially all knowledge should be consumed. If nothing else, Rabelais helped break through the narrow constraints that had characterized the curriculum of the earlier period.

The second humanistic strain derived from the Renaissance is represented principally by the work of Erasmus. There is much in Erasmus that at least superficially resembles the unbridled appetite for learning that characterizes Rabelais's curriculum; but the list of authors to be studied that Erasmus drew up is not nearly as long nor as eclectic as is Rabelais's. Here one is not simply gobbling up everything in sight, but selecting certain delicacies with a purpose in mind beyond the mere satisfaction of the intellectual appetite. That purpose is expressed in the development of the *orationis facultas*, the ability to use language elegantly and expressively. "There is nothing," says Erasmus, "more magnificent and more worthy to be admired than discourse (*oratio*) which, when it contains a wealth of words and phrases, flows in abundance like a river of gold."[4] Unlike Rabelais, then, there is for Erasmus as well as for other educational theorists of the Renaissance, such as Vives, a hierarchy of studies with language in its several manifestations clearly at the top. The way of achieving the great purpose of education—elegance and precision in the use of language—was accomplished mainly by immersing the student in those masterpieces of literature that can serve as models. To humanist educators of the Renaissance, this meant intensive study of the classics of Greece and Rome, and hence the persistent legacy linking humanism to the study of Greek and Latin. As Durkheim expressed it, education in the Middle Ages was an intellectual fencing match; for Rabelais, it was a vast luxurious banquet; and for Erasmus it was the supreme development of the literary faculty.[5] For Erasmus, literature was not simply one of an array of subjects. It was the vehicle par excellence for shaping mind and character. Contemporary versions of what constitutes the humanistic studies are traceable to that vision; the Rabelais tradition seems to have become submerged.

With all the appeal that that vision held and continues to hold today, it also contained the seeds of the decline of humanism in educational practice. The rise of humanism as an educational ideal coincided, not accidentally, with the rise of a highly restricted class of cultivated aristocracy, a class capable of rarified tastes, who was removed from the world in which the vast majority of Europeans lived. Humanistic education had its origins in a world where education served mainly as an adornment to courtly life. Without denying the value of that adornment to those privileged to enjoy it, humanistic education was never an education for power or even, for that matter, for survival. Individual feats of learning during the Renaissance are indeed astounding, but given the course of political and social events over the next three or four centuries, humanism as an educational ideal restricted to an elite class had to adapt or die. It did a little of both.

The Humanistic Curriculum in Nineteenth-Century America

The challenge of Rousseau and the Romantic movement notwithstanding, humanism continued its firm hold on the American curriculum through most of the nineteenth century. More than any other in this country, Yale's course of study embodied the curriculum orthodoxy that had evolved over the previous two hundred years. The first three years were devoted mostly to Latin, Greek, and mathematics, the traditional classical subjects, but with a smattering of such other subjects as astronomy, history, geography, and English grammar and rhetoric. The final year was devoted primarily to moral philosophy, metaphysics, English composition, and *belles lettres*.[6] The only options that existed were noncredit ones, but even these were sometimes alarming to college authorities. When Anglo-Saxon, for example, was introduced as a noncredit option, the outraged President Jeremiah Day announced: "It might soon be necessary to appoint an instructor in *whittling*."[7]

By contrast, other American colleges of the period were beginning to experiment with modifications of the traditional humanistic curriculum. After some mainly unsuccessful attempts to modify the course of study at the College of William and Mary, Thomas Jefferson was able to introduce a certain measure of choice for students in electing departments of study in the University of Virginia. In 1827, at the urging of George Ticknor, the Harvard College curriculum was revised to permit students to substitute work in a modern foreign language for up to half of the requirement in Greek and Latin (although, in practice, such substitutions were rare). Three years earlier, in 1824, Hobart College was established as the first college in the United States (or England for that matter) with no instruction in Greek or Latin. There appeared to be a modest but decided movement among some of America's leading colleges away from rigidly prescribed curricula with Latin, Greek, and mathematics at the core. A minor rebellion among Yale under-graduates in 1825 led, ultimately, to what became the first coher-ent attempt to justify the time-honored curriculum of Yale College and hence the mainstream of curriculum theory in early nine-teenth-century America.

Two years following the rebellion, at the 1827 commencement, State Senator Noyes Darling, a former student at Yale College, proposed the elimination of the "dead languages" and the substi-tution of modern languages. At almost the same time, the Con-necticut legislature, taking into account the apparent dissatisfac-tion of students with the Yale program of studies, called for similar reforms along practical lines. President Day sensed the danger, and on September 11, 1827, the President and Fellows of Yale College passed a resolution that a committee "inquire into the expediency of so altering the regular course of instruction in this college as to leave out of said course the study of the *dead languages*, substi-tuting other studies therefor."[8] Also to be considered was the pos-sibility of eliminating those "dead languages" as a basis for ad-mission to Yale.

Published originally in 1828 under the title, *Reports on the Course of Instruction in Yale College: By a Committee of the Corporation and the Academic Faculty*, and a year later as "Original Papers in Relation to a Course of Liberal Education," the report is at once the most comprehensive account of the conventional wisdom on the undergraduate curriculum in the early nineteenth century and the most spirited defense in its time of the humanistic curriculum against the onslaught of modernity. The report was divided into two sections with President Day himself mainly responsible for Part I, a general defense of Yale's course of study, and with Professor James K. Kingsley, probably America's leading classical scholar, undertaking the defense of the study of Latin and Greek in Part II. By the nineteenth century, humanistic education had become closely associated with faculty psychology, and much of President Day's defense was based on the idea that certain subjects of study had the power to invigorate the various faculties of the mind, such as memory, imagination, and reasoning. (President Day himself had earlier published two books on faculty psychology.)

Day began his defense by admitting that Yale's "present plan of education admits of improvement."[9] He also expressed surprise that there were reports to the effect that the program of studies was "unalterable" and alluded to the fact that many alumni have remarked upon return visits that the college had changed considerably. Day thus established that he was not opposed to change per se. What concerned him particularly was the persistent cry that "our colleges must be new-modeled; that they are not adapted to the spirit of age; that they will soon be deserted, unless they are better accommodated to the business character of the nation."[10] What he seemed to fear most was an abandonment of the humanist ideal in favor of the immediately practical.

After asserting that the chief purpose of any college is to "Lay the Foundation of a Superior Education," Day presented, in what has become the most famous passage of the report, the chief defense for the continued validity of the humanist curriculum.

> The two great points to be gained in intellectual culture, are the *discipline* and the *furniture* of the mind; expanding its powers, and storing it with knowledge. The former of these is, perhaps, the more important of the two. A commanding object, therefore, in a collegiate course, should be to call into daily and vigorous exercise the faculties of the student. Those branches of study should be prescribed and those modes of instruction adopted, which are best calculated to teaching the art of fixing the attention, directing the train of thought, analyzing a subject proposed for investigation; following with accurate discrimination, the course of argument; balancing nicely the evidence presented to the judgment; awakening, elevating, and controlling the imagination; arranging with skill, the treasure which memory gathers; and guiding the powers of genius.[11]

Thus, by using the standard mental disciplinarian argument, Day was able to deflect the persistent concern expressed by educational reformers and at least some students regarding the usefulness of certain of the traditional subjects. Their usefulness lay not in any immediate practicality but in their ability to develop certain highly valued habits of thought, habits of thought that, in the long run, were the foundation of what we mean by education.

The notion that the mind was composed of a discrete set of identifiable faculties waiting there to be exercised constituted the most powerful justification for a curriculum that incorporated the traditional disciplines of knowledge. Almost miraculously, there appeared for each of the identified faculties a subject perfectly suited to its development. As Day put it:

> From the pure mathematics, he [the student] learns the art of demonstrable reasoning. In attending to the physical sciences, he becomes familiar with facts, with the process of induction, and the varieties of probable evidence. In ancient literature, he finds some of the most finished models of taste, by English reading he learns the powers of the language in which he is to speak and write. By logic and mental philosophy, he is taught the art of thinking; by rhetoric and oratory, the art of speaking. By frequent exercise on written composition, he acquires copiousness and accuracy of expression. By extemporaneous discussion, he becomes prompt, fluent, and animated.[12]

Along with the development of the individual faculties, mental discipline theory placed great emphasis on the harmonious development of all faculties, leaving none to wither. "The mind," Day declared, "never attains its full perfection, unless its various powers are so trained as to give them the fair proportions which nature designed."[13] The traditional branches of learning and faculties of the mind not only presented a certain correspondence, they also exhibited a certain "symmetry and balance" which ought to be brought to the fullest perfection. The root metaphor in mental discipline theory is, of course, mind and body, and Day expressed in those metaphorical terms his ideal education: "As the bodily frame is brought to its highest perfection, not by one simple and uniform motion, but by a variety of exercises; so the mental faculties are expanded, and invigorated, and adapted to each other with the different departments of science."[14] By departments of science, Day was referring not specifically to the natural sciences but to what today we would call the disciplines of knowledge. His appeal was for balance and against a high degree of specialization, an argument for what later became known as general education.

Professor Kingsley's defense of Latin and Greek in Part II of the report was equally impassioned and also infused with mental discipline as the chief object of higher education. He began his section of the report, for example, by defining liberal education as "such a course of discipline in the arts and sciences, as is best calculated, at the same time, both to strengthen and enlarge the faculties of the mind, and to familiarize it with the leading principles of the great objects of human investigation and knowledge,"[15] almost a paraphrase of Day's famous discipline and furniture of the mind. In addition, however, Kingsley refused to concede the commonly held notion that the study of French and German was more practical than Latin and Greek. "The literature of every country of Europe," he claimed, "is founded more or less on classical literature, and derives from this source its most important illustrations."[16] To engage in any sort of literary inquiry, then, required a familiarity with these classical sources. Without mastery of the classical languages any scholar "immediately feels a deficiency in his education, and is convinced that he is destitute of an important part of practical learning."[17] Moreover, as a preparation for the professions, particularly divinity and law, a classical education was unrivaled. As for the modern languages, they simply did not provide sufficient mental exercise. "To acquire the knowledge of any of the modern languages," Kingsley argued, "is chiefly an effort of memory,"[18] and, although they may be "recommended on their own merits,"[19] they certainly do not provide a substitute for the kind of mental gymnastics that Greek and Latin provide. "To establish this truth," Kingsley asserted, "let a page of Voltaire be compared with a page of Tacitus."[20]

A humanistic curriculum justified in mental disciplinarian terms remained practically unchallenged for about half a century. It would be to overemphasize the impact of the Yale report to attribute this continued success to the arguments of Day and Kingsley in particular. But if these arguments did not actually influence the course of the American curriculum during the next five decades, they accurately reflected mainstream thinking as to what constituted a proper education. If humanistic subjects were not immediately practical in the sense that surveying or French might be, they had great potential for indirect utility. The subjects that comprised the humanistic curriculum, with only minor modifications, had the power to strengthen the individual faculties of the mind, and, properly balanced, they created a mental harmony, a mind ready to undertake the work of the world. Nothing could be more practical than that. Even so momentous an event as the emergence of the American common school in the mid-nineteenth century offered little immediate threat to the established order of school subjects except, perhaps, insofar as it helped create a population of persons whose children and grandchildren would be prepared to move to the next step on the educational ladder; and, in the long run, mass education on the secondary level profoundly affected the course of the humanistic curriculum. Moreover, the rise of experimental psychology, which coincided with a dramatic increase in the population of secondary schools, served to weaken the psychological foundations of mental discipline, a theory that had served so well as a justification for humanistic subjects.

The Challenge to the Old Order of Subjects

Around 1880, when the high school surpassed the academy as the most populous form of secondary education, a major threat to the humanistic curriculum emerged. It was not the fact of the new population itself that changed the course of the American curriculum, but that fact as interpreted by a variety of pedagogical reformers and leaders. There had been, after all, an industrial revolution which had profoundly affected the social fabric and a Darwinian revolution that, for a while at least, had rent the intellectual world apart. One could hardly cling, many reformers reasoned, to a mode of education tied to aristocratic origins and to a curriculum that only minimally reflected the rise in scholarly status of scientific inquiry.

It was not simply that more scientific subjects ought to be added; the curriculum itself had to be determined scientifically rather than by vague speculation. Moreover, the social institutions, such as family and church, that had served so well to socialize the young in a preindustrial society no longer functioned successfully. The school as a social institution, it was felt, had to take a stronger hand in the socialization process. Vice and corruption in the cities, a problem presumably exacerbated by waves of immigrants from Southern and Eastern Europe, had to be controlled. "We find," said Edward A. Ross, the noted sociologist, "*an almost worldwide drift from religion toward education as the method of indirect social restraint.*"[21] The problem as Ross saw it was that education had "become less an instrument of social control than an aid to individual success."[22] It was not that an intellectual education was "without a moral value"; but it was not enough merely to "open a range of new and healthy interests" that would divert the young from vice. "The cry goes up," he proclaimed, "for a secular civic and moral education that shall effectively minister to peace and order."[23] What we find in the last two decades of the nineteenth century is a heightened perception of a profound change in American society, in many cases an apocalyptic vision, and with that perception a demand for a new role for the schools. The role and function of the American school had to be redirected away from simply purveying intellectual culture or the development of the faculties of the mind, and toward direct and conscious social well-being. That new role, many reformers argued, could be accomplished by nothing less than a thorough transformation of the outmoded curriculum.

It would be easy to exaggerate the degree of consensus that was reflected in the 1890s, particularly in secondary schools. The decade of the 1890s, after all, marked the beginning of a massive influx of new students, the secondary school population rising from a mere six or seven percent of the population fourteen to seventeen years old in 1890 to more than fifty percent by 1930.

But, while the desire to reform the curriculum was virtually universal, there was wide disagreement as to what direction that reform should take. There were those, like Ross, who took their cue from the demands of a modern industrial society and particularly from the feeling that the school should undertake the functions of social control once performed by other, now decaying, social institutions. There were those, like G. Stanley Hall, who drew their inspiration from Rousseau, and who saw in an education according to nature the possibility of a new, scientifically determined curriculum that would be in tune with the true interests and needs of children and adolescents. Even such leading defenders of humanism in this period as Charles W. Eliot, the patrician president of Harvard University, and William Torrey Harris, the powerful Commissioner of Education, were themselves reformers, in essence, seeking modest reforms in the American curriculum that would retain and revivify the humanistic ideal. And, hovering over the battle, there was the figure of John Dewey, critical not only of the old education but of the reformers of the period as well, while at the same time beginning to forge his own proposals for the reconstruction of American schooling.

Around the turn of the century, the principal antagonists were humanists like Eliot and Harris and the child-study educators under the leadership of Hall. By the second decade of the twentieth century, social efficiency emerged as the predominant educational ideal, and while humanism showed surprising resilience, its decline was inevitable.

The most important single event in the battle for control of the school curriculum during the 1890s was the National Education Association's report of the Committee of Ten.[24] The immediate reason for the creation of the Committee was the desire on the part of high school principals for greater uniformity in the curriculum. With different colleges varying widely in their admissions requirements (such as the ability to translate particular works in Latin and Greek), high schools had a virtually impossible job. But beyond this sticky practical problem, there loomed the distinct possibility that the high school would be transformed from a rather elite institution serving a tiny minority of the adolescent population into a mass popular institution. The profound question that the committee had to deal with, therefore, was whether the curriculum that had held sway in this country, practically since its founding, could continue to serve in the period beyond elementary school.

The Committee was headed by Eliot whose reputation as an educational reformer had extended beyond his support of the elective system as president of Harvard University to various changes he recommended in elementary and secondary schools. Like Day and Kingsley, Eliot was a mental disciplinarian, but, perhaps because of his training as a scientist, his version of mental discipline took a somewhat unusual turn. Eliot believed that any subject, so long as it were capable of being studied over an extended period (thereby excluding practical subjects), had the power to train the mind. It was possible, therefore, to broaden the curriculum, including even elective subjects, and still preserve the humanist ideal (or one form of it). The full development of the innate human capacities, then called faculties, could be accomplished by intensive study, not of a highly restricted set of subjects, but of a wider range of studies. This broadening of the range of subjects appropriate for the curriculum was more in the tradition of Rabelais than Erasmus. At least in principle, French thus had as much disciplinary value as Latin (although Eliot himself seems to have had some doubt about that claim in practice). The actual recommendations of the Committee of Ten for the high school curriculum can best be interpreted through this set of fundamental assumptions.

The main feature of the Committee's report when it was published in 1893 was four recommended "programmes," each acceptable both for college admission and for what was then called "life," that is, for those who did not go beyond their high school education. The four courses of study, the Classical, the Latin-Scientific, the Modern Languages, and the English, probably did not go as far as Eliot would have liked in the direction of electivism, but at least they offered students an option as to course of study. By modern standards, each of these courses of study would be considered highly academic. In fact, in the contemporary mythology of the education world, the recommendations of the Committee of Ten are regarded anachronistically as designed to impose college domination on the high school curriculum. Eliot is seen as an arch-conservative who vainly sought to fend off an appropriate adaptation of the high school curriculum to the new high school population. Actually, however, modest, even significant, changes are apparent in the report. Considered as a whole, only the Classical program retained Greek as a requirement, and even there, it was reduced from the customary three years to two. (Professors of Greek back at Harvard were outraged.) Even more significant was the fact that in two of the programs, the Modern Languages and the English, there was no Latin requirement at all. Had these two programs been recommended only for the non-college-going population, there probably would have been little controversy, but the Committee unanimously refused to make any distinction between preparation for college and preparation for life. In the mental disciplinarian context, such a distinction was unnecessary because the ultimate purpose of education was the fullest possible development of native capacities, and this was true whether one went on to college or not.

By far the greatest criticism of the report came from those who saw the need for a much more thoroughgoing reform of the high school curriculum. Led by G. Stanley Hall, one of America's foremost psychologists, the criticism centered on the conviction that the committee had underestimated the impact of the new high school population. The impact, as seen by critics of the report, was not so much the implication of sheer numbers, but that the new population was qualitatively different; these new students simply lacked the ability to cope with the programs the Committee recommended. Referring to the new population as a "great army of incapables,"[25] Hall chided the Committee for failing to recognize the huge differences in mental capacities of high school students. For Hall, high school programs of study had to be sharply differentiated according to students' mental capacities and therefore indirectly according to their future places in society and their occupational roles. Eliot, while recognizing that differences in ability did exist, did not regard those differences as being so significant as to require different curricula for different identifiable groups in the school population. At the heart of Eliot's position was his fundamental optimism with regard to human intellectual capacities. Essentially all human beings were capable of studying and profiting from the subjects now regarded as academic. In this sense,

Eliot represented a position that regarded the basic humanist curriculum, expanded and with a few modifications here and there, as appropriate not only for an elite, but for the great mass of people as well.

Whatever may have been the merits or defects of the Committee of Ten report, it was eventually the position represented by Hall, combining as it did the idea that a curriculum could be scientifically constructed with what might be called a pessimism about human intellectual capacities, which became ascendant in twentieth-century curriculum thinking. A crushing blow to the mental disciplinarian justification for the humanist curriculum was delivered by growing experimental evidence that seemed to contradict some of the fundamental assumptions of faculty psychology. Without specific faculties to be trained, it would hardly be possible to maintain that certain subjects had the special power to train them. As early as 1890, William James reported as a result of a modest experiment he conducted with his students at Harvard that the faculty of memory was not improved by continued practice in memorizing.[26] By the turn of the century, Edward L. Thorndike and other psychologists brought experimental evidence to show that abilities developed in one context were not easily transferred to new situations.[27] The implication that professional educators drew from this evidence was that, in the absence of broad faculties to be developed, education had to be directed toward the development of highly specific skills pertinent to very specific situations. These new beliefs about the workings of the mind, combined with a new sense of what schools were for, posed a formidable threat to what remained of humanistic studies.

Humanism as the Preservation of the Cultural Heritage

If humanistic subjects did not have the power to develop thinking ability in its several manifestations, what good were they? A new justification had to be found, and the chief spokesperson for that new justification was the United States Commissioner of Education, William Torrey Harris. Harris was undoubtedly the preeminent figure in education during the last quarter of the nineteenth century. The fact that he never produced a *magnum opus* may lead us to underestimate the significance of his position and the pivotal role he played in the pedagogical world of the time. During his long career, he addressed national meetings of the National Education Association scores of times, and one attempt to compile his bibliography listed 479 publications.[28] The force of his intellect and his incredible energy were undoubtedly vital ingredients in Harris's national stature, but beyond the question of his personal influence, which was considerable, he gave voice to that large constituency of school teachers and administrators who were made uneasy by the threat of massive reform then looming on the horizon.

In particular, Harris helped build a plausible platform for the segment of the educational world that resisted the idea of a massive change in the schools of the nation presumably reflective of the great social transformation that had taken place in American society or, for that matter, the intellectual transformation through the rise of science. He was able to strike a tone of moderation in the midst of cries for a revolution in education. Harris, in a sense, was one of the last great spokespersons for a humanistic curriculum that education was to produce from within its midst. Educational leaders in the twentieth century were essentially arguing for change of various sorts, while the banner of humanism in educational policy, usually identified with the school's role in the development of the intellect, was carried by academicians and intellectuals drawn from outside the professional education establishment. Although Harris's position began to lose some ground among the leaders who regularly assembled at major educational conferences and who wrote for prestigious pedagogical journals, it is likely that Harris's basic approach to curriculum continued to hold sway in the schools across the nation for years to come.

Born in 1835 when America was still an agrarian country, Harris was keenly aware of the changes that had been wrought in American society, but he did not regard these changes as dictating a drastic reordering of the school's curriculum. Although certain modest adaptations to modern society could be incorporated, the basic function of the school, the development of reason, remained the same. In fact, the restructuring of American society made it even more imperative that the schools perform their distinctive function effectively. Harris's interpretation of Hegelian philosophy permitted him to see industrialization, with its profound effect on America's social institutions, not in any apocalyptic sense but as part of the unfolding of the Divine Will. Harris could, at one and the same time, be an advocate of rugged individualism and believe that the individual achieves realization only by subordinating himself or herself to social institutions, institutions that embody the fruits of civilization. It was through these institutions that the wisdom of the race would be transmitted. A consistent advocate of what he like to call "self-activity," Harris identified that activity with the rational through the exercise of will,[29] and it was his persistent emphasis on rationality in children that put him into direct conflict with the advocates of "education according to nature," such as Hall. The school, according to Harris, must train children to gain control over their natural impulses, not to submit to them. "Rousseau's doctrine of a return to nature," Harris once said, "must seem to me the greatest heresy in educational doctrine."[30]

As early as 1880, Harris was proclaiming the centrality of the curriculum in educational matters. "The question of the course of study," he said, "is the most important the educator can have before him."[31] The curriculum, in Harris's mind, should take its cue, not from the vagaries of children's interests, nor their spontaneous impulses, but from the great resources of civilization. For Harris, psychological inquiry into child growth and development had its place, but it could never, in itself, direct the course of a proper education. "Self-activity," he said, "is in every newborn soul as a spontaneity—a possibility of unlimited action, good or bad;"[32] and, essentially, it was the function of the curriculum to direct the development of self-activity in the interest of "a knowledge of truth, a love of the beautiful, a habit of doing good. . . ."[33] Considering the maxim of "the self-styled 'New Education' . . . learn to do by doing,"[34] (a maxim he attributed to the prominent German pedagogue, Friedrich Adolph Wilhelm Diesterweg), Harris was careful to point out that it was incomplete without some "guiding direction." That direction would be provided by a properly constructed course of study. Each branch of study in the curriculum (or, as he liked to call them, "coordinate groups of study"), he felt, could open the way for an ever more adequate appreciation of the Western social and intellectual tradition. His "five windows of the soul," represented by arithmetic and mathematics, geography, history, grammar, and literature and art, were chosen because to him they represented the best ways of initiating the child into the kind of self-activity that would lead to a command of the resources of that civilization.

Harris claimed that the school should first provide the command of language in reading and writing that goes beyond the "colloquial vocabulary" the child acquires in the home.[35] That increased command of language opened up the wisdom of the race that is contained on the printed page, thus emancipating the child from "the thraldom of dependence on the spoken word,"[36] and once that command were achieved, the child could reach beyond the world of personal experience and oral language, and the first of the "windows," arithmetic, could be opened. Arithmetic permitted entry into the abstract relationships that govern the physical world. Arithmetic, especially exact measurement, represented for Harris a first step in the conquest of nature, and he favored proceeding expeditiously from basic arithmetic to those mathematical operations that were useful in the natural sciences, opposing extensive drill in arithmetic operations as well as "numerical conundrums and other useless mathematical exercises."[37] Geography, the second of the windows, served to relate the inorganic world to the human world. Harris opposed what he called "sailor geography," the memorization of the names of rivers, islands and cities, in favor of the "dynamics of geography," the interrelationship between natural forces and human beings that led to different forms of commerce and industry in different parts of the world. History focused directly on the unfolding of the will "realized in institutions rather than in mere deeds of the individual."[38] In historical studies, the State and how collectivities made civilization possible should be emphasized. A particular enthusiast for the study of grammar, Harris, waxing poetic, claimed that the window of grammar "lets in a flood of light for the explanation of all problems which human experience can enunciate."[39] For Harris, the logical structure of language was a kind of model for the nature of thinking itself. And finally, literature opened up that window that permitted us to see life as a totality and to appreciate what is essential in human character. That understanding of human experience, according to Harris, could best be instilled through careful study of standard literary works. These works not only led to an understanding of the root of human action, but provided the principal form of aesthetic appreciation available in the curriculum.

These basic components of the curriculum, Harris claimed, were "the five great lines of study that radiate from the center and relate to the five great departments of human learning."[40] Other subjects were not exactly excluded; they were simply subordinate. Industrial drawing, for example, "should have its place in the common school side by side with penmanship."[41] While his position permitted him to support certain changes in the curriculum of the nineteenth century, such as systematic instruction in art, he was probably the leading champion of the continued study of classical literature and never wavered in his support of Greek and Latin, then becoming a lost cause. Harris's defense of the study of classical languages, however, differed in its rationale from that of the typical mental disciplinarian. While Harris seems to have given qualified support to the proposition that mental power could be developed through use, he was skeptical of the mental disciplinarian's belief that mental power developed in one field could be transferred to another. He was more interested in what the subjects had to offer directly than in their alleged value as vehicles for strengthening innate powers. Thus, memorizing dates may have some positive effect on "the health of the nervous system," but that activity derived its most immediate justification "on account of the intrinsic usefulness of the data themselves."[42]

Although, almost inevitably, Harris found himself using the vocabulary of formal discipline on occasion, especially in connection with the development of the will, his fundamental justification for retaining Greek and Latin in the curriculum lay in the fact that Greece and Rome were seminal to Western civilization, and no understanding of modern society would be complete without an appreciation of that heritage. For Harris, it was the content of the subjects rather than the form that was crucial in determining their value. Thus, unlike a mental disciplinarian such as Eliot, Harris opposed the substitution of French and German for the classical languages. While Eliot could argue that French, properly taught, could discipline the mind as well as Latin, Harris would hold that a knowledge of French simply was not as valuable as a resource of our culture as was Latin. Unlike Eliot, too, Harris was deeply suspicious of electives, advocating substitutions only within each of his five coordinate groups of study, where content was sufficiently similar. By emphasizing the virtues of the content of what was learned instead of disciplinary value, Harris was reconstructing the justification for a curriculum that preserved the humanist ideal.

The distance that Harris was able to create between his version of a humanist curriculum and the doctrine of mental discipline was particularly important in an era when the psychological underpinning of that doctrine, faculty psychology, was under serious attack by respected psychologists. William James's experiment on the ability to train memory in 1890, crude though it was, was only one in a series of studies that cast doubt on the idea that a mental ability, such as memory, trained in one setting could function successfully in another.[43] The rise of experimental psychology was seriously undermining the rationale that mental discipline had successfully

provided during most of the nineteenth century for the continu-
ance not only of Greek and Latin, but of other humanistic subjects
in the curriculum. Undoubtedly, part of the appeal of Harris's educational position was that the basic organizational structure of
the school required no radical alteration since essentially the same
things were to be taught, but for different reasons. Moreover, the
central role of the school, the development of the intellect, remained substantially unchanged. What remains of humanistic studies
in the twentieth-century American curriculum follows, at least in
broad outline, the program that Harris enunciated.

Humanism in the American Curriculum of the Twentieth Century

During the nineteenth century, humanistic subjects in the American school curriculum were defended, basically, on two grounds.
The first, as developed by such leaders in higher education as Day,
Kingsley, and in a modified form by Eliot, was that the study of
humanistic subjects (with some additions and modifications) had
the power to improve the ability to think. As it happened, the ability to think in this context was accomplished primarily by the vigorous exercise of innate faculties of mind. Since the function of
the school, throughout most of the nineteenth century, was seen
as intellectual development, the vital importance of these traditional subjects was, for the most part, taken for granted. The second major justification, as represented mainly by the work of Harris, was that humanistic subjects conveyed the vital core of the
Western cultural heritage. To be educated in the modern world
meant to be educated in the finest expressions of that civilization.

In the context of twentieth-century American education, both
these justifications were thought to be seriously flawed. First, faculty psychology as a theory of mind had collapsed and with it
mental discipline as an educational ideal. The vast majority of educators no longer believed that certain subjects had the power to
train the mind. Not only Latin and Greek, but eventually modern
foreign languages and even literature were left without that defense for their existence. Secondly, with the advent of mass education, particularly at the secondary level, the conviction grew that
the cultural heritage could only be passed on to a relative handful,
while for the great majority of youth, education had to concern
itself primarily with social and vocational functions. Ross and his
influential contemporaries in the educational world saw the pri-

mary function of schools as producing law-abiding citizens properly trained for efficient functioning in their destined social roles. A prominent part of that role was occupational, and vocational education had, by the second decade of the twentieth century, already begun to assume a prominent place in the curriculum.

Humanistic studies, in short, were increasingly being seen as remote and irrelevant to the children and youth now attending the schools. Additionally, such early twentieth-century events as the arrival of the IQ test and the mental measurement movement that followed served to provide persuasive evidence (however spurious) that only a small segment of the school population was capable of the study of such subjects as literature, languages, history, and higher mathematics. Most of the school population had to be trained to perform efficiently in the social roles that their native capacities dictated.

Three unresolved problems faced the defenders of humanism in the twentieth century, none of which they addressed adequately. The first, going back to its origins in the courtly life of Renaissance Europe, was the fact that humanism was associated with a highly restricted elite. The great defenders of humanism in the twentieth century, such as Irving Babbitt, were never able to reconcile their doctrine to the fact of mass public education. In the main, they simply decried it. Second, by restricting the doctrine of humanism to that which they took to be distinctly human in origin, such as literature, humanists set up an unwarranted opposition between humanistic studies and the sciences, an unnecessary dualism between the doctrines of humanism and naturalism which Dewey, for example, continually tried to dispel. The real enemy of humanism in the modern era was not science, but a certain pessimism about the human intellect, particularly the idea that only a relative handful were capable of intellectual development. By directing their arguments against such doctrines as naturalism, the principal advocates of humanism simply picked the wrong enemy. Contrary to popular impression, for example, Dewey, one of modern humanism's principal targets, was probably America's leading spokesperson in the twentieth century for the development of the intellect as the central function of education, an ideal he pursued in the face of powerful tendencies within the technological society marshalled against it. In an odd way, Dewey can be seen as attempting to rekindle the mental disciplinarian ideal, although his version of what intellectual functioning consisted of was, of course, vastly different from that of his nineteenth-century forebears. Finally, most humanists continued to insist that the study of certain subjects in themselves had the power to develop desirable habits of thought. Thorndike's experimental evidence notwithstanding, it is still plausible to assume that the prolonged and intensive study of certain subjects results not simply in the gaining of knowledge or skills (the furniture of the mind), but in enhancing certain ways of thinking (the discipline of the mind). What is implausible is that the study of these subjects in itself has that effect.

The key to a modern version of mental discipline as a justification of humanism lies not in identifying allegedly disciplinary subjects and then proceeding dutifully to study them. The key lies in *how* the subjects are studied. History, as a record of names, dates, and events, is just a lot of shabby and mostly useless furniture; history as giving order and meaning to human experience is thinking in a certain way. In fact, in a modern sense, what makes any field of study humanistic is not its identification with literature or the arts, but its potential for enlarging and deepening human experience.

The decline of the humanities in the modern American school curriculum is, at least in part, a matter of record. As a percentage of public high school students in grades nine through twelve, the study of Latin declined from a high of over fifty percent in 1900 to less than eight percent in 1949. Greek as a high school subject has been virtually extinguished in this century. Even French, the "modern," whose place Eliot sought to raise to the status of the classical languages, has declined from over fourteen percent in 1900 to under five percent in 1949.[44] The decline in the study of other subjects traditionally defined as humanistic is more difficult to document. Subjects like literature (English) and history have not so much suffered a decline in enrollments as they have undergone internal transformations. What we mean by English and what we mean by history are no longer quite the same. Additionally, although the sheer number of public schools in the United States is so large as to make it difficult to generalize, it seems clear that such recent educational fashions as career education and "back to basics" have helped move the center of gravity in the educational enterprise from its place in the development of the intellect to immediate utility and mindless drill in the rudiments. One should not be deluded into thinking, however, that education in the United States before the turn of this century represented some kind of golden age. Most of the evidence that exists indicates that what went on in the schools of the nation was, by and large, not only dull and lifeless, but utterly devoid of intellectual stimulation. Mental discipline as a defense of humanism, noble as that ideal may have been, was translated, more often than not, into monotonous drill and inhumane treatment of pupils. It was these defects that the best of the twentieth-century reformers in education tried to correct.

The rescue of humanistic study from its present state of decay in elementary and secondary schools (and perhaps in colleges as well) lies not in a return to an imagined nirvana in the pre-modern era, nor does it lie simply in a quantitative shift in the balance of humanities and science in the curriculum. It lies primarily in reconstructing all the studies that comprise the curriculum so that their origins in human purposes and human activity are restored and made the focal point of study. The contemporary American curriculum is not anti-humanistic because music, art, literature, and foreign languages are given a secondary role to mathematics, physics, chemistry, and industrial arts. It is because the so-called academic subjects (usually characterized curiously as "college-entrance" subjects, as if that were their only function) are set against the practical subjects; and they have become so abstracted from the world that children and adolescents inhabit, that these studies are no longer recognizable as being themselves forms of experience. The problem, as Dewey repeatedly emphasized, is one of restoring the subjects of study to their place *in* experience.

The study of the sciences, no less than the study of the humanities, suffers from the abstraction of these studies from their origins in human interests and human purposes. The mechanical dissection of frogs in a so-called laboratory and the routine combining of chemical elements to make a mixture turn blue is as anti-intellectual as the familiar recitation of *amo, amas, amat* or the recounting of the bare plot of a novel. The vague association of these activities with the aura of scholarly activity serves only to mask their fundamentally anti-intellectual character. The marks of scholarship imposed from without, as they so often are, quickly degenerate, as Dewey said, "into a miser's accumulation, and a man prides himself on what he has, and not on the meaning he finds in the affairs of life."[45] The school subjects, whether they are conventionally categorized as humanities or sciences, if they are perceived and presented merely as badges of scholarship, will remain not only anti-humanistic but anti-intellectual, precisely because they have lost their human meaning.

One of the salient factors in the decline of the humanities in the American school curriculum is the common perception, reflected in the work of detractors and even many defenders, that, while science and practical subjects concern themselves with the serious business of living, the humanities are to be identified with leisure and vaguely frivolous pursuits. That distinction is rooted partly in the common dualism in ancient Greece between labor and leisure. Thus, their association with leisure makes humanities a luxury only a few can afford, and then only after we have taken care of the really important work. The identification of the humanities with a small, cultured, leisure class, which is a legacy of the Renaissance, inevitably will work to the disadvantage of the humanities if they are ever to function effectively in an era of mass public education. If the office of education is primarily the cultivation of intelligence, then the humanities, no less than the sciences, must be reintegrated into their place in intelligent action. As such, the power of humanistic studies to invest in ordinary experience what Dewey called "a depth and range of meaning . . . which otherwise might be mediocre," lies at the core of their value.[46] The humanities in this sense should not be seen as enjoyable appendages to the real work of education. The humanities, as Dewey said, "are not luxuries of education, but emphatic expressions of that which makes any education worthwhile."[47]

Notes

1. John Dewey, "Whither Humanism?" *The Thinker* 2 (1930), pp. 9–12.
2. Émile Durkheim, *The Evolution of Educational Thought: Lectures on the Formation and Development of Secondary Education in France* trans. Peter Collins (London: Routledge and Kegan Paul, 1977), pp. 177–226.
3. Ibid., p. 187.
4. Quoted in ibid., p. 194.
5. Ibid., p. 197–98.
6. Frederick Rudolph, *Curriculum: A History of the Undergraduate Course of Study Since 1636* (San Francisco: Jossey-Bass, 1977), pp. 65–66.
7. Brooks Mather Kelley, *Yale: A History* (New Haven: Yale University Press, 1974), p. 165. Quoted in Rudolph, *Curriculum*, p. 66.
8. "Original Papers in Relation to a Course of Liberal Education,"

American Journal of Science and Arts 15, No. 2 (1829), pp. 297–351.

9. Ibid., p. 299.

10. Ibid., p. 300.

11. Ibid., p. 301–2.

12. Ibid.

13. Ibid., p. 301.

14. Ibid., p. 303.

15. Ibid., p. 324

16. Ibid., p. 328.

17. Ibid.

18. Ibid., p. 332.

19. Ibid., p. 335.

20. Ibid., p. 332.

21. Edward A. Ross, *Social Control* (New York: Macmillan, 1901), p. 176.

22. Ibid.

23. Ibid., p. 177.

24. National Education Association, *Report of the Committee on Secondary School Studies* (Washington, DC: Government Printing Office, 1893).

25. G. Stanley Hall, *Adolescence*, vol. II (New York: D. Appleton and Co., 1904), p. 510.

26. William James, *Principles of Psychology*, vol. I (New York: Henry Holt and Co., 1890), pp. 666–67.

27. Edward Lee Thorndike and R. S. Woodworth, "The Influence of Improvement in One Mental Function upon the Efficiency of Other Functions," *Psychological Review* 8 (May, July, November 1901), pp. 247–61, 384–95, 553–64.

28. *Report of the Commissioner of Education for the Year Ended June 30, 1907*, vol. I (Washington, DC: Government Printing Office, 1908), pp. 37–72.

29. William T. Harris, "The Pedagogical Creed of William T. Harris," in *Educational Creeds of the Nineteenth Century*, ed. Ossian H. Lang (New York: E. L. Kellogg and Co., 1898), p. 43.

30. Ibid., p. 37.

31. William T. Harris, "Equivalents in a Liberal Course of Study," *Journal*

of *Addresses and Proceedings* (Washington, DC: National Education Association, 1880), p. 174.

32. William T. Harris, "Psychological Inquiry," *Journal of Addresses and Proceedings* (Washington, D.C.: National Education Association, 1885), p. 157.

33. Ibid.

34. Ibid., p. 156.

35. William T. Harris, "What Shall the Public Schools Teach?", *Forum* 4 (1888), p. 574.

36. Ibid., p. 575.

37. William T. Harris, "Preface." in James A. McLellan and John Dewey, *The Psychology of Number*, International Education Series, vol. 33 (New York: D. Appleton and Co., 1895), p. 5.

38. Harris, "What Shall the Public Schools Teach?" p. 576.

39. Ibid., p. 576.

40. Ibid., p. 579.

41. Ibid.

42. William T. Harris, *Psychologic Foundations of Education*, International Education Series, vol. 37 (New York: D. Appleton and Co., 1898), p. 178.

43. Harold Ordway Rugg, *The Experimental Determination of Mental Discipline in School Studies* (Baltimore: Warwick and York, 1916).

44. John Francis Latimer, *What's Happened to Our High Schools?* (Washington, DC: Public Affairs Press, 1958), p. 26.

45. John Dewey, *Democracy and Education* (New York: Free Press, 1916), p. 288.

46. Ibid., p. 238.

47. Ibid.

2

The Liberal Arts Curriculum and its Enemies: The Effort to Redefine General Education

Accounts of the rise and/or fall of the liberal arts as an educational ideal usually begin quite appropriately either with the glories of ancient Greece or with the revival of learning in Europe which we have come to call the Renaissance. While these time-honored beginnings of a kind of education that is supposed to exalt the human spirit and express many of the central values of Western civilization have much to tell us about how that venerable ideal of education came to prominence, they are less illuminating on the question of how it fell into a kind of undeclared disfavor. (Hardly anyone is willing to admit being against a liberal education.) We know little about what the challenges to the liberal arts were or what accounts for its decline in twentieth-century American schooling. In the case of ancient Athens, the most potent challenger was reputed to be barbarism (which everybody is against) or perhaps Spartan education, and, in the Renaissance, it was probably scholasticism or even that great antagonist to sustained intellectual pursuit, Eros[1].

The roots of the decline of the liberal arts curriculum are probably more proximate than either ancient Greece or the Renaissance. They are most likely to be found in the great controversies over educational policy that erupted in Victorian England. There is no question that, in that period, education was getting public attention. Controversy over educational policy tends to erupt as the perception of significant social change becomes acute, and it was apparent that the changes wrought by the Industrial Revo-

First appeared in *Cultural Literacy and the Idea of General Education*, edited by Ian Westbury and Alan C. Purves, Eighty-seventh Yearbook of the National Society for the Study of Education, Part II (Chicago: University of Chicago Press, 1988), pp. 29–51.

lution in England were profound indeed. Not only were the lives of the working classes massively transformed, but the newly powerful middle class was beginning to flex its muscles.

By common agreement, education in England from at least the mid to late nineteenth century was a mess. The great figures of Victorian intellectual society, Thomas Carlyle, John Ruskin, John Henry Newman, John Stuart Mill, and Matthew Arnold were aware of its shortcomings and frequently expressed their criticisms in their writings. One of the most potent of the critics of formal education in his time was Charles Dickens. Among other unflattering portraits of schooling in Victorian England, Mr. Gradgrind's address at the opening of his school in *Hard Times* conveyed Dickens's bitter impressions of the prevailing pedagogy of the day:

> Now, what I want is facts. Teach these boys and girls nothing but the facts. Facts alone are wanted in life. Plant nothing else, and root out everything else. You can only form the minds of reasoning animals upon facts; nothing else will ever be of any service to them. This is the principle on which I bring up my own children, and this is the principle on which I bring up these children. Stick to the facts, sir!

When "girl number twenty" (Sissy Jupe), a girl who has grown up with horses, is declared by Mr. Gradgrind as unable to define a horse, he proceeds in his recitation until he finds one that satisfies him:

> Quadruped. Graminivorous. Forty teeth, namely, twenty-four grinders, four eyeteeth, and twelve incisors. Sheds coat in spring; in marshy countries sheds hoofs too. Hoofs hard, but requiring to be shod with iron. Age known by marks in mouth.

To that response, Mr. Gradgrind remarks triumphantly, "Now, girl number twenty . . . you know what a horse is." With accounts of education like this reaching hundreds of thousands of Dickens's readers, the controversy over the direction that education should follow was reaching beyond an inner circle of intellectuals. To be sure, what Dickens described in *Hard Times* and several other of his novels was anything but what a liberal education was supposed to be, but his criticisms, like those of his contemporaries, opened the way for a serious reexamination of the standard fare for the curriculum of his time.

What Knowledge Is of Most Worth?

Hovering over the brewing controversy as to the course that the curriculum should take was the pervasive influence of Charles Darwin. While the theory of evolution was popularly conceived primarily as a challenge to the reigning theology of the day, its most lasting impact was in terms of what it said about science itself and in terms of how the new conceptions of science, as well as its enormously increased status, would have on what knowledge people thought to be valuable. To a considerable extent, this reexamination had economic roots and is connected to the prominence of commerce and trade in industrial England. Increasingly, for example, critics of English society were observing that England no longer produced enough food for its citizens, and, to maintain its position of power and influence in the world, she needed to achieve preeminence in technology and manufacture. Classical studies, linguistic elegance, and masterpieces of literature as the centerpieces of the liberal arts curriculum were being challenged, and they were being challenged on a number of fronts. Illustrative of the kinds of challenges that were being directed at the traditional liberal arts were the positions of two of the most eminent Victorians and influential educational reformers, Herbert Spencer, whose "synthetic philosophy" was perceived to be at least consistent with Darwinism, and "Darwin's bulldog," Thomas Henry Huxley. The impact of their efforts to change the traditional curriculum of the time was ultimately to be felt in the schools of twentieth-century America.

Spencer, of course, is best known in the educational world for his 1859 essay, "What Knowledge is of Most Worth?," that title having since been appropriated and paraphrased many times, practically taking on the status of being the most central of all the questions that can be raised about the curriculum. His answer to that question, like that of many of his descendants, was influenced by his interpretation of the theory of evolution. Spencer's speculative anticipation of Darwinian theory led him to carry forward the principle of natural selection into such areas as the development of knowledge and social relationships. Evolutionary theory, in other words, became not just a way of explaining the development of species in a physical world, but became the basis for a cosmic understanding of society, psychology, ethics, and education. Spencer's 1854 essay "On the Genesis of Science," for example, posited a kind of sympathy between the development of mental concepts within the individual and the evolution of knowledge. His main point, however, was that everyday knowledge cannot be distinguished in any significant way from scientific knowledge. The latter was merely the evolutionary extension of the former. Part of the appeal of that doctrine was that it made the lines between aristocratic and ordinary knowledge less distinct. As the study of the world around us, the natural sciences were not as arcane or as exclusionary as ancient languages and classical literature. Nor were they as specialized: "The sciences are as branches of one trunk," he said, "and . . . were at first cultivated simultaneously" with differentiation only occurring later. In fact, science may be said to have a "common root" with language and art as well. Spencer predicted that, "Whenever established, a correct theory of the historical development of the sciences must have an immense effect upon education."[2]

In that same year (1854), Spencer's "Intellectual Education" turned his theory of the evolution of knowledge into the principle of curriculum: "The genesis of knowledge in the individual must follow the same course as the genesis of knowledge in the race."[3] In general terms, that principle is a rough extrapolation of the commonly held scientific truth of the time that "ontogeny recapitulates phylogeny." The mental development of the individual, in other words, recapitulates the development of the species over the course of history. This is one of the senses in which Spencer can be seen as an advocate of "natural education." According to this view, the course that the curriculum should take is one that follows scientific principles, which, when discovered and followed, lead inevitably to a desirable curriculum. This was an argument not simply in favor of a place for science in the curriculum but for a scientific curriculum. Education would proceed along evolutionary lines in the same way that the various plant and animal species, including the human species, proceeded.

Several versions of a scientifically determined curriculum that were rife in the latter part of the nineteenth century incorporated the idea of a recapitulation of human history within the child, thus setting out not only the sequence but actually the content of the course of study. Like Spencer's version, many others were, potentially at least, antagonistic to the ideal of the liberal arts. Although the particular subjects that have been proposed as comprising the liberal arts have varied according to time and place, on a fundamental level, the liberal arts ideal has always involved the effort consciously to select those elements of the culture that serve to make one fully human. Traditionally, the elements involved are presumed to make one sensitive to beauty, intellectually alive, and humane in outlook. The idea of a natural education substituted for that the notion that education was deterministic in the sense that the search for the good curriculum did not involve casting about for the cultural elements of highest value. Rather, it consisted of *discovering* the laws that the human being followed over the course of development in the same way that Darwin discovered the laws that governed the descent of the human species. Once those natural laws of development were discovered, they could be used to determine the curriculum.

Spencer's "What Knowledge is of Most Worth?," which first was published in 1859 and then appeared as the initial chapter of his *Education: Intellectual, Moral, and Physical,* offered an even more formidable challenge to the traditional conception of a liberal arts education. In his opening paragraph, Spencer noted with a suggestion of amusement if not condescension that "an Orinoco Indian, though quite regardless of bodily comfort, will yet labor for a fortnight to purchase pigment wherewith to make himself admired" or that an Indian woman would leave her hut unclothed but never unpainted. His point was to illustrate the curious phenomenon that "the idea of ornament predominates over that of use," and he then went on to argue that this principle seemed to hold true in terms of mental as well as bodily acquisitions."[4] In English schools, for example, Latin and Greek, which had no functional value, were the equivalent of the Orinoco Indian's ornamental paint. And ornamental education predominated equally in the education of women: "Dancing, deportment, the piano, singing, drawing—what a large space do these occupy!"[5] "Before there can be a rational *curriculum*," he concluded, "we must settle which things it most concerns us to know," and, "to this end, a measure of the value is the first requisite."[6]

The requisite step in this process, according to Spencer, was to classify in their order of importance the activities that comprise human life. In order of importance, he listed them as follows:

1. Those activities which directly minister to self preservation;

2. Those activities which, by securing the necessaries of life indirectly minister to self-preservation;

3. Those activities which have for their end the rearing and discipline of offspring;

4. Those activities which are involved in the maintenance of proper social and political relations;

5. Those miscellaneous activities which make up the leisure part of life, devoted to the gratification of tastes and feelings.[7]

The substitution of these functional criteria in the development of curricula for those that emphasized criteria drawn from some conception of what comprised the great cultural resources of Western culture constituted nothing short of a major revolution in thinking as to how a curriculum should be determined.

For one thing, Spencer set up an aim of education (self-preservation) to which education itself would be subordinate. Education, in other words, became an instrument to achieve something that lay beyond it. Specifically, there were categories of activities for which a good education prepared one to perform successfully. Music, poetry, and painting were no longer to be studied as the finest expressions of human aspirations and emotions but in order to "fill up the leisure left by graver occupations."[8] Leisure as an activity, ranking number five and last on Spencer's list of activities, needed to be performed, and the study of certain subjects could help one perform that function successfully. The task of developing a curriculum would then be seen in terms of "Life as divided into several kinds of activity successively decreasing in importance; the worth of each order of facts as regulating these several kinds of activity, intrinsically, quasi-intrinsically, and conventionally; and their regulative influences estimated as knowledge and discipline."[9]

Quite simply, the subject most suited to the proper preparation for "complete living" was science. Although nature itself provided much of what is needed for self-preservation, deliberate education in the interest of self-preservation was also necessary. Nature could help us instinctively ward off such dangers as "want of food, great heat, [and] extreme cold,"[10] but the absence of "an acquaintance with the fundamental principles of physiology as a means to complete living"[11] led to all sorts of infirmities and chronic disabilities. "Hence, knowledge which subserves direct self-preservation by preventing this loss of health, is of primary importance."[12] Mathematics plays a vital role in everything from ordinary carpentry to making a railway. Physics has given us the steam engine and has shown us how to make our smelting furnaces more efficient. Chemistry is vital to the work of the bleachers and dyers. Biology is intricately connected with the production of food. And the "Science of Society"[13] helps us to understand money markets, consider intelligently the chances of war, and improve mercantile operations. Science, in short, is the subject *par excellence* for maintaining the vital function of self preservation.

Other subjects needed to be examined in similar fashion, according to Spencer, in terms of their role in fulfilling the other vital purposes. The absence of attention in the curriculum to the proper raising of children needed to be corrected. Spencer imagined that a future antiquary surveying the curriculum of the mid-nineteenth century would have concluded that "This must have been the *curriculum* for their celibates."[14] The functions of the citizen must be addressed not by biographies of kings and queens but on what is necessary for the general welfare. As to poetry, that staple of the liberal arts curriculum, Spencer granted that taste may be improved through its study, but, he argued, "it is not to be inferred that such improvement of taste is equivalent in value to an acquaintance with the laws of health."[15] Those subjects that Spencer called "the efflorescence of civilization," the arts and *belles letters* for example, should be subordinated to the knowledge really vital to our civilization. Even appreciation of the arts requires such scientific understanding as the theory of equilibrium and how the effects of nature are produced. Referring to the fate of what we usually call the humanities, he recommended, *"As they occupy the leisure part of life, so should they occupy the leisure part of education."*[16] Science, in its various forms, became that subject that was associated with the real work of the world, whereas the humanities became associated with mere leisure.

Spencer concluded his revolutionary essay in dramatic and unequivocal terms:

> What knowledge is of most worth?—the uniform reply is—Science. This is the verdict on all the counts. For direct self preservation, or the maintenance of life and health, the all-important knowledge is—Science. For that indirect self preservation which we call gaining a livelihood, the knowledge of greatest value is—Science. For the due discharge of parental functions, the proper guidance is to be found only in—Science. For that interpretation of national life, past and present, without which the citizen cannot rightly regulate his conduct, the indispensable key is—Science. Alike for the most perfect production and highest enjoyment of art in all its forms, the needful preparation is still—Science. And for the purposes of discipline—intellectual, moral, religious—the most efficient study is, once more—Science.[17]

Spencer's, "What Knowledge Is of Most Worth?" turned the traditional conception of the liberal arts on its head. In the first place, the humanities, which had in the liberal arts curriculum been accorded the central place in the curriculum, were relegated in no uncertain terms to a distinctly inferior position to that of science. Secondly, both the sequence and the content of the curriculum could be determined scientifically rather than simply representing a judgment as to the most valuable resources of the culture. A "natural education" was one that followed the laws that governed the process. And finally, the purposes of the curriculum could no longer be described in such terms as "liberating the human spirit" or "initiation into the life of the mind" but in terms of the curriculum's contribution to the performance of specific and vital activities. In fact, the preservation of life itself became the supreme function of education. Education was seen as having a purpose beyond itself. In Spencerian terms, education could no longer be seen as an adornment, like the pigment on the Orinoco Indian, but as an instrument necessary for the performance of life-preserving functions like the clothes that shield us from the vicissitudes of weather. The apparent good sense of such a position must had an enormous appeal to the rising mercantile and manufacturing class.

The Prophet of Science

Spencer's contemporary, Thomas Henry Huxley, was a considerably more formidable public speaker and effective advocate of science than Spencer and an even greater celebrity in the upper echelons of the Victorian scientific community, but, as an educational reformer, he was far less revolutionary. In a significant sense, however, his interest in educational reform was more abiding and more profound than Spencer's. He was, after all, a working educator for a good part of his life and took a particular interest in the education of the working class. He had served as a Professor of Natural History at the Royal School of Mines, an examiner for the Government's Science and Art Department, a member of the School Board for London and chairman of its influential Scheme of Education Committee, and was the author of several widely praised textbooks in science.

Huxley's best-known expression of his educational ideals was contained in the inaugural address he delivered when he was made principal of the South London Workingman's College, an address he called, "A Liberal Education; and Where to Find It." As is implied in the title, Huxley took this occasion to redefine what was meant by a liberal education. Huxley reviewed briefly several of the extant justifications for providing a liberal education. For the politicians, educating the masses was essential because they would one day become masters; the clergy's hopes were built on the idea that education would halt the drift toward infidelity; the "manufacturers and the capitalists" claimed that "ignorance makes bad workmen" and that the market for English goods would suffer. Huxley rejected these positions in favor of the view that "the masses should be educated because they are men and women with unlimited capacities of being, doing, and suffering, and that it is as true now, as ever it was, that the people perish for lack of knowledge."[18] Huxley's emphasis on the intrinsic need to know as the justification for education as opposed to purposes that lie beyond education made his position consistent with the *ideal* of a liberal arts education, although his notion of what the components of that education would be departed significantly from the traditional one.

Huxley scorned the argument that education should be instrument to some larger good. If the masses in power without an education would be so disastrous, why is it, he asked, it that "such ignorance in the governing classes in the past has not been viewed with equal horror?"[19] As to the manufacturers' and the capitalists' position, he asked whether we really want the English educational system "diverted into a process of manufacturing human tools?"[20] Furthermore, Huxley went on, it was not simply the education of the masses that was a matter of concern. To him, it appeared that even the most exclusive of the English schools ought to be made to "supply knowledge" rather than simple performing their traditional function of inculcating "gentlemanly habits, a strong class feeling, and eminent proficiency in cricket."[21] The knowledge that Huxley sought to include in a modern curriculum, to be sure, included a strong dose of science, but one that was balanced by other factors:

> Education is the instruction of the intellect in the laws of Nature, under which name I include not merely things and their forces, but men and their ways; and the fashioning of affections and of the will into an earnest and loving desire to move in harmony with those laws. For me, education means neither more nor less than this.[22]

In Huxley's view, the main thrust of a liberal education could be found in the development of the intellect and not something that

lay beyond it, such as producing high quality workers, as many in
the rising middle class of the time were advocating. Huxley saw
the function of education as something much broader than "a process of manufacturing human tools, wonderfully adroit in the exercise of some technical industry, but good for nothing else."[23]

There is no question that Huxley was a passionate and, as it
turned out, effective advocate for the introduction of a much
stronger measure of science into the curriculum of his day. There
were even times when his passion on the subject led to exaggerated
claims for science and something close to a denigration of the traditional humanist curriculum. (Huxley's tendency toward hyperbole and embroidered rhetoric has even been the subject of some
study.[24]) Unlike Spencer, however, he was not claiming that one
study was actually more valuable than another. His position essentially was that, given the prominence and significance of science
in Western civilization, science was getting short shrift in the education of English youth. He was arguing for a redress of an imbalance that had existed in the liberal arts curriculum for some
time, not for a new set of criteria by which the worth of subjects
would be determined. Opposition to the introduction of the sciences into the standard curriculum of Victorian England, in Huxley's view, was not only opposed by business interests but by the
"Levites in charge of the ark of culture and monopolists of liberal
education" who essentially ignored the significance of science in
the modern world and its potential role in the liberal education of
youth.[25] But in his eagerness to define a major role for natural
sciences in the curriculum, Huxley was not ready to assert unequivocally its superiority to the traditional humanities nor any of
the other subjects as did Spencer.

Some indication of Huxley's basic moderation on the issue of
redefining the general education of his time may be illustrated
through his skirmish with his friend, Matthew Arnold, on educational policy. Arnold, of course, was one of the great defenders
of high culture in Victorian society, and as one of Her Majesty's
Inspectors of Schools was powerfully situated to influence the curriculum. His leadership in the defense of the traditional liberal arts
against the onslaught of crass materialism in education was widely
recognized. In his *Culture and Anarchy*, Arnold had sought to answer the question of what use is culture by arguing that real culture in its highest form not only "reminds us that the perfection
of human nature is sweetness and light," but serves to infuse in
us "the passion to make them prevail."[26] Rejecting the idea that

culture must be adapted to the condition of the masses in order for them to appreciate it, Arnold argued passionately for what he called the "social idea" of culture. Culture, he said,

> . . . does not try to teach down to inferior classes; it does not try to win them for this or that sect of its own, with ready-made judgments and watchwords. It seeks to do away with classes; to make the best that has been thought and known in the world current everywhere; to make all men live in an atmosphere of sweetness and light, where they may use ideas, as it uses them itself, freely—nourished and not bound by them."[27]

It was in this sense that the upholders of true culture were "the true apostles of equality."[28]

In his "Science and Culture," Huxley really did not take issue with Arnold's well-known definition of culture as "the best that has been thought and said in the world." Culture, Huxley agreed, was something quite different from simply learning or a technical skill. But he took issue with the implication that culture is to be equated with the works of classical antiquity along with a smattering of the modern classics. "The Humanists," he argued, "take their stand upon classical education as the sole avenue of culture" despite the fact that, even in the Renaissance, that period commonly referred to as the "Revival of Letters" was also a revival of science and learning generally.[29] Insofar as the ancients were concerned, Huxley went on,

> . . . we cannot know all the best thoughts and sayings of the Greeks unless we know what they though about natural phenomena. We cannot fully apprehend their criticism of life unless we understand the extent to which that criticism was affected by scientific conceptions.[30]

Although he remained a passionate advocate of the sciences and was even wont to exaggerate the merits of his case on occasion, Huxley's chief concern was that the monopoly on culture that had been traditionally exercised by the Humanists had given us a truncated version of true culture as the basis of a liberal education.

Arnold ultimately did find it necessary to reply to Huxley's attack on traditional Humanism as the basis for the liberal arts curriculum, but his argument indicated a broader area of agreement on the nature of culture than disagreement. He objected to Huxley's equation of Humanism as a fundamental belief with superficial knowledge of *belles lettres*, but he went on to emphasize that

"There is . . . really no question between Professor Huxley and me as to whether knowing the great results of modern scientific study of nature is not required as a part of our culture, as well as knowing the products of literature and art."[31] Rather, Arnold parted company with the reformers of the liberal arts when they proposed "to make the training in natural science the main part of education for the great majority of mankind."[32] The appeal to experience which the humane letters provided was for Arnold a far more universal appeal than the desire to understand how the universe worked. Implicitly rejecting the approach that Spencer took in "What Knowledge Is of Most Worth?," he proposed instead: "Let us . . ., all of us, avoid indeed as much as possible any invidious comparison between the merits of humane letters, as a means of education, and the merits of the natural sciences."[33] Arnold's commitment to humanistic studies, however, eventually came through. He recalled from one of his own school reports that a young man in an English training college paraphrased the line in *Macbeth*, "Can't thou not minister to a mind diseased?" as "Can you not wait upon the lunatic?" Arnold confessed in the end that he would rather have someone ignorant about the moon's diameter than unable to provide a better rendering of Shakespeare's line than that one.[34]

The Curriculum Debate in America

Both Spencer's radical challenge to the way the curriculum was traditionally structured and Huxley's advocacy of a balance in the liberal arts between science and humanities as comprising Western culture found their advocates in the American context. Both men, after all, had made triumphant tours of the United States. But the political and social climate of the times led Spencer's position to take root and flourish in late nineteenth-century America and to become a burgeoning movement in the twentieth century, strongly influencing the course that the curriculum would take. Of enormous appeal to many Americans was Spencer's application of such biological principles as "survival of the fittest" to the conduct of social as well as economic affairs. With such ardent and influential disciples as John Fiske and Edward Livingston Youmans (the founder of *Popular Science Monthly*), Spencer soon became, in Richard Hofstadter's characterization, "the metaphysician of the homemade intellectual, and the prophet of the cracker-barrel agnostic."[35] The idea of a laissez-faire society that was somehow self-regulating made social legislation and economic regulation not only unnecessary but positively dangerous as an unwarranted intrusion on natural law and therefore an impediment to true progress. The law of the jungle became an accepted way of perceiving and justifying inequality in terms of wealth and differentiated social functions.

Through the work of such intellectual leaders as William Graham Sumner, one of the founders of American sociology and a professor of political and social science at Yale University, Spencer's Social Darwinism achieved wide popularity. Like Spencer, Sumner saw not only the jungle but society generally as governed by the laws of survival. He argued, for example, that the struggle of various interest groups for their share of the fruits of industry should be left "to free contract under the play of natural laws" and that interference would result only in the diminution of the spoils that were left to be divided.[36] The choice, in Sumner's terms, was between "free social forces" on the one hand and "legislative and administrative interference" on the other.[37] In general, societal functions such as the concentration of wealth, according to Sumner, should be seen as the product of evolutionary forces. "The concentration of wealth," he said, "is but one feature of a grand step in societal evolution."[38] In an early version of "trickle down" economics, Sumner argued that "No man can acquire a million without helping a million men to increase their little fortunes all the way down through all the social grades."[39] Millionaires are merely the "naturally selected agents of society for certain work" and should be seen as the product of natural selection in the same way that Darwin saw the evolution of the species.[40]

With Spencer's ideas enjoying such significant acceptance in the social and political spheres, it should not be surprising that his conception of what knowledge is of most worth should begin to gain popularity with respect to the American curriculum. Basically, Spencer's conception of a worthwhile curriculum is reflected in three directions that the American curriculum began to take in the latter part of the nineteenth century: First, there was the elevation of the natural sciences to a more prominent role in programs of general education (although that tendency in itself could easily have reflected Huxley's more moderate as well as Spencer's more radical conception of how a curriculum should be constructed). Secondly, there was the notion that the curriculum was not merely to be a selection of the finest elements of the culture as Arnold or even Huxley would have seen it, but as a reflection of natural laws governing both the course of human history and the development of the individual. And finally, there was the Spencerian conception of the curriculum as instrumental to some purpose beyond itself. In Spencer's case, that purpose was first and foremost self-preservation, and this made the development of those functions that would achieve that purpose, rather than those elements that would merely add to the stock of high culture, the most desirable as elements in a program of general education.

The new prominence that the natural sciences would enjoy was at least symbolically represented by the elevation of Charles William Eliot, a chemist and an admirer of Spencer's, to the presidency of Harvard University in 1869. Although some contemporary interpretations of Eliot's work tend to depict him as a stodgy conservative who used the Committee of Ten report[41] to impose college domination on the high school curriculum, he was in his own time regarded as a radical innovator and representative of the "new education." Eliot was not simply interested in including a measure of science in the American curriculum. He argued in general for the doctrine of the equivalence of school subjects (a position that was incorporated into the Committee of Ten report). This meant that other subjects would have equal status with the time-honored triumvirate of the classical curriculum, Latin, Greek, and mathematics.

First and foremost, Eliot sought that status for English language and literature, which had at best only a subordinate place in American schools and colleges in the late nineteenth century.[42] Secondly, he tried to achieve "academic equality" for French and German, arguing that there is no reason for modern languages to be slighted in favor of the classical ones.[43] Thirdly, Eliot saw a larger place for the study of history and the social sciences in the form of political economy (or, as it was sometimes called, public economics).[44] And finally, Eliot sought the inclusion of the natural sciences in what he called "the magic circle of the liberal arts."[45] To some extent, as in the case of modern foreign languages, Eliot's arguments were somewhat utilitarian in character, but, for the most part, he framed his justification for the inclusion of new subjects into the liberal arts curriculum on the doctrine of mental discipline, which had in the nineteenth century formed an association, albeit an unnecessary one, with the liberal arts. Eliot argued, for example, that the student of the natural sciences "exercises his powers of observation and judgment [and] acquires the precious habit of observing appearances, transformations and processes of nature."[46] Despite his unfortunate attachment to mental discipline, however, Eliot's overall position can be seen mainly as an effort to open up the concept of the liberal arts to a new array of significant elements of the culture, including science.

The success of the effort to redefine the liberal arts is difficult to gauge in terms of school practice. During the period between 1871 and 1875, the Bureau of Education collected figures only on the three types of general curricula then in vogue—English, classical, and modern languages. The English curriculum actually was the most popular, with enrollments roughly double that of the other two, but curriculum data on individual subjects are incomplete, since only Latin, Greek, French, German, and English were tabulated in the period between 1876 and 1885–86. It was not until 1887–88 that data became available, although on a sporadic basis, for mathematics, physics, chemistry, and other sciences.[47] Although the data are incomplete, they indicate a rather spotty performance on the part of the natural sciences, beginning with the 1890 Bureau of Education report. In 1890, for example, physics as a percentage of total enrollments in grades 9–12 were reported as 22.8, with a drop to 19.0 in 1900 and a further drop in 1910 to 14.6. By 1949 (the height of the life adjustment era), the percentage of physics enrollments had declined sharply to 5.4, and that figure included not only advanced physics, but applied physics, fundamentals of electricity, radio and electronics, and fundamentals of machines. Although the initial reported percentages in such subjects as chemistry, geology, astronomy, and earth science were not nearly as high to begin with, they experienced similar declines in percentages of high school enrollments. The first percentage figure reported for physical geography in 1900 was 23.4, but by 1934 this had dropped to a minuscule 1.6.

Reconstruction of the liberal arts through the inclusion of the so-called "moderns" into the American school curriculum, as advocated by reformers such as Eliot, apparently met with marked success in one sense, but only restricted success in another. Indeed, the sciences, for example, began to enjoy roughly equal status with the classical subjects, with about 54 percent of secondary school students enrolled in any science course by the 1948–49 academic year. It is noteworthy, however, that that figure is somewhat below the 59 percent registered by the combination of business courses in the same year. (Of some significance also is the fact that in 1949, 72 percent of the total science enrollments were in general science and biology.) Likewise, modern foreign languages not only began to enjoy academic respectability, but eventually surpassed the classical languages in terms of enrollments. That success is tempered, however, by the fact that only 22 percent of students were enrolled in any kind of foreign language study in 1949.[48]

This means, of course, that while the traditional liberal arts curriculum had indeed undergone something of a transformation during the first part of the twentieth century, the "modernized" form of the liberal arts was reaching only a select segment of the school population. If anything, that tendency toward curriculum differentiation, by design or default, has become accelerated in the 1980s, with the "shopping mall" becoming the most pervasive model of high school studies.[49] In effect, there is no program of general education in the United States (defined as liberal arts or anything else); there is only a potpourri of hundreds of subjects from which students make sometimes considered and sometimes haphazard choices as to what subjects they will "buy." The laissez-faire doctrine advocated by Spencer and later Sumner in social and economic relationships has somehow taken a firm hold in the curriculum of American schools.

Spencer's other vision of a curriculum governed by scientific principles also met with mixed success. Clearly, the early leader in the American drive to create a program of studies governed by natural law was G. Stanley Hall. After a period of intellectual struggle, Hall ultimately rejected the philosophical idealism of Kant and Hegel in favor of the naturalism of Spencer. Like Spencer, he sought to extend evolutionary theory to mental life, even aspiring to become the "Darwin of the mind." As the acknowledged leader of the child-study movement in the late nineteenth century and founder of such influential journals as the *American Journal of Psychology* and *Pedagogical Seminary*, Hall attracted thousands of followers to his idea of an educational system controlled by scientific principles. Insofar as the curriculum was concerned, Hall, like Spencer, subscribed to the position that individuals recapitulate in their development the historical stages through which the human race had passed, and this principle guided many of his pronouncements as to how the course of study should be reformed. "The principle that the child and the early history of the human race are each keys to unlock the nature of the other," he said, "applies to almost everything in feeling, will, and intellect. To understand either the child or the race we must constantly refer to the other."[50]

Based on his studies of the child in relation to the human race, Hall became basically suspicious of efforts to develop the intellect, particularly in the early years of schooling. Health became for him the all-controlling factor in directing educational policy, and he feared that early intellectual training might be detrimental to the health of children and even adolescents. Since natural laws were to govern the education of children, Hall felt that the safest course was to "strive first of all to keep out of nature's way."[51] As such, education according to nature began to take on an almost anti-intellectual character. More particularly, the development of the intellect began to lose its traditionally central place in educational debates. If fully realized, that doctrine would have supplanted the idea that the curriculum should consist of the finest expressions of our culture (as, say, Arnold, expressed it so eloquently) with a curriculum allegedly derived from scientific laws. In time, the specific doctrine that the developmental stages through which the child passed somehow recapitulated historical epochs began to lose its credibility, but the more general idea that a science of education could redirect the purposes of education continued to have wide appeal, and thus served to undermine to some extent the central role that the traditional liberal arts assigned to freeing the intellect.

The Triumph of a Spencerian Alternative to Liberal Studies

Besides the predominant emphasis on science and the idea of a curriculum controlled by natural law, the third implication of Spencer's educational reform was that the curriculum could be finely tuned to the functions that needed to be performed in order to survive in the modern world. It was both revolutionary in its potential impact on the liberal arts ideal and substantially, although not altogether, realized as an alternative to the liberal arts as the foundation of general education. Like the other two reforms, this one was linked to science, at least in the sense that it was alleged to be consistent with Darwinian theory applied first to society and by extension to education. Unlike the other two, however, its success was more visible and more enduring. Even though the victory of a curriculum reform proposing substitution of the efficient performance of social functions for the ideal of a curriculum that embodied the main intellectual resources of our culture was anything but complete, it nevertheless stands as the most potent enemy today of the liberal arts.

Although the reconstruction of the modern American curriculum along directly functional lines was one of the principal motivations of educational reform generally in the twentieth century, its significance can probably best be illustrated through the work of one of its major exponents, David Snedden. Born in a tiny cabin and educated in a one-room schoolhouse in late nineteenth century California, Snedden eventually completed a classical course at St. Vincent's College in Los Angeles, but as a young schoolteacher he undertook to study the complete works of Spencer in his spare time, an experience that led him to reject the standard curriculum of his time in favor of one that was directly tied to self-preservation.[52] To Snedden, this meant that a truly functional education could be derived scientifically from the analysis of human activity and its translation into a socially efficient curriculum that, in effect, repudiated completely the ornamental trappings of education that Spencer so much deplored. Later, as State Commissioner of Education in Massachusetts and a Professor of Educational Sociology at Teachers College, Columbia University, he was in a position to reach a large and predominantly receptive audience for his ideas.

Although Snedden is sometimes identified particularly with vocational education, his influence was far more pervasive. In fact, he saw himself primarily as someone who was redefining general education in the twentieth century. Human functioning, according to Snedden, could be roughly classified into two major categories: production and consumption. Vocational education derived its legitimacy from its role in creating efficient producers, and liberal education would constitute that part of education that aims at making human beings effective consumers or users. "The liberally educated man," he said, "utilizes the products and services of many producers; but because of his education he uses them well, both in the individual and social sense."[53] Together, vocational education for the producer and liberal education for the consumer would create the fully functioning human being. In this sense, liberal education would be as functional and as vital to human survival as vocational education.

Within a few years, Snedden's protege, Clarence Darwin Kingsley, translated that conception of general education into the famous seven aims of the Cardinal Principles Report.[54] Consciously or unconsciously, those seven aims—health, command of fundamental processes, vocation, worthy use of leisure time, worthy home membership, citizenship, and ethical character—followed in rough outline Spencer's efforts more than half a century earlier to base the curriculum on categories of vital life activities (with the possible exception of the second of the aims). Kingsley stopped short, however, of actually recommending the abandonment of the traditional subjects; instead, his Commission recommended that subjects reorganize themselves so as to achieve at least one of those indispensable life functions. Those subjects, in other words, were no longer in the curriculum because they represented the major intellectual resources of our culture; they now became *instruments* by which future adults would acquire the skills to function efficiently in their daily lives. So far had the idea of a directly functional education progressed by 1918, when the Cardinal Principles Report was published, that its recommendations were considered by some educational reformers as unduly moderate. By that time, scientific curriculum makers such as Franklin Bobbitt and W. W. Charters, as well as Snedden, were calling for the substitution of functional categories for the subjects themselves. Snedden, in fact, declared Kingsley's report to be "almost hopelessly academic."[55]

The concept of general education was being massively redefined by American educational leaders in the first quarter of the twentieth century. All education was specific and was directed toward specific purposes. Even vocational education had very limited generality. Snedden declared in 1924, for example, that

> two . . . delusions yet persist in much of our unanalyzed educational theory. One is that somehow there can be some general education that is valuable for any and all vocations. The other, a much more modern one, is that vocations or even a vocation can be so taught as to produce large amounts of culture or of civilism.[56]

Even in the realm of vocational education, Snedden argued, we make the mistake of trying to prepare general farmers instead of poultry producers. He was critical, for example, of John Dewey's failure to articulate a program of vocational education suited to modern social needs. "The modern world," he said, "divides and again subdivides its vocations," and a modern educational system will reflect that great specificity. The same could be said of civic education, cultural education, moral education and "educations in the uses of foreign languages." Each requires its own specific form of preparation. "Only educational mystics or obscurantists or, shall we say, 'fools' can say other otherwise," Snedden insisted.[57] Not only are there thousands of different kinds of education, but "every distinguishable species of education and, of each species, each distinguishable degree is or should be designed 'to meet a need' " with each need to be met being controlled by "foreseen ends."[58]

As if such specificity were not enough, Snedden argued further that each education had to be designed particularly to fit the characteristics of the person to be educated (what he liked to call the "educand"). A truly scientific education could not be designed until the curriculum was adapted to the traits of those who would be educated, particularly to the social functions that they would one day perform as adults. Since people perform different functions according to such attributes as gender, class, and occupation, the skills to perform those functions had to be anticipated and ultimately incorporated into a supremely differentiated curriculum. Under these conditions, the idea of a general education was, practically speaking, a self-contradiction.

To be sure, Snedden's vision of a minutely differentiated curriculum was never completely realized, but the general idea of different educations for different population groups, variously defined, has taken firm root in modern American education.[59] Moreover, the idea persists that education should be designed with very specific purposes in mind (hence the continued emphasis on stating educational objectives in highly specific terms.) It is clear that, despite the call to create a common curriculum by such influential groups as the Carnegie Foundation,[60] diversity and particularity reign supreme in terms of school practice. It would be an obvious oversimplification to say that Snedden's curriculum ideology merely prevailed over the idea that an education should be common to all regardless of future destination. It is more likely that an educational ideology controlled by specific but differentiated social and individual purposes was more congenial to an industrial society itself highly specialized and differentiated. Snedden was probably merely articulating (albeit in extreme form) basic twentieth-century values. And one should not overlook the very real obstacles that school officials would face in declaring one form of education to be suitable for all, a policy that would fly in the face of such sacred American values as autonomy and choice.

Conclusion

The idea of a liberal education in American schools is alive, but barely. The incorporation of science and other "moderns" into a conception of the liberal arts, in itself, was not sufficient to maintain its place in general education. In the first place, even the "new" liberal arts competed rather unsuccessfully with a curriculum directly tied to the real business of life. The liberal arts maintained its status as fit for a social elite who had the leisure to pursue it, whereas a general education tied to efficient performance of life's tasks predominated for the many. The ancient dichotomy between labor and leisure, with its implications for strong class divisions, was thus maintained. Secondly, the internal reconstruction of the elements of a liberal education proceeded only haphazardly. For liberal education to be successful in an era of mass public education, not simply the addition or substitution of subjects, but a massive reconstruction of what we mean by the arts, literature, history, political economy, and even science had to be accomplished. What had to be created was a path which the masses could also follow to the kind of intellectual liberation that modern advocates such as Arnold and Huxley foresaw.

In place of such a reconstruction, educational leaders such as Snedden advocated a differentiated curriculum designed to fit people specifically for the tasks they needed to perform, and specificity is the great enemy of a liberal education. As Charles Bailey recently expressed it, "The first justification for engaging people in liberal general education . . . is that its very rejection of *specific* utility, and its espousal of intrinsically worthwhile ends, provides the maximum and most general utility. . . ."[61] In rejecting specificity, then, the liberal arts does not reject utility; it seeks a broader and grander utility than is represented by the specific and the immediate. It is a utility that lies, broadly speaking, in the development of rationality and the freedom that rationality provides to discover *why* I should believe and act as I do. Moreover, the espousal of intrinsically worthwhile ends should not be equated with education that has no purpose. Ends that are intrinsic to knowing literature, history, and science are ends that can reasonably associated with their study. They are not external to them. Spencer's convictions to the contrary, knowing Newton's second law of thermodynamics is no more necessary for self-preservation than a knowledge of Homer's *Iliad*. Science is a vital element in a liberal education, not because we as individuals survive through our knowledge of it, but because it is an extension of our need to know about the natural world. It is on principles such as these that a modern conception of the liberal arts may be rebuilt.

Notes

1. See, for example, Ayers Bagley, *Study and Love: Aristotle's Fall* (Minneapolis: Society of Professors of Education, 1986).

2. Herbert Spencer, "On the Genesis of Science" in *Essays on Education* (New York: E. P. Dutton & Co., Inc, 1910), p. 296.

3. Herbert Spencer, *Education: Intellectual, Moral and Physical* (New York: D. Appleton and Company, 1860), p. 117.

4. Ibid., pp. 1–2.

5. Ibid., p. 4.

6. Ibid., p. 11.

7. Ibid., pp. 13–14.

8. Ibid., p. 15.

9. Ibid., pp. 19–20.

10. Ibid., p. 22.

11. Ibid., p. 23.

12. Ibid., p. 25.

13. Ibid., p. 36.

14. Ibid., p. 40.

15. Ibid., p. 62.

16. Ibid., p. 63.

17. Ibid., pp. 84–85.

18. Thomas Henry Huxley, "A Liberal Education; and Where to Find It," in *Science and Education: Essays* (New York: D. Appleton and Company, 1896), p. 77.

19. Ibid., p. 78.

20. Ibid., p. 70.

21. Ibid.

22. Ibid., p. 83.

23. Ibid., p. 79.

24. See, for example, Charles S. Blinderman, "Semantic Aspects of T. H. Huxley's Literary Style," *Journal of Communication* 12 (September 1962) pp. 171–178; Walter E. Houghton, "The Rhetoric of T. H. Huxley," *University of Toronto Quarterly* 18 (January 1949) pp. 159–175.

25. Thomas Henry Huxley, "Science and Culture," in *Science and Education* (New York: D. Appleton and Company, 1899), p. 137.

26. Matthew Arnold, *Culture and Anarchy*, (Cambridge: Cambridge University Press, 1960 [1869]), p. 69.

27. Ibid., p. 70.

28. Ibid.

29. Ibid., p. 149.

30. Ibid., p. 152.

31. Matthew Arnold, "Literature and Science," in *Discourses in America* (London: Macmillan and Co., 1885), pp. 94–95.

32. Ibid., p. 99.

33. Ibid., p. 125.

34. Ibid., p. 127.

35. Richard Hofstadter, *Social Darwinism in American Thought* (Boston: Beacon Press, 1944, 1955), p. 32.

36. William Graham Sumner, "State Interference," in *Social Darwinism*, ed. Stow Persons (Englewood Cliffs, NJ: Prentice-Hall, 1963), pp. 105–106.

37. Ibid., p. 109.

38. William Graham Sumner, "The Concentration of Wealth: Its Economic Justification," in *Social Darwinism*, ed. Stow Persons (Englewood Cliffs, NJ: Prentice-Hall, 1963), p. 151.

39. Ibid., p. 156.

40. Ibid., p. 157.

41. National Education Association, *Report of the Committee on Secondary School Studies* (Washington, DC: Government Printing Office, 1893).

42. Charles William Eliot, "What Is a Liberal Education?" in *Educational Reform* (New York: The Century Company, 1898), pp. 97–101.

43. Ibid., pp. 101–104.

44. Ibid., pp. 104–109.

45. Ibid., p. 110.

46. Ibid.

47. John Francis Latimer, *What's Happened to Our High Schools?* (Washington, DC: Public Affairs Press, 1958), pp. 12–15.

48. Ibid., pp. 21–57.

49. Arthur G. Powell, Eleanor Farrar and David K. Cohen, *The Shopping Mall High School: Winners and Losers in the Educational Marketplace* (Boston: Houghton Mifflin, 1985).

50. G. Stanley Hall, "The Natural Activities of Children as Determining the Industries in Early Education, II," National Education Association, *Journal of Proceedings and Addresses* (1904), p. 443.

51. G. Stanley Hall, "The Ideal School as Based on Child Study," National Education Association, *Journal of Proceedings and Addresses* (1901), p. 475.

52. Walter H. Drost, *David Snedden and Education for Social Efficiency* (Madison, WI: University of Wisconsin Press, 1967), p. 5.

53. David Snedden, "The Practical Arts in Liberal Education," *Educational Review* 43 (April 1912), p. 379.

54. National Education Association, *Cardinal Principles of Secondary Education: A Report of the Commission on the Reorganization of Secondary Education* (Washington, DC: Government Printing Office, 1918).

55. David Snedden, "Cardinal Principles of Secondary Education," *School and Society* 9 (May 3, 1919), p. 522.

56. David Snedden, "The Relation of General to Vocational Education," National Education Association *Journal of Addresses and Proceedings*, 62 (1924), pp. 1003–1004.

57. David Snedden, "Progress Towards Sociologically Based Civic Education," *Journal of Educational Sociology* 3 (April 1930), p. 493.

58. Ibid., pp. 485–486.

59. See, for example, Jeannie Oakes, *Keeping Track: How Secondary Schools Structure Inequality* (New Haven: Yale University Press, 1985).

60. See, for example, Ernest Boyer, *High School* (New York: Harper & Row, 1983).

61. Charles Bailey, *Beyond the Present and Particular: A Theory of Liberal Education* (London: Routledge & Kegan Paul, 1984), p. 35.

3

Keeping Out of Nature's Way:
The Rise and Fall of Child-Study as the
Basis for the Curriculum, 1880–1905

Even as enthusiasm for the child-study movement was beginning to wane, G. Stanley Hall aggressively reiterated what to him was the central principle of child-study: "The guardians of the young should strive first of all to keep out of nature's way. . . ."[1] Proponents of that principle proudly traced its ancestry as far back as Comenius, most prominently to Rousseau, and then to the work of Pestalozzi and Froebel. These ancestors of the child-study movement in America, to be sure, had done much to redirect interest to the child as the center of the pedagogical process and to mitigate the excesses of drill and regimentation. Some of the force of those earlier reforms was also derived from their association with science, but events in the latter part of the nineteenth century gave science new significance as a basis for deciding what to teach. The intellectual revolution that had been most visibly manifested by the publication of Darwin's *Origin of the Species* in 1859 was moving out of its immediate arena of controversy, the alleged conflict between science and widely held religious beliefs, and becoming a potent force in human affairs. Particularly in the last two decades of the nineteenth century, science was beginning to transcend the arena of the natural world in a very visible way.

In the industrial world, for example, Frederick Winslow Taylor initiated his campaign in what later came to be known as scientific management with a paper delivered in the mid-1880s.[2] In the same period, William Graham Sumner at Yale University was also beginning to extrapolate some of Darwin's ideas on natural selection into laws of society. Scientific management and Social Darwinism, both buttressed by the potency of science, were profoundly conservative in social terms. As Taylor developed the concept of scientific management, for example, science became a force through which industry could extract a much larger output in terms of production by efficiently controlling the behavior of laborers. Through science, management could also overcome conflict between management and labor and resistance on the part of workers to some of the effects of the Industrial Revolution. At roughly the same time, Social Darwinism was evolving into a plausible rationale for the wide discrepancies in wealth and for governmental restraint in the regulation of big business. "Survival of the fittest," widely proclaimed as an immutable law of the jungle in terms of Darwinian evolution, was becoming a credible way of perceiving the workings of the social machinery, and included an explicit justification of social inequality. The use of science in the realm of human affairs was not always liberating in a social or political sense.

From a pedagogical perspective, however, a science of child development was a powerfully attractive one in at least two senses: first, it proposed to liberate education from its preoccupation with the written word, whether sacred or secular, that had dominated the curriculum at least since the days of Erasmus; secondly, it held out the promise that a new developmental psychology could provide the truly scientific basis for the curriculum that was so lacking in earlier forms of psychology. In the judgment of many founding leaders of the child-study movement, earlier attempts to apply psychology to educational practice were not only scientifically invalid but infused with vaguely speculative and hence fatally flawed philosophical ideas. In fact, under Hall's leadership, child-study developed a barely concealed antagonism toward philosophy and theory which may in the end have contributed to its collapse as a coherent movement.

To be sure, there were portents of a child-study movement in America well before Hall appeared on the scene. It was not until Hall returned from a period of study in Germany early in 1880, however, that the incipient child-study movement found a knight-errant who was able to carry its banner. After suffering some initial disappointment in being unable to secure a regular academic position, Hall was offered a temporary lectureship in pedagogy at Harvard University later in that year. Favorable publicity regarding the success of Colonel Francis Parker's experimental curriculum in nearby Quincy, Massachusetts made Hall's arrival on the scene especially propitious. Parker, whose studies in Europe had included the works of both Froebel and Pestalozzi, had broken with the traditional formalism that had characterized American public schooling and successfully advanced the ideas of the European Romantic educators in the Quincy schools.[3] But Parker's innovations, while favorably received, remained largely unarticulated, and Hall's series of lectures delivered in Boston in 1881 gave voice and scientific respectability to the Quincy reforms. Hall's lectures, in fact, were such a resounding success that he was reappointed in the two succeeding years and then invited to The Johns Hopkins University for a similar lectureship. The theme of the authority of science in pedagogical matters that Hall had sounded in his lectures had obviously struck a responsive chord with a significant segment of American educators.

The Saturday series of lectures at Harvard not only launched Hall on a highly successful academic career, culminating in his appointment as president of Clark University in 1888, but cast him in the role of leading spokesperson and publicist for the burgeoning child-study movement. Indeed, there was some internal disagreement in the child-study movement (such as the methodological dispute between the advocates of the "anthropological" study of children in natural settings as advocated by Hall, and the study of children under laboratory conditions favored by Joseph Jastrow and E. P. Scripture), but the main outlines of the doctrine that emerged from the movement are evident even in Hall's early work. The implications he drew from it, as to how child-study could become the instrument through which a curriculum appropriate to the natural development of children could be fashioned, became widely heralded, and in those precepts lay both the seeds of child-study's widespread appeal as well as, ultimately, the sources of its rejection. The quarter-century or so beginning with his arrival from Germany encompassed both the rise and fall of the child-study movement in America, although half-conscious relics of it reappear from time to time, and contemporary critics of American education sometimes treat Hall's version of developmental psychology as a continuing and potent force in American education.

Basic Tenets of Child-Study

Hall's first major article, published in 1883, exhibited many of the methodological and substantive assumptions that lay behind Hall's drive to build a curriculum around natural laws. Hall took his cue for his investigation of the content of children's minds from a study done at the Pedagogical Society of Berlin in 1869.[4] That earlier study, sometimes facetiously referred to as an "entrance examination" to primary school, was designed to see how children entering school from different sections of the city differed with respect to their knowledge of such things as street names, Grimm's tales, and hymns or prayers. Hall was obviously intrigued by the idea of discovering what children actually knew upon entering school but was skeptical of some of the techniques used in the Berlin study. In the main, the children were questioned in fairly large groups, and given children's tendency to imitate one another, Hall felt that the results were questionable. He was also suspicious about the extent to which the questioners may have been "brusque, lacking in sympathy or tact, or real interest or patience in the work . . . "[5] Nevertheless, the general precept—that the construction of a curriculum for children just starting their schooling should begin with an explicit awareness of the knowledge they already possessed—was an especially appealing one to Hall.

For his own study of the contents of the minds of Boston children, Hall obtained the services of "four of the best trained and experienced kindergarten teachers,"[6] and only three children were questioned at a time. Later about sixty other teachers were recruited. Schools where children were deemed to have come from either too cultured or too ignorant households were excluded, apparently in an effort to tap a typical population. Although the study was presented as merely providing a catalog of what children knew, the choice of questions to ask the sample of Boston schoolchildren is one indication of what knowledge Hall believed to be most valuable. It is evident that Hall's own preferences as to what knowledge ought to exist in children's minds leaned strongly to the bucolic. "As our methods of teaching grow natural," he declared, "we realize that city life is unnatural, and that those who grow up without knowing the country are defrauded of that without which childhood can never be complete or normal."[7] Thus, it was of considerable concern to him that some kindergarten children had said that cows go bow-wow, that pigs purr, and that butter comes from buttercups. To Hall, this was an indication that the city was simply a bad place for children pedagogically and psychologically. The child of the country, having more solitude, was more likely to develop independence, while the child of the city was more likely to become "prematurely caught up into the absorbing activities and throbbing passions of manhood. . . ."[8] Just as unnatural city life was believed to have a pernicious effect on young children, so the contrived and artificial aspects of schooling as it was conventionally practiced became the source of definite harm. According to

Hall, the remedy was to discover the natural inclinations of children through scientific data gathering.

Although Hall conspicuously and self-consciously carried the banner of science throughout his career, the romantic, even mystical, side to his ideas and by extension to the child-study movement generally were evident even in his initial foray into experimental child-study after his return from Germany. First, there is an unconscious or even a deliberate conflating of at least two meanings of natural. The idea of an education according to nature derived much of its potency from its scientific connotations. Natural laws were scientific laws. Instead of teaching simply what came to mind, education according to the immutable laws of nature would provide a valid basis for the course of study; but education according to nature also referred to country life and the virtues of growing up in rustic settings. Civilization as represented by urban living in particular was antagonistic to an idealized rustic upbringing. Reflecting its roots in European Romanticism, child-study embodied the idea that 'nature' had at one and the same time scientific and pastoral connotations, and the ambiguity in the term contributed to its appeal. Science represented power and certainty; urbanization was regarded with suspicion and distrust by many Americans.

Secondly, beneath Hall's reverence for life in the country lay an almost mystical concern for health. One side of this concern was reflected in the idea that cities were unwholesome places. The other was that schools themselves were potentially dangerous to children's health. Hall warned parents, for example, to send their children "to good and hygienic as distinct from most fashionable kindergartens,"[9] and there are even suggestions here and there that premature book-learning, what Hall liked to refer to as "word cram," was detrimental to the child's physical and mental well-being. In fact, because of Hall's preoccupation with health, there emerged almost an antipathy toward the cultivation of the intellect in young children. Insofar as young children were concerned, there seemed to exist in Hall's mind a positive antagonism between school and physical vitality.

Finally, as also exhibited in "Contents of Children's Minds," Hall believed fervently that "the mind can learn only what is related to other things learned before. . .,"[10] a belief closely related to the Herbartian concept of apperception. Hence, child-study derived much of its credibility from claiming that what the child already knew could become the basis for determining what to teach, but apart from the commonsensical notion that teachers should not make unwarranted assumptions as to what children of a given age actually know, it was never exactly clear how a curriculum would emerge from strictly scientific evidence on what knowledge children actually possessed or what their natural propensities were.

Nevertheless, Hall's continued enthusiasm for and optimism about the practical results emanating from massive collection of data on child life was evident in much of his early work as well as in his later career. It also extended beyond the confines of early childhood. In 1885, for example, Hall published an inventory of the collecting habits of Boston's fifteen- and sixteen-year-old boys. What emerged from this study was another inventory and the conclusion that boys possessed a collecting "instinct" that amounted to a "universal force."[11] Naturally, schools were encouraged to capitalize on this universal instinct, in this case by encouraging collections in such areas as science, and in creating scrapbook collections of favorite stories. In terms of improving school practice, however, the almost indiscriminate amassing of data once again yielded little more than prosaic, even trivial, recommendations for teachers.

An Organizational Structure for Child-Study

Hall's agenda for the child-study movement wavered between two overweening ambitions. One was nothing less than to create an exacting science of human nature. Hall, for example, confessed in his autobiography to aspiring to the title of "Darwin of the mind."[12] If the evolution of the human spirit could once and for all be exposed, then perhaps even the ultimate purpose of life could be revealed. Secondly, he dreamed of revolutionizing the practice of schooling by firmly rooting school practice in science rather than in speculation and tradition. These two ambitions were obviously interrelated. In Hall's mind, a fully realized psychology would become the unfailing handbook for teaching practice. In his magnum opus, *Adolescence*, for example, Hall referred to psychology as nothing less than "the teacher's Blackstone."[13] As critics would eventually point out, both these ambitions, as Hall embodied them, were not only fundamentally flawed but almost certainly incompatible.

Some of that criticism emerged as Hall tried to position himself in the absolute forefront of child-study. Hall played a leading role not only in articulating the basic tenets of what a scientific study of the child would consist of and how this could be applied to educational practice; he also sought to place himself in the vanguard of the organizational structure that would support those ideas. Among his major achievements in that regard was the founding of the *American Journal of Psychology* with himself, of course, as editor. Hall's major purpose in founding the journal was to promote the advancement of psychology as a true science, but all did not proceed according to plan. In the very first issue in October of 1887, Hall's desire to put his personal imprint on psychology in America set eccentric limits on the journal's scope, which led to dissention and even some rancor within the ranks of prestigious psychologists of the time. For one thing, virtually all of the articles in the inaugural issue were either by Hall's students or others closely associated with him. Hall himself undertook most of the book reviews, and in them he was especially critical of anything that smacked of philosophy rather than psychology as Hall conceived it.[14] Even John Dewey's *Psychology*, which was somewhat more favorably treated than other books in Hall's review, was criticized for its Hegelian overtones. Dewey's preoccupation with Hegelianism (and, by extension, philosophy), in Hall's view, was simply "a stage of development which minds that come to full scientific maturity are certain to transcend."[15]

Perhaps even more inflammatory to some of the major figures in the world of psychology of the time was Hall's "Editorial Note," designed to initiate a new series. The *Journal*, Hall declared, would be restricted entirely to "psychological work of a scientific, as distinct from a speculative character."[16] This meant that even psychologists whose primary orientation was toward experimental research would be excluded from publishing their theoretical reflections on that work in Hall's new journal. Like other emerging disciplines in the late nineteenth and early twentieth century, psychology in Hall's hands was assertively seeking to delineate itself. As the semi-official organ of the new science, the *American Journal of Psychology*, through its editorial policy, was being launched on a distinctive note of scientism. In a sense, though, Hall was overplaying his own scientific credentials as well as those of the budding discipline. His extravagant claims as to the promise of a purely scientific psychology as well as a pedagogy governed by those scientific principles were becoming evident to a growing number of eminent psychologists.

One of Hall's efforts at self-promotion in particular offended some of the leading psychologists of the day and made Hall's sometimes exalted claims for his own leadership open to widespread criticism. In October of 1895, Hall's editorial in the *American Journal of Psychology* was devoted to extolling its influence in the psychological world. Hall was anything but modest about his own contributions to the success of the *Journal*. "For years," he said, "the struggle for existence was severe, and the editor himself did a good part of the review and other unsigned work, and made good the large annual deficit from his own pocket."[17] More provocatively, he went on to claim that members of the Clark University faculty and its students, upon whom he depended for scholarly contributions to the *Journal*, then went on to found "departments of experimental psychology and laboratories at Harvard, Yale, Pennsylvania, Columbia, Toronto, Wisconsin and many other higher institutions of learning. . . ."[18] The impression was created that scientific psychology had been initiated at other prominent universities primarily through Hall's own students and colleagues at Clark.

Hall's editorial prompted a series of letters to the editor of *Science*. In the first, William James, obviously annoyed, said that he could not let Hall's "extraordinary statements" appear without objection.[19] James was unequivocal in stating that "I, myself, 'founded' the instruction in experimental psychology at Harvard in 1874–5, or 1876, I forget which."[20] Even more elaborately, George Trumbull Ladd took issue with another of Hall's claims: "Inasmuch as Yale University has an institutional interest in the truthfulness of this surprising claim, and inasmuch as I have reason to suppose that my influence and not President Hall's led to the founding of its laboratory, I wish publicly to contradict him."[21] There followed another letter by J. Mark Baldwin stating that "the Toronto Laboratory was founded by myself. . .,"[22] and James McKeen Cattell similarly disavowed Hall's influence at Columbia University, saying that he began the study of experimental psychology there "with the cooperation of Professor [Nicholas Murray] Butler."[23] Cattell even took issue with Hall's claim that no periodical other than the *American Journal of Psychology* served the function of publishing experimental studies in psychology. Obviously having taken the trouble actually to count articles, Cattell pointed out that *Psychological Review* had published 42 such articles while *American Journal of Psychology* had published only 27 over the previous two years. Hall seemed once again to be overreaching himself. His aggressive campaign for taking the reins of leadership in the drive to remake psychology into an experimentally based science had aroused spirited opposition from other prominent psychologists in decidedly personal terms.

Hall's other ambition, to make psychology a dependable handbook for guiding teaching practice, was made manifest in the founding in 1891 of another journal, *Pedagogical Seminary*, again with himself as editor. The reasons for his decision to return to education as a major focus in the 1890s were undoubtedly complex. Hall's reputation as an experimental psychologist was already beginning to fade, and it may be that he foresaw that his desire to transform psychology in his own terms was on the road to failure. On the other hand, the world of education was in turmoil in the 1890s. American Herbartians, disciples of the German philosopher Johann Friedrich Herbart, for example, were making a concerted and highly visible effort to overturn what they regarded as the old order in education, and the crusading journalist, Joseph Mayer Rice, had called national attention to widespread abuses in the educational systems in several large cities. While Hall took pains at times to distance himself from the Herbartians, many of his ideas were actually compatible with theirs. At the least, there was the common desire to focus directly on the child as the center of the educational process. It may be that the Herbartians represented to Hall rivals for the leadership of what were regarded as the progressive forces in American education. The fact that there seemed to be a changing of the guard taking place in the educational world of the 1890s presented an opportunity for Hall to make a decided imprint in the direction that education was to take over the course of the twentieth century. In many respects, however, that course was driven by Hall's own idiosyncracies rather than by scientific evidence.

An editorial written by Hall inaugurating the second volume of *Pedagogical Seminary* not only set forth one of Hall's favorite themes, health, as its keynote, but also illustrated Hall's penchant for incorporating his own deeply felt personal beliefs and preconceptions into what was purported to be scientifically-based practical advice.[24] He decried, for example, the inclination of some teachers to "seek a triumph"[25] by focusing on slow students, students Hall asserted belonged in a special school for "dullards."[26] He also expressed renewed concern on one of his favorite themes, the effect of women teachers on the wholesome development of boys. While he conceded that "women are natural trainers of young children and have certain advantages in their vocation," he felt that since they "lack the body of voice and the muscle of men" a certain robustness is lost insofar as the maturation of boys is concerned.[27] Although Hall pointed with pride to what he regarded as promising developments in the introduction of school gardens, school excursions and school baths, he also alluded to the fact that fatigue was the source of many forms of disease, and, therefore, schools need to give more attention to the length of the school day and academic year. Insofar as the curriculum was concerned, he demanded that each branch of study be "judged from the standpoint of health" and concluded with one of his favorite aphorisms, "what shall it profit a child if he gain the whole world of knowledge and lose his own health?"[28] Hall's conviction that schooling and health were fiercely antagonistic at times took on mythic overtones.

Child-Study in Decline

Mobilized by some of Hall's excesses in his claims not only for his own accomplishments but for child-study in general, a new generation of psychologists began to develop certain criticisms which contributed in a visible way to the decline of child-study as a coherent movement. The major themes of these criticisms went to the heart of Hall's most crucial ambitions for the movement. The first line of criticism was that child-study as it developed under Hall's leadership was not psychology at all; the second was that Hall had grossly misconceived the relationship between a science of psychology and pedagogical practice.

One of the earliest of the expressions of disapproval was voiced by John Dewey in 1897. In a short address to the National Education Association, entitled "Criticisms Wise and Otherwise on Modern Child-Study,"[29] Dewey alluded to problems associated with "exaggerations incident to all large movements" and found the claim for "a certain, positive and scientific basis for education" to be at least "premature."[30] Here Dewey seemed to be voicing his own reservations about the power of child-study to provide usable guidelines for teaching practice. Dewey also expressed his misgivings about child-study as a movement isolated from the disciplines with which it ought to be most closely allied, presumably psychology itself. In becoming "a thing by itself," child-study was removing itself from the self-correcting context in which scientific findings are usually imbedded. Compounding that problem was the fact that those ignorant of the parent disciplines are plunged unawaringly into child-study, undoubtedly an allusion to Hall's persistent use of untrained teachers and lay persons to collect data. "The method," he said bluntly, "is quackery, and the outcome confusion." Finally, Dewey, at least implicitly, attacked Hall's position (as embodied in the editorial policy of *The American Journal of Psychology*) that indiscriminate study of "facts" would somehow evolve into scientific findings. "The mere collection of facts uncontrolled by working hypotheses, unenlightened by generalization," Dewey argued, "never made a science and never will."[31] Mere inventories of the contents of children's minds or their collecting habits, in others words, added little or nothing to our understanding of the child or to the educational process. In voicing these criticisms, Dewey was challenging some of Hall's most cherished methods and beliefs.

A student of Wilhelm Wundt's, Hugo Münsterberg, whom William James brought to Harvard from Germany to lead the psychology program there, emerged in the 1890s as Hall's principal antagonist. Münsterberg was representative of a new breed of psychologist whose interest in psychology as a science seemed deliberately devoid of traces of romanticism, and this made him particularly contemptuous of the claims of child-study to scientific respectability. In his most concerted attack, Münsterberg maintained that what passed for child-study was not psychology at all.[32] He deplored the fact that some of his earlier attempts to condemn child-study had been interpreted as an attack on experimental psychology. To the contrary, Münsterberg proclaimed, he was trying to prepare the way for a true science of psychology unfettered by unsound and unscientific practices. "If I denounce a dangerous misuse of experimental psychology," he asked, "do I attack with that experimental psychology?."[33] He was particularly skeptical of the many statistical reports that had appeared in *Pedagogical Seminary* (many patterned after Hall's "Contents of Children's Minds"), such as a "splendid collection of teasing and bullying phrases" and that among 845 children "exactly 191 preferred wax dolls. . . ."[34] To Münsterberg, these were not psychological facts at all but merely a collection of curiosities about children. If we were to repeat that type of experiment with adult men, he asserted contemptuously, we would find, for example, how many prefer cigarette holders and meerschaum pipes. Münsterberg's point, of course, was that the vast bulk of what passed for scientific child-study consisted of minute collections of data uninformed by psychological theory. Hall had at times claimed that these accumulated data would eventually yield scientific findings through what he called the "Baconian" (inductive) method. Münsterberg pointed out, however, that the science of physics did not advance in this way and neither would psychology.

Münsterberg's second source of criticism was the child-study movement's use of untrained teachers as collectors of data. The teacher, Münsterberg felt, was being required to accomplish something without the necessary training, but more importantly, was being asked to adopt an attitude inimical to good teaching. The teacher, he asserted, is "hampered by this new way of looking on the children, not as friends but as interesting results of psychological laws."[35] "I detest this mingling of the teacher with psychology just because I do not wish to destroy in him the powers of sound and natural interest" he added later.[36] The attitude of the teacher and the attitude of the psychologist were fundamentally different, he felt, and their commingling was deleterious to good teaching. More importantly, Münsterberg launched into an extended examination of what he regarded as the three branches of psychology—child psychology, experimental psychology, and physiological psychology—and then asked of what use psychology is for the individual teacher. "My answer is simple and the same for all the three branches," he said, "I maintain they are not of the slightest use."[37]

Münsterberg's attacks on child-study as Hall had fashioned it could hardly have been more devastating. Moreover, Münsterberg was representative of an emerging conception of psychology that would become dominant in America for most of the twentieth century. Edward L. Thorndike, who was to become the most prominent educational psychologist of the twentieth century, voiced similar criticism is his very first book. In general, Thorndike was more optimistic than Münsterberg as to the ultimate value of psychology, including child-study, for classroom purposes, but he was critical of the students of child-study for their lack of precision in making assertions as to psychological truths. Instead of stating their findings as absolute truths, he contended, it would be far better to state them in terms of numerical probability or variation from the average. Because of the lack of scientific precision in statements emanating from the child study movement, Thorndike said, "this book will be largely bare of them." Even more pointedly, he added, "that child-study has few exact statements thus carefully made as yet is due to the incompetence or thoughtlessness of its students. . . ."[38] Such blunt and devastating criticism could hardly have been lost on Hall.

If Thorndike continued to entertain hopes that a properly constituted and appropriately precise science of psychology would ultimately enhance the practice of teaching, the dean of American
psychology, William James, did not. In a work bearing the title
*Talks to Teachers on Psychology: and to Students on Some of Life's
Ideals,*[39] one would have expected an exposition on the direct relevance of psychology to teaching practice. In fact, James explicitly
rejected such a connection. James began his first lecture by stating
that "the desire of schoolteachers for a completer professional
training, and their aspiration toward the 'professional' spirit in their
work, have led them more and more to turn to us for light on
fundamental principles," but then he added, "I feel a little anxious
lest, at the end of these simple talks of mine, not a few of you may
experience some disappointment at the net results."[40] Alluding to
what he referred to as a "boom" in psychology, he concluded that
"it does seem as if there were a certain fatality of mystification
laid upon the teachers of our day," a charge that could easily have
been laid at Hall's doorstep. In his most telling statement on the
relevance of psychology to teaching practice, James proclaimed that
"I say moreover that you make a great, a very great mistake, if
you think that psychology, being the science of mind's laws, is
something from which you can deduce programmes and schemes
and methods of instruction for immediate classroom use."[41] James
went on to ally himself with his colleague, Münsterberg, in arguing
that the attitude of the teacher is fundamentally different from the
attitude of the psychologist when viewing classroom phenomena.
In taking this position, America's foremost psychologist was as-
sociating himself directly with the developing forces of opposition
to Hall and his confederates in the child-study movement. Such
formidable opposition was likely to have its effect.

Conclusion

The child-study movement with Hall assuming the helm in the
1880s had aspired not just to scientific respectability but to a science of human behavior that would guide the process of education
with a sure hand. In the mood of that time, this meant abandoning
theory and speculation in favor of empirical accumulation of data
on child life as the basis for a true science of human behavior. In
many respects, Hall was an admirable choice to lead the movement. His energy was boundless, and he had a remarkable ability
to attract devoted disciples. Moreover his founding of the *Amer-*

ican Journal of Psychology and *Pedagogical Seminary* provided a concrete basis for the sustenance of the movement and the dissemination of its ideas.

On the other hand, his vision for the new science of child-study was fatally overambitious, even misguided. This was true of his claims for the movement itself as well as in terms of his personal contributions. The latter in particular put him into conflict with the established figures as well as the rising stars in psychology and education. Although criticisms were voiced in terms of professional differences, a few exhibited a clear personal animosity. Partly as a result of Hall's own personal ambition, but more conspicuously as an outcome of developments within psychology and education itself, Hall's dream began to evaporate. What, then, were the emerging factors in psychology, education, and society generally that served to erode a reform movement once so full of promise?

In the first place, the development of psychology simply outpaced the way Hall (and by extension the entire child-study movement) perceived that discipline. Despite Hall's promotion of science as applied to education, his version of science was still prominently laced with a strong dosage of romanticism. The idealization of nature and pastoral life was simply not part of the thinking of the new psychology as represented by the likes of Hugo Münsterberg and Edward L. Thorndike; neither were the mystical parallels that Hall like to draw between the development of the individual and the historical development of the human race. Moreover, the psychologists representing the new order were keenly self-conscious of their professionalism. It was in their interest to distance themselves from ordinary and hence unprofessional ways of observing and understanding human behavior. The indiscriminate collecting of data by untrained observers was to them simply no way to go about creating a science of human behavior patterned on the natural sciences. In that regard, they were equally disdainful of the collection of data in the absence of theory and hypothesis. What Hall liked to call the "Baconian method" of deriving generalizations was thus widely rejected.

Secondly, at least some of Hall's most powerful contemporaries, such as William James and John Dewey, were openly skeptical of the extent to which psychology could become "the teacher's Blackstone" as Hall envisioned. To be sure, they agreed that the study of psychology by teachers could contribute some insight into pedagogical processes, but psychology could by no means provide a blueprint for determining either what to teach or how to teach. As issue after issue of *Pedagogical Seminary* was published, it must have become increasingly evident that Hall and his disciples simply could not deliver on the promise of immediate utility deriving from a science of child-study. As is the case with other applied fields such as engineering and medicine, the practice is far more encompassing and more diverse that can be represented by a single discipline. Engineers do not function as engineers simply by applying the principles of a solitary discipline like physics any more than physicians merely apply the discipline of anatomy in their practice. The study of those disciplines is relevant but far from determinant. It is difficult to say from our present vantage point whether this realization actually became part of the thinking of teachers of the day. Probably not. It is more likely that teachers and other school practitioners simply became disillusioned by more than two decades of unfulfilled promises. In either case, however, Hall's vision of child-study as providing teachers with the key to practice remained monumentally unrealized.

Finally, the child-study movement in the quarter-century of its existence failed to exhibit a vital ingredient of its legacy. Eminent forerunners of the child-study movement, like Rousseau and Pestalozzi, were first and foremost social and political reformers. Each in his own way saw an education according to nature as a way of liberating the human spirit from the misery and degradation that an unjust social system had imposed. Their emphasis was on a common humanity rather than differentiation and determinism. By contrast, Hall's decidedly deterministic approach to education became increasingly evident as the child-study movement evolved. Furthermore, as industrialization and urbanization proceeded apace in the late nineteenth and early twentieth centuries, the lack of a social ideal which somehow addressed those profound changes became keenly felt. Education in the twentieth century was emerging as a self-consciously social enterprise. While certain of the education movements that were to vie for dominance in the twentieth century, such as social efficiency, were patently conservative in terms of their social policy, others were liberal, even radical. In either case, the social dimension to their pedagogical ideology was conspicuous and reasonably consistent. While leaders of the child-study movement spoke out from time to time on the social issues of the day, the movement as a whole lacked a coherent social outlook. This absence of a recognizable social agenda made an educational policy of keeping out of nature's way plainly irrelevant as a force in twentieth-century American education.

Notes

1. G. Stanley Hall, "Ideal School Based on Child Study," *Journal of Proceedings and Addresses of the National Education Association* (1901), pp. 474–488.

2. Frederick Winslow Taylor, "A Piece-rate system, being a step toward partial solution of the Labor Problem," *Transactions of the American Society of Mechanical Engineers* 24 (1895), pp. 1337–1480.

3. Michael B. Katz, "The 'New Departure' in Quincy 1873–1881: The Nature of the Nineteenth Century Educational Reform," *New England Quarterly* 40 (March 1967), pp. 3–30.

4. G. Stanley Hall, in "The Contents of Children's Mind," *Princeton Review* 2 (May 1883), 249–272.

5. Ibid., p. 251.

6. Ibid., p. 251.

7. Ibid., p. 255.

8. Ibid., p. 257.

9. Ibid., p. 272.

10. Ibid., p. 271.

11. G. Stanley Hall, "A Study of Children's Collections," *Nation* 41 (September 1885), p. 190.

12. G. Stanley Hall, *Life and Confessions of a Psychologist* (New York: D. Appleton, 1923), p. 360.

13. G. Stanley Hall, *Adolescence* (New York: D. Appleton, 1904), p. 496.

14. G. Stanley Hall, "Psychological Literature," *American Journal of Psychology* 1 (November 1887), pp. 128–164.

15. Ibid., pp. 154–159.

16. G. Stanley Hall, "Editorial Note," *American Journal of Psychology* 1 (November 1887), pp. 3–4.

17. G. Stanley Hall, "Editorial," *American Journal of Psychology* 7 (October 1895), p. 3.

18. Ibid., p. 4.

19. William James, "Correspondence," *Science* 2, (November 1895), p. 626.

20. Ibid.

21. George T. Ladd, "Correspondence," *Science* 2, (November 1895), pp. 626–627.

22. J. Mark Baldwin, "Correspondence," *Science* 2, (November 1895), p. 627.

23. J. McKeen Cattell, "Correspondence," *Science* 2, (November 1895), p. 628.

24. G. Stanley Hall, "Editorial," *Pedagogical Seminary* 2 (June 1892), pp. 3–8.

25. Ibid., p. 4.

26. Ibid., p. 5.

27. Ibid.

28. Ibid., p. 8.

29. John Dewey, "Criticism Wise and Otherwise on Modern Child Study," *Journal of Proceedings and Addresses of the National Educational Association* (1897), pp. 867–869.

30. Ibid., p. 867.

31. Ibid., p. 868.

32. Hugo Münsterberg, "Psychology and Education," *Educational Review* 16 (September 1898), pp. 103–132.

33. Ibid., p. 106.

34. Ibid., p. 114.

35. Ibid., p. 118.

36. Ibid., p. 125.

37. Ibid., p. 123.

38. Edward Lee Thorndike, *Notes on Child Study*, Columbia University Contributions to Philosophy, Psychology and Education, Vol. 8, Nos. 3–4 (New York: Macmillan, 1901), p. 20.

39. William James, *Talks to Teachers on Psychology: and to Students on Some of Life's Ideals* (New York: Henry Holt and Company, 1899/1915).

40. Ibid., p. 5.

41. Ibid., p. 7.

4

Dewey and the Herbartians:
The Genesis of a Theory of Curriculum

When, at the age of twenty, John Dewey was offered a teaching position in Oil City, Pennsylvania by his cousin, the principal of the high school, he readily accepted. It is likely, however, that this decision was reflective of a young man uncertain about himself and his future, rather than an early manifestation of Dewey's interest in education. During the time that he held the position in Oil City High School, between 1879 and 1881, Dewey taught Latin, science and algebra. It was in 1881 that Dewey submitted his first article to the *Journal of Speculative Philosophy* accompanied by a letter to the editor, William Torrey Harris, America's leading Hegelian, describing himself as a "young man in doubt as to how to employ my reading hours" and asking Harris for advice as to whether his article on metaphysics showed "ability enough of any kind to warrant my putting much of my time on that sort of subject."[1] After he left Oil City, Dewey taught for a while in a village school in Charlotte, Vermont near his home of Burlington.

Dewey did not mention his early experiences as a schoolteacher in his only published autobiographical account,[2] and it remains a relatively obscure chapter in his life. Although he appears to have been a rather successful high school teacher, there is still no reason to believe that, at this point in his life, he seriously entertained the idea of devoting a major portion of his career to professional education. Rather, Dewey's interest in education as a major scholarly pursuit seems to have had its inception in his graduate work in psychology, particularly in his second year at The Johns Hopkins University, as well as in certain opportunities that were available to him as a faculty member at the University of Michigan.

First appeared in *Journal of Curriculum Theorizing* 3, number 1 (1981).

Dewey began his graduate work at Johns Hopkins in 1882 working under George Sylvester Morris, but when Morris returned to his regular academic post at the University of Michigan in 1883, Dewey concentrated his graduate study in psychology under G. Stanley Hall. Dewey's choice of a Ph.D. dissertation topic, "The Psychology of Kant," a dissertation completed early in 1884, reflected Dewey's growing identification with psychology as a major scholarly focus. Dewey is known, for example, to have delivered a paper entitled "The New Psychology" to the Metaphysical Club at Johns Hopkins in March of 1884, and later published it in the *Andover Review*.[3] Although this article, unlike Dewey's four earlier philosophical articles, has been described as "incomprehensible,"[4] it does reflect a high optimism, almost a euphoria, about the future of psychology.

Dewey's Appointment at the University of Michigan

There is little doubt that George Sylvester Morris was responsible for an offer of an appointment as instructor in philosophy and psychology at the University of Michigan when Dewey completed his Ph.D. degree in 1884. Apart from Morris's apparent recognition of Dewey's ability, he was probably concerned about the growing dissatisfaction among the students at Michigan over the philosophy faculty's preoccupation with German idealism and the neglect of what was regarded as "the whole modern scientific school of philosophy."[5] Although philosophically committed to idealism himself, Dewey also possessed the "scientific" credentials that the students apparently felt were needed, and it was this feature of Dewey's scholarly interests, rather than as a Hegelian, that seems to have been his early professional identification at the University of Michigan. Morris himself taught the course in History of European Philosophy, Ethics, Aesthetics, and Real Logic, while Dewey's teaching responsibilities included Empirical Psychology, Experimental Psychology, Speculative Psychology, and Special Topics in Psychology (Physiological, Comparative, and Morbid).[6] Dewey's work in these courses undoubtedly led to the publication of his first book, *Psychology*, which he began writing within a year of his arrival at Ann Arbor.

Apart from his work in psychology, Dewey participated in at least two other major activities during his tenure at the University of Michigan. His principal extracurricular activity seems to have been in the field of religion. Dewey became a trustee of the Students' Christian Association and involved himself actively in their work.[7] His numerous lectures on religious topics on behalf of the Association led one Ann Arbor newspaper to comment, "no one can afford to miss the privilege of hearing him."[8] One of these lectures, entitled "Christianity and Democracy," drew an audience of about 400.[9] While these activities did not lead to an abiding interest in theological issues, one of Dewey's other university activities did, his gradual and tentative involvement in education, which reached its peak in the period of the Laboratory School at the University of Chicago between 1896 and 1904.

The University of Michigan, in the late nineteenth century, offered its faculty a rare opportunity to see education beyond the university setting. In 1869–70, the university had undertaken a program of admissions based on the observations and evaluations of its faculty in secondary schools. In essence, this was an attempt to assess the preparation of applicants to the university through direct examination of the secondary schools they attended. The University of Illinois and the University of Wisconsin adopted similar plans, and by 1895 this approach to college admission culminated in the creation of the North Central Association, a voluntary association of secondary schools and colleges designed to provide "accreditation" for the secondary schools that met their standards. In this respect, its functions were similar to other regional associations such as the Association of Colleges and Preparatory Schools of the Middle States and Maryland and the Preparatory Schools of the Southern States. In 1886, two years after Dewey's arrival at the University of Michigan, the Michigan Plan, as it was then called, evolved into the Schoolmaster's Club, and Dewey was a founding member. At its first meeting Dewey, still reflecting his fascination with psychology, read a paper entitled "Psychology in High-Schools from the Standpoint of the College."[10] (His first article related to education and his only publication of the previous year was a brief commentary on a study conducted by the Association of Collegiate Alumnae on the question of the effects of college life on the health of women.)

During the remainder of his tenure at the University of Michigan, Dewey published almost nothing concerned directly with education. Although he is listed as a co-author of *Applied Psychology*, originally published in 1889, and while it is true that book is subtitled, *Principles and Practice of Education*, it is difficult to find in it much that reflects Dewey's distinctive psychological interpretations or any educational ideas not directly tied to the standard psychology of the period. The book is a typical, even pedestrian, normal-school textbook of the period. It appears to be almost entirely the work of James A. McLellan, a director of normal schools in Ontario, Canada, rather than Dewey. In fact, Dewey was not listed as co-author in the first edition of the book but is thanked for his contribution and cited by McLellan in the preface as someone "whose work on Psychology has been so well received by students of philosophy."[11] It is likely, as Boydston has suggested, that Dewey's name was added as a co-author in later printings in order to take advantage of his then established position in education.[12]

If *Applied Psychology*, a popular textbook, is indeed only nominally attributable to Dewey, then it is difficult to find any concrete basis for the outstanding reputation he was unquestionably building in education. There is some evidence to indicate that Dewey, despite his shy manner, had a powerful effect on people with whom he came into contact, and it may have been through his personal associations with teachers' groups, professional education associations, and speaking engagements rather than through his published writings or formal teaching, that Dewey's reputation in the field of education became established in this early period.

One particular event during his tenure at the University of Michigan seems to have had a profound effect on the course of Dewey's evolving theory of education. When the National Education Association met in Saratoga Springs, New York in 1892, a prominent group of educators, including Charles DeGarmo, Frank and Charles McMurry, Elmer E. Brown, Nicholas Murray Butler, and Joseph Mayer Rice organized the Herbart Club. By becoming a charter member of the group and later involving himself actively in its affairs, Dewey aligned himself with a particularly zealous group of educational reformers who had undertaken to challenge the existing order in American education. Several of the leading Herbartians had studied pedagogy in Germany, particularly at Leipzig and Jena. By 1895, they reorganized into the National Herbart Society for the Scientific Study of Education and in that same year they used the occasion of the Committee of Fifteen's subcommittee report to mount an attack on the dominant figure and conservative spirit in American education, William Torrey Harris, who was the principal author of the report. The atmosphere at that meeting was so charged and the clash of ideologies so strong that thirty-eight years later, DeGarmo, at the age of 85, was moved to write his friend Nicholas Murray Butler, "No scene recurs to me more vividly than on that immortal day in Cleveland, which marked the death of the old order and the birth of the new."[13] In America, the Herbartians were regarded as the major force for progressive educational ideas, and Dewey's association with them set in motion a lifelong commitment to educational reform.

Dewey's Criticism of American Herbartianism

Apart from the sheer zeal they brought to the cause of reforming American education, the Herbartians came equipped with a particular set of concepts and ideas which they used to challenge "the old order." Whether these ideas were faithful to the work of the German philosopher, Johann Friedrich Herbart, who died about a half a century before, is open to serious question,[14] but they did present a more or less coherent system of thought with respect to education. At the very least, the Herbartians were successful in introducing a new vocabulary into the educational discourse of the late nineteenth and early twentieth centuries, and Dewey became involved in the controversies surrounding the definition of their key terms and the clarification of the concepts they represented. Dewey, for example, was drawn into the fray over the Herbartian concept of interest. The concept of interest had become a focal point in the clash between Herbartian psychology and the then dominant faculty psychology. Characteristically, Dewey found fault on both sides.

Dewey also became involved in the controversy over the meaning and utility of the central Herbartian concept in curriculum, culture epochs. His attempt to reinterpret the concept of culture epochs provides the best illustration of how his early involvement with the American Herbartians profoundly influenced his thinking in curriculum matters. The first Yearbook of the National Herbart Society included a long and presumably definitive article on the subject by C. C. Van Liew, a major American Herbartian theorist. Van Liew reviewed the historical development of the idea that "the individual recapitulates the experience of the 'race' " through the work of such philosophers as Kant, Goethe, and Pestalozzi with particular attention, however, to the application of the idea to curriculum by Tuiskon Ziller, a leading German disciple of Herbart.[15] The parallelism that Ziller and others perceived between the historical stages in the development of the human race and the stages of development in the individual human being were seen as being applicable to certain major curriculum questions. "This parallelism, applied to curriculum," said Van Liew, "suggests not only a

[handwritten margin note: Once again, someone believes that they have the answers to everything.]

motive for the approach to the study of nature, but also the general character of the material in the various grades. . . ."[16] In other words, the Herbartian concept of culture epochs provided not only a justification for teaching certain things at various levels of schooling, but the very materials from which these things would be taught. Thus, "the superstitious fear of the savage race . . . finds its parallel in the fears of the child in its earliest years,"[17] and the products of this epoch in race history provide the materials for the child to study while undergoing that stage in his development. This was generally interpreted to be a "natural" order of studies in which the interest of the child could be evoked. As Van Liew put it, "the principal [*sic*] of succession in the curriculum must be sought in the humanistic institutional movement in culture; that material which is selected on the principal [*sic*] of culture epochs will be able to call forth lasting interest in the child."[18]

Dewey took issue with this position on at least two counts. First, Dewey argued that unless the parallel were exact (which admittedly it was not), it made a great difference, educationally speaking, if we start with the history of the human race and make inferences to child development or vice versa. To Dewey, it was obvious that the sequence of development in the child was the critical factor whether or not a parallel could be found in race history. Dewey put it this way:

> We must, in all cases, discover the epoch of growth independently in the child himself, and by investigation of the child himself. All the racial side can do is to suggest questions. Since this epoch was passed through by the race, it is possible we shall find its correlate in the child. Let us, then, be on the look-out for it. Do we find it? But the criterion comes back in all cases to the child himself.[19]

Dewey also objected to the inferences the Herbartians were drawing from culture epochs regarding the amount of time devoted to the various stages. Even if we were to accept the idea that there is a stage in individual development which corresponds to the hunting epoch in human history, do we have a right, Dewey asked, to "condemn" children to a whole year of study corresponding to that epoch?

Dewey's second major objection to the culture epochs curriculum pertained to its assumption that the products of each of the historical stages were the appropriate objects of study for the child undergoing the parallel stage in individual development. Herbartians assumed, in other words, that a child who is experiencing the "agricultural" phase in his or her development should study the products—particularly the literary products—of the parallel historical epoch. If the theory makes any sense at all, Dewey argued, "the agricultural instinct requires . . . to be fed in just the same way in the child in which it was fed in the race—by contact with earth and seed and air and sun and all the mighty flux and ebb of life in nature."[20] In this sense, Dewey's objection was not to the general idea of a parallelism between individual development and the historical development of the human race, or to the interpretation of this parallelism, but to its interpretation as a kind of mystical union between the individual and his ancestors through the works of those ancestors. What was implied by that parallelism, according to Dewey, was direct participation in the activities that characterized the historical period.

Dewey's criticism of the central Herbartian concept of culture epochs evoked no less than three published replies. Charles McMurry, a leader of the Herbartian movement, was the first to spring into the fray. He conceded one of Dewey's major points—that the child, not the historical epoch, is the proper "center" from which to draw curricular inferences. He denied, however, that present manifestations of a particular epoch are to be preferred over historical ones. "First find out," McMurry argued, "what present society has to offer that the child needs. If the child is the center, the argument against imposing materials on him or her is just as strong on one side as on the other. Present society, just as past history, has a great many things for which the child has no use at all."[21]

McMurry's argument against Dewey's notion of substituting direct experiences for cultural products was a much weaker one. He suggested that since the child comes to school already having experienced much direct activity through his or her senses, the school should provide the influence from history and literature that the child presumably lacks. Naturally, these "cultural products" should be tested so as to ascertain their relationship to children's interests.

A second response to Dewey's criticism of culture epochs was wholly laudatory. The superintendent of schools of Great Bend, Kansas wrote the editor to say that the article "by Professor Dewey is worth a whole year's subscription to The [Public School] Journal."[22] He went on to speculate that the "greater part of the culture epochs theory comes from the inner consciousness of the pedagogical philosopher"[23] rather than from the true instincts and interests of the child, a noteworthy insight. Van Liew's own response initially criticized Daum, the school superintendent, for interpreting culture epochs doctrine in terms merely of the interest that children allegedly show in the products of historical epochs, such as myths or fairy tales. In turning to Dewey's criticism, Van Liew accused Dewey of not actually attacking the theory of culture epochs "rightly understood,"[24] referring rather mysteriously to a letter he received from "Dr. Dewey" in which culture epochs theory is "viewed in the light of [Dewey's] philosophy." According to Van Liew, Dewey's letter revealed him to be "not an opponent of the doctrine in question. . . ."[25]

Van Liew's puzzlement regarding Dewey's position on this key curriculum issue is probably due to an assumption that Dewey's criticism of the master's teaching amounted to a rejection of the concept of culture epochs as the basis of curriculum organization. Dewey's writing on curriculum during the period of his direct association with the Herbartians indicates that, while he was obviously critical of certain features of the theory, he accepted the overall framework of recapitulation along with most of his fellow Herbartians. Acceptance of this basic frame of reference is especially significant, since this was the period in Dewey's development when he was beginning to move away from the mere translation of psychological concepts into educational terms and starting to consider the curriculum principles that were later to form the basis of the program of studies at the Laboratory School at the University of Chicago.

Dewey's Brigham Young Lectures

Dewey's early fascination with Herbartian educational theory was also reflected in a little-known series of ten lectures that Dewey delivered at Brigham Young Academy in 1901.[26] They were published by the Brigham Young Summer School under the title, *Educational Lectures by Dr. John Dewey*. The lectures reflected not only Dewey's early interest in psychology, and the application of psychology to educational affairs (which was actually the major thrust of the lectures), but also the new directions in which his interaction with Herbartian concepts was leading him.

In line with Dewey's predominantly psychological approach to education during this early period, his summer session lectures were drawn heavily from his maturing psychological theory. In his very first lecture, for example, Dewey announced that his lectures would deal with "psychological topics in their bearing upon education."[27] Indeed, most of the lectures deal with the conventional psychological topics of the day including "How The Mind Learns," "Imagination," and "Habit." Interestingly, Dewey's ideas on these psychological matters did not reflect direct Herbartian influence; for example, in evoking an image of the mind, he specifically rejected the idea that "the mind is like a piece of blank paper, to which it is sometimes compared, nor like a waxed tablet on which the natural world makes impressions." [28] Instead, Dewey invoked a digestive metaphor, declaring the child's "hunger to be an active thing, so active that it causes him to search eagerly for food."[29] In extending the metaphor, Dewey asserted that "the child supplies the hunger but he does not supply the food."[30] Why, then, Dewey asked, do children so often find their schools studies so repulsive? The answer Dewey supplied is that, "The food is not being presented in the shape they recognize as food."[31] Such an active concept of mind is more reflective of Hegel than it is of Herbart.

In two of the lectures, however, (the second and the eighth) Dewey departed from the basic psychological orientation of the course and dwelt on curriculum matters. In these instances, the influence of a Herbartian frame of reference was unmistakable. In his lecture on the "Social Aspects of Education," for example, Dewey dealt with the curriculum question of how the school subjects may be interrelated. In this context, Dewey introduced the Herbartian concept of correlation, first in connection with tying the educational opportunities in the home with those in the school. Pointing out that the school is only one of the educational agencies within a community, Dewey applauded the introduction of cooking, sewing, and household management into the school's curriculum, seeing it as a way of correlating family life with the work of the school.[32] Here, Dewey, characteristically, took a familiar educational concept and twisted it. By correlation, the Herbartians meant, generally, the interrelationship among school subjects. Thus, a single topic could be used to "correlate" the various schools subjects around a central theme: For example, if fish were the theme, a day's activity in geography, arithmetic, science, and literature would all revolve around the topic thus achieving, presumably, a unifying effect. Dewey conceived of this unity in terms of the child's overall experience rather than in traditional Herbartian terms.

Of even greater significance to Dewey was that the connection between home and school afforded an opportunity for the child to understand and experience the social origins of school subjects.

People did not invent arithmetic, Dewey pointed out, in an advanced abstract form. Arithmetic, like all school subjects, arose out of practical necessity. As Dewey put it, "we may trace one study after another to a period where it grew originally out of the actual necessities of social life."[33] Ultimately, this epistemological development from basic social activities to abstract subject matter became the core of Dewey's curriculum theory.

As soon as Dewey introduced this principle, he turned to the general notion of recapitulation, which was then already popular as a basis for curriculum—one particularly favored by the Herbartians. Dewey described the position as holding that "just as the race goes step by step from the lower to the higher plane, so the child must go through similar stages of evolution."[34] Dewey twice described this idea as "absurd" but was careful to qualify this judgment on both occasions by indicating that this opinion was confined to those who took it too literally. Obviously, the young child was not actually a savage comparable in any literal sense to the "savage" stage in human history. In fact, when Dewey returned to the question of the value of school subjects, he asserted a qualified, but unmistakable, endorsement of the theory. "So far as these branches [of study] are concerned," Dewey said, "we might accept the statement of the race development theory."[35] What Dewey seemed to be reaching for, but which he did not enunciate fully until later in his career, was a refinement and reinterpretation of the recapitulation metaphor as central to his curriculum theory, a metaphor which he recognized was constantly being misinterpreted as a literal statement.

When Dewey turned his attention once more to curriculum issues in his eighth lecture, his starting point was again Herbartian doctrine, this time referring to it explicitly by name. Using the terms correlation and concentration more or less interchangeably, Dewey objected particularly to the use of literature as the integrating core around which the school subjects should be concentrated. (In later years, Dewey expressed the idea that geography as a study possessed such integrating properties.) Dewey regarded the Herbartian emphasis on literature as leading toward artificiality, pointing out that in German schools, where the race development theory had both a religious and secular side, German children, at one stage in the curriculum, "get their arithmetic by adding, dividing, multiplying, and subtracting the Twelve Tribes, and by dealing numerically with the various incidents of history, the number of people engaged in battle, the number of miles in Palestine from this point to that and so on."³⁶ Apart from the sheer artificiality of this organization of the curriculum, Dewey again objected to the attempt merely to correlate subjects with one another. Correlation must be achieved not only among the various school subjects, Dewey insisted, but between the school subjects as a whole and the life experiences of the child.

It is in the context of trying to explicate this idea that Dewey first used the term, "occupations," a concept that was crucial in developing the curriculum of the Laboratory School in Chicago. As Dewey introduced the concept here, occupations were to be pursued not for specific didactic purposes, but for their own sake. Children Dewey said, "cook for the fun of cooking . . . not for the sake of making a scientific study of the chemistry of foods."³⁷ Occupations such as cooking, furthermore, not only "follow out the child's own end," but "recapitulate" the social world that surrounds the child. Dewey argued that if such fundamental human activities as woodwork, ironwork, cooking, and weaving "were to be made part of the curriculum they would give the child a chance to reflect from within the school and social interests and activities of the home."³⁸ As yet, Dewey did not seem to have incorporated the notion of occupations fully into his general recapitulation theory. Against the possible charge that these activities may be too utilitarian, for example, Dewey argued only that much of the activity of mankind is directed toward utilitarian pursuits and that the school may be a good place to "idealize" them. Later, he would have denied that occupations, as part of the curriculum, had any direct utilitarian purpose.

Apparently, however, Dewey did have in mind an overall plan for the curriculum based on three distinct groups of studies which would be arranged more or less sequentially. The first group, "hardly studies in the technical sense," would be those occupations which "the child must shortly follow for a livelihood,"³⁹ a characterization which Dewey would not have used in more sophisticated versions of his curriculum theory. Even here, however, Dewey argued that the basic occupations "can be made to teach a broader view of the evolution of civilization down the avenues of history."⁴⁰ As an example of the first group of studies, Dewey cited the making of clothing from the raw wool of sheep through the various stages required to bring it to a refined and useful state. Accounts of the activities of the Dewey School actually report this as a major activity of the youngest age groups.

The second group of studies would be directed mainly to providing the background for social life and comprised, essentially, history and geography (including nature study). Dewey deplored the emphasis in history on the "military side" arguing that its proper focus should be on "finding out how people lived, and how they came to live as they did—I mean the common people—the difficulties they were laboring under, the struggles they had to make, the victories they won—not the military victories so much as the human victories—the artistic advances, the educational movements, and the moral and religious conquests."[41] History, Dewey said, ought to be "a sort of moral telescope"[42] through which we can gain a perspective on the present. In the same vein, geography should be seen as "a study of the theatre of life" with an emphasis on human value. One of the problems here, according to Dewey, was that the specialist so influences what should be taught in the fields like history and geography that technicalities begin to dominate what is taught instead of elements of our common experience. The child, Dewey argued, does not even need to know the particular names of the subjects he is studying. "The very moment you put one of those labels on the study," Dewey said, "you isolate it."[43]

The third and final group of studies rounding out Dewey's curriculum would be those that deal with symbols and forms. While the first group of studies, the occupations, dealt directly with social life and the second group, history and geography, provided the background for social life, the third group would be one step further removed from direct social participation. Although Dewey was vague here in actually spelling out what these studies consist of, it is clear that language, particularly language defined as social communication, as a form of social intercourse, formed the basis of this third group of studies. As Dewey expressed it, through mastery of symbols we become "initiated" into the social experience of the community. Thus, one's individual consciousness becomes social by absorbing into it the thought and consciousness of the ages. The medium of the school curriculum was becoming, for Dewey, a principal way in which individual and social aims were harmonized.

The Herbartian Influence on Dewey's Curriculum Theory

Dewey's interaction with the ideas of the American Herbartians had not only earned him a reputation as a promising educational leader and reformer, but provided him with the anvil on which he was to forge his major educational theories. Herbartian concepts such as correlation, concentration, and culture epochs represented ways by which central curriculum issues could be addressed. His early work at the University of Chicago Laboratory School gave him a chance to test these theoretical concepts in an actual school setting. Although Dewey ultimately did not accept the traditional Herbartian interpretations of these concepts, he did accept them as potent ways of considering those issues that almost inevitably arise when one undertakes to construct a curriculum.

Of particular significance was Dewey's acceptance of recapitulation as the central frame of reference for his curriculum theory. Although he rejected any kind of strict or literal notion of race recapitulation in the individual, he seems to have accepted the idea of a temporally ordered curriculum paralleling stages of individual growth. Delivered a year before Dewey's major essay on curriculum, "*The Child and the Curriculum*," the Brigham Young lectures indicate that Dewey was thinking in terms of individual stages in human development on one hand, and on the other, the stages by which the human race moved from one state of knowing to a higher one. While Dewey saw no special merit in a curriculum that simply recapitulated the history of the human race, he began to see some promise in the idea that, through the curriculum, children may recapitulate the stages in which the human race *created and acquired knowledge*, from the most primitive and direct ways of knowing to the most sophisticated and abstract.

Dewey's reconstruction of the theory of culture epochs began to take concrete shape shortly after his appointment at the University of Chicago. In particular, Dewey took the first tentative steps toward substituting a social and epistemological basis for the historical and literary one that the Herbartians favored. It seems clear that Dewey did not reject the fundamental metaphor by which an individual's growth and development are seen as paralleling an historical dimension of the human experience. It was the particular conception of the historical side of that analogy and not the recapitulation analogy itself that Dewey rejected. In fact his own theory of curriculum rests on almost the same metaphor. Instead of the naive conception of discrete stages in human history, which the Herbartians favored, Dewey took as his parallel to individual development the growth of ever more refined ways of knowing over the course of social history.

Notes

1. John Dewey to William T. Harris, 17 May 1881, quoted in George Dykhuizen, *The Life and Mind of John Dewey* (Carbondale: Southern Illinois University Press, 1973), p. 23.

2. John Dewey, "From Absolutism to Experimentalism," in *Contemporary American Philosophy*, eds. George P. Adams and William P. Montague, vol. 2 (New York: Macmillan, 1930), pp. 13–27.

3. John Dewey, "The New Psychology," *Andover Review*, 2 (September, 1884), pp. 278–289.

4. Neil Coughlan, *Young John Dewey* (Chicago: University of Chicago Press, 1973), p. 42.

5. George Dykhuizen, *Life and Mind of John Dewey*. (Carbondale: Southern Illinois University Press, 1973), p. 45.

6. Ibid., p. 46.

7. John A. Axelson, "John Dewey," *Michigan Educational Journal*, 43 (May 1966), p. 13.

8. Ibid., p. 14.

9. Ibid.

10. John Dewey, "Psychology in High-Schools from the Standpoint of the College," Michigan Schoolmaster's Club, *Papers* (Lansing, MI: H.R. Pattengill, 1886).

11. James A. McLellan, *Applied Psychology* (Toronto: Copp, Clark and Company, 1889), p. vi.

12. Jo Ann Boydston, "A Note on Applied Psychology," in *John Dewey: The Early Works, 1882–1898 III: 1889–1892* (Carbondale: Southern Illinois University Press, 1969), pp. xiii–xix.

13. Charles DeGarmo to Nicholas Murray Butler, 15 December 1933, Butler Papers, Columbia University, quoted in Walter H. Drost "That Immortal Day in Cleveland—The Report of the Committee of Fifteen," in *Educational Theory*, 17 (April 1967), p. 178.

14. Harold B. Dunkel, *Herbart and Herbartianism* (Chicago: University of Chicago Press, 1970).

15. C. C. Van Liew, "Culture Epochs," in *First Yearbook of the National Herbart Society* (Bloomington, IL: The Society, 1895), pp. 70–123.

16. Ibid., p. 97.

17. Ibid., p. 106.

18. Ibid., p. 117.

19. John Dewey, "Interpretation of the Culture-Epoch Theory," *Public School Journal*, 15 (January 1896), p. 234.

20. Ibid., p. 235.

21. Charles A. McMurry, "The Culture-Epochs," *Public School Journal*, 9 (February 1896), p. 298.

22. N. F. Daum, "Culture Epoch Theory," *Public School Journal*, 15 (May 1896), p. 509.

23. Ibid., pp. 509–10.

24. C. C. Van Liew, "Culture Epoch Theory," *Public School Journal*, 15 (June 1896), p. 546.

25. Ibid.

26. John Dewey, *Educational Lectures* (Provo, UT: Brigham Young Academy Summer School, n.d.)

27. Ibid., p. 1.

28. Ibid., p. 3.

29. Ibid., p. 4.

30. Ibid., p. 6.

31. Ibid., p. 7.

32. Ibid., p. 38.

33. Ibid., p. 45.

34. Ibid., p. 45.

35. Ibid., p. 46.

36. Ibid., p. 175.

37. Ibid., p. 180.

38. Ibid., p. 181.

39. Ibid.

40. Ibid., p. 186.

41. Ibid., p. 188.

42. Ibid., p. 189.

43. Ibid., p. 192.

5

The Rise of Scientific Curriculum-Making and its Aftermath

When Boyd Bode published *Modern Educational Theories* in 1927,[1] he took on what had already become the entrenched establishment of the curriculum world. With his penetrating criticism of Franklin Bobbitt in the chapter, "Curriculum Construction and Consensus of Opinion" and of W. W. Charters in the succeeding chapter, "Curriculum Making and the Method of Job Analysis," Bode was attacking not only the work of two men who had established themselves as the prototypes of the curriculum specialist, but the very foundations on which curriculum as a field of specialization had been based. Bode probably did not suspect, however, that the notion of careful prespecification of educational objectives (with variations in terminology and technique) and the notion of activity analysis as the means toward their "discovery" (also with variations in terminology and technique) would become the foundations on which, almost half a century later, many books would be written, Ph.D.s awarded, careers established, and millions of dollars expended. Certainly Bode never dreamed that legislation embodying these principles would be enacted across the United States and that the very ideas he was attacking would become semi-official doctrine in federal and state agencies as well as in many educational institutions.

The Scientific Curriculum Making of Bobbitt and Charters

Bobbitt and Charters lived in auspicious times. Mental discipline as a theoretical basis for the curriculum was almost dead by the early twentieth century. The bright flame of American Herbar-

---

First appeared in *Curriculum Inquiry* 5, number 1 (1975).

tianism, which had for a time captured the imagination of the educational world, was flickering. An educational ideology true to the times was needed, and nothing was more appropriate than scientific curriculum-making. This doctrine, with its promise of precision and objectivity, had an immediate appeal. Certainly there was no reason why scientific principles applied to education would not meet the same success as science applied to business in the form of scientific management. The general notion of applied science, as well as the particular model of scientific arrangement, is in fact evident throughout the work of Bobbitt and Charters.

Of the two, Bobbitt was perhaps the first to strike this rich vein. As a young instructor in educational administration at the University of Chicago, he effectively drew the parallel between business techniques and education in a lengthy article in the Twelfth Yearbook of the National Society for the Study of Education.[2] But Bobbitt, unlike other educators who turned to scientific management, was not content merely to apply certain management techniques to education, such as maximum utilization of the school plant; he provided the professional educators in the twentieth century with the concepts and metaphors—indeed, the very language—that were needed to create an aura of technical expertise without which the hegemony of professional educators could not be established. Science was not simply a tool with which to carve out exactitude in educational affairs generally and in the curriculum in particular; it was a means by which one could confer professional status and exclude the uninitiated. Even the term "curriculum specialist" implied a particular set of technical skills unavailable to the untrained. While the notion of science implies a certain aura of exclusiveness, Bobbitt was probably not explicitly aware of such a political use of his technical language. In his two major works, *The Curriculum* and *How to Make a Curriculum*,[3] as well as in numerous articles on the techniques of curriculum making, he seems simply to have believed that science had the key that idle speculation and even philosophy failed to provide.

Like Bobbitt, Charters was already a major leader in education by the time Bode's work was published. Charters had written *Methods of Teaching* in 1909 and *Teaching the Common Branches* in 1913,[4] both popular books; but with *Curriculum Construction* in 1923,[5] he established himself in the forefront of curriculum thinking. (In the preface to this book, Charters gives particular thanks to his "former colleague, B. H. Bode" for "his criticism of theoretical principles.") Like Bobbitt also, Charters approached the problems of curriculum from the perspective of functional efficiency. Through the method of activity analysis (or job analysis, as it was also called), Charters was able to apply professional expertise to the development of curricula in many diverse fields, including secretarial studies, library studies, pharmacy, and especially teacher education (with *The Commonwealth Teacher-Training Study* in 1929).[6] Activity analysis was so universally applicable a technique of curriculum development that Charters was even able to use it do develop a curriculum for being a woman. As with other occupations, one simply had to analyze the particular activities that defined the role and then place these in relationship to the ideals that would control these activities. The training involved in performing the activities well would then become the curriculum.[7] Out of the work and thought of Bobbitt and Charters, as well as their contemporaries and disciples, arose a new rationale and a modus operandi for the curriculum field that were to prevail to the present day. So dominant did scientific curriculum making become that Bode's *Modern Educational Theories* stands as one of the few direct assaults on some of its principal tenets and certainly the most important.

Preparing for Adulthood

One of the most basic tenets of scientific curriculum making is a principle enunciated early in Bobbitt's *How to Make a Curriculum*: "Education is primarily for adult life, not for child life. Its fundamental responsibility is to prepare for the fifty years of adulthood, not for the twenty years of childhood and youth."[8] Education, in other words, consists in preparing to become an adult. There is probably no more crucial notion in the entire theory. Without it, there would be no point, for example, in such careful analysis of adult activities and their ultimate transformation into minute and explicit curricular objectives. Moreover, much curriculum policy, such as the strong emphasis on curriculum differentiation with its basis in predicting the probable destination of children as to their adult lives, rests squarely on education as preparation. If education is for what lies ahead, then it becomes of utmost importance to state with reasonable accuracy what that future holds. Bode's criticism is most telling in making the distinction between a prediction by, for example, an astronomer as to the curve of a comet and an educator constructing a future ideal in schooling. Curriculum-making, in other words, is a form of utopian thinking, not of crystal ball gazing.

But Dewey, whom Bode cites favorably in this context, had gone even further in attacking the notion of preparation. In "My Pedagogic Creed," Dewey took pains to define education as "a process of living and not a preparation for future living,"[9] and he undertook specifically in *Democracy and Education* to point up other deficiencies in the idea. To think of children as merely getting ready for a remote and obscure world, Dewey thought, is to remove them as social members of the community. "They are looked upon as candidates," he said; "they are placed on the waiting list."[10] Furthermore, since children are not directed and stimulated by what is so remote in time, the educator must introduce, on a large scale, extrinsic rewards and punishments. Bode's criticism of education as preparation rests largely on the assumption that it would lead to a social status quo rather than social improvement. While Dewey would no doubt agree, his criticism is more far-reaching and devastating. He considered not only its social significance but its impact on the child and the pedagogical process itself.

A curious sidelight to the importance of education as preparation in scientific curriculum making is Bobbitt's own developing ambivalence toward the idea. In setting forth his curriculum theory in the epic Twenty-Sixth Yearbook of the National Society for the Study of Education, Bobbitt says, "Education is not primarily to prepare for life at some future time. Quite the reverse; its purposes to hold high the current living, . . . In a very true sense, life cannot be 'prepared for.' It can only be lived."[11] Later, when asked to write his summary theory of curriculum, Bobbitt declared, "While there are general guiding principles that enable parents and teachers to foresee in advance the long general course that is normally run, yet they cannot foresee or foreknow the specific and concrete details of the course that is to be actualized."[12] In these passages, he sounds more like Kilpatrick than himself.

But if Bobbitt was ambivalent, even self-contradictory, on the subject of education as preparation, his disciples and present intellectual heirs are not. If anything is ingrained in curriculum thinking today, it is the notion that it is the job of curriculum planners to anticipate the exact skills, knowledge, and—to use one of today's most fashionable term—"competencies" that will stand one in good stead at an imagined point in the future. These predictions about what one will need in the future become the bases of curriculum planning.

Specificity of Objectives

A concomitant of the emphasis on preparation is the insistence that the end products of the curriculum be stated with great particularity. Vague Delphic prophecies simply won't do. " 'Ability to care for one's health'. . ." declared Bobbitt, "is too general to be useful. It must be reduced to particularity: ability to manage the ventilation of one's sleeping room, ability to protect one's self against micro-organisms, ability to care for the teeth, and so on."[13] If science is to be identified with exactitude, then scientific curriculum-making must demonstrate its elevated status through the precision with which objectives are stated. It is at this point that Bode's criticism is both astute and telling. He points out, for example, that under the guise of scientific objectivity, Bobbitt inserts a submerged ideology. Scientific objectivity, it turns out, becomes a way of preserving the tried and true values of the society as well as making explicit the prevailing practical skills of the contemporary world.

Bode, of course, would not object to a philosophy of education governing curriculum; his objection is that the values of the scientific curriculum makers are disguised and covert. Furthermore, even a cursory examination of Bobbitt's most famous list of objectives would indicate wide latitude in the degree of specificity with which the objectives are stated. Alongside "the ability to keep one's emotional serenity, in the face of circumstances however trying,"[14] "an attitude and desire of obedience to the immutable and eternal laws which appear to exist in the nature of things," and "confidence in the beneficence of these laws,"[15] we find "ability to read and interpret facts expressed by commonly used types of graphs, diagrams, and statistical tables,"[16] as well as "ability to care properly for the feet."[17] Although the injunction to be specific and explicit is unqualified, there seems to be some difficulty in carrying it out simply as a practical matter. In considering the efficient functioning of the human body, for example, we have no guidance as to whether to begin with the leg, the foot, the toe, or the toenail. The same problem would arise if we were dealing with the ability to swing a hammer or the ability to solve quadratic equations. The scientific curriculum makers' allegiance to specificity was allied to Thorndike's conception of the mind as consisting of "multitudinous separate individual functions,"[18] whereas Bode seems committed to a much broader conception of thought processes as well as a more optimistic view of transfer of training.

Making a Choice

If the practical problem of specificity were somehow resolved, perhaps by extending the list of objectives into the thousands or the hundreds of thousands, another issue would become even more apparent: how would we decide, objectively of course, which objectives to keep and which to leave out? As Bode indicates, one of Bobbitt's solutions was to throw the matter open to a vote or at least to a panel. In his famous Los Angeles study, Bobbitt asserted that his list of objectives "represent[ed] the practically unanimous judgment of some twenty-seven hundred well-trained and experienced adults,"[19] a claim about which Bode is clearly skeptical. As Bode points out, the twelve hundred Los Angeles teachers, who were charged with reviewing the list drawn up by the fifteen hundred graduate students at the University of Chicago, were in a dilemma. All of the objectives listed unquestionably represented desirable traits and skills, from "keeping razor in order"[20] to "ability to tell interesting stories interestingly—and many of them."[21]

The wide agreement, Bode suspects, was probably achieved by a combination of specificity when practical and clearly desirable skills were involved and vagueness or ambiguity when value issues were broached. Inspection of Bobbitt's list of objectives indicates that Bode is essentially correct, thereby accounting in part for the obvious discrepancies in the level of specificity with which the objectives are stated as well as the near unanimity of agreement among twenty-seven hundred adult human beings. State legislators, educators, and the general public frequently find themselves in the same position today when they are asked to give their assent to such educational goals as "self-realization" and "mental health." One can hardly be against them.

A Standard for Living

Although Bode's criticism of the method of consensus is certainly convincing, he considers only indirectly another of Bobbitt's ways of dealing with the seemingly limitless scope of a curriculum defined by the full range of human activity. While the task of the "curriculum discoverer" did involve, according to Bobbitt, a full catalog of the activities of mankind, Bobbitt was careful to indicate that much of what has to be learned is acquired by "undirected experience." "The curriculum of the directed training," Bobbitt insisted, *"is to be discovered in the shortcomings of in-*

dividuals after they have had all that can be given by the undirected training" (original emphasis).[22] Bobbitt's understanding of "shortcomings," actually, is quite similar to the contemporary notion of "needs." A standard is set, a norm; and the curriculum consists of the ways of treating deviations from the standard. Thus the curriculum seems cut down to manageable proportions without resorting to the method of consensus. (It is a deceptively simple solution.) The fundamental issue, however, is not whether the list of objectives is derived from this or that method: more basic is the question of whether objectives ought to be prespecified at all. One might argue, therefore, that Bode, in skillfully demolishing the method of consensus, did not quite strike the jugular vein of scientific curriculum making. The central question is whether the curriculum should be a blueprint for what people should be like, not how the blueprint is drawn.

But even if one were to concede prespecification of objectives in such areas as arithmetic, grammar and spelling, how far could one go in justifying the "social shortcomings" of which Bobbitt speaks?[23] As many of Bobbitt's objectives imply, there was literally no human activity—social, intellectual or practical—that was not potentially, at least, a curricular objective. Bode correctly identified Herbert Spencer as having anticipated the trend toward specificity in stating objectives, but of at least equal importance is Spencer's role in identifying the scope of the school curriculum with life itself. Spencer, like Bobbitt and Charters, considered the best curriculum to be the one that demonstrated the highest utility. Spencer, it should be remembered, asked the question, "What knowledge is of most worth?", not merely, "What shall the schools teach?" In a subtle way, then, he was reconstructing a basic curriculum question. To the scientific curriculum makers, the two questions were essentially the same. Thus, by posing their question in this way, scientific curriculum makers were determining the kind of answer that could be given.

The answer to the scientific curriculum maker is likely to be phrased in terms of high survival value and functional utility rather than in terms of intellectual virtues. In this sense, the curriculum became the ultimate survival kit for the modern world. For example, in the state of Oregon today, certain districts have instituted requirements for high school graduation of such "survival" skills as listing birth control methods in order of effectiveness, or demonstrating ability to officiate at two different sports and to perform two basic dance steps.[24] Any sense of a distinctive function for the schools is lost.

Limitations of the School

Two serious but often unexamined questions are raised by such a conception of the school curriculum. The first relates to the extent to which the school as one institution of society can as a purely practical matter devote itself to the full range of activity that human beings engage in. A second question, perhaps even more fundamental than the first, is whether all activity can be reduced to particular components.

From the days of the *Cardinal Principles* report[25] to the present, the conventional way to begin the process of curriculum development has been to agree on a set of broad goals which in fact represents a categorization of human activity generally. The next step, of course, is to "operationalize" these goals by translating them into numerous minute and specific objectives—in effect, creating a catalog of human activity. Surely if Charters were able to identify the activities that constitute being a secretary or a librarian, it was only a step further to identify all the other human activities. In this way the most urgent of these activities may be identified (*e.g.*, earning a living) and the most pressing social problems addressed (*e.g.*, drug addiction).

The missing ingredient in all this is some attention to the nature of the school. If there is one serious omission in Bode's analysis, it is the failure to recognize the limitations of the institution of schooling. The knowledge that is of the most worth may not be the kind of knowledge that can be transmitted in a school context. The place of the school in the social structure, the makeup of its inhabitants, and the characteristic activities that take place within its boundaries must be considered along with the power of schooling as we know it to produce fundamental and direct changes in human attitudes and behavior. Hence, if curriculum makers do not temper the question of what is most important to know with the question of what schools can accomplish, their claims for programs designed to reduce crime, improve human relations, prevent drunken driving, ensure economic independence, or remove sex inhibitions are subject to serious examination.

Furthermore, while it may be true that a limited number of human activities may be anticipated and therefore practiced in advance, the extension of the method of job analysis from the limited realm of routine and replicative behavior into the full universe of human activity represents perhaps the most fundamental fallacy in the whole scientific curriculum-making movement. The source of this assumption, as is the case with other elements of scientific curriculum-making, is the example of industry. Just as the global and complex process of building an automobile can be broken down into a series of minute and simple operations, so presumably can the activities of a mother or a teacher. But we do not learn language, for example, by anticipating all of the sentences we will utter in our adult lives and then rehearsing them as part of our preparation to become adults. Instead, we learn or assimilate or perhaps even inherit the governing principles of language that permit us to create or invent sentences that we have never before heard expressed. Similarly, in mathematics we do not scientifically catalog all of the mathematical operations we will perform as adults as a direct rehearsal for the performance of those mathematical operations.

Here Bode's criticism of job analysis as the universal technique of curriculum making is particularly cogent. The analogy between definite operations which imply simple replicative activity and activities that involve, let us say, judgment, simply will not hold. As he puts it, friendliness, courtesy, and honesty "are not reducible to 'definite operations'. "[26] The process of educating a teacher to conduct himself or herself wisely and judiciously in the classroom is not, as current programs of teacher training so often imply, a process of first anticipating the particular situations that will arise in the classroom and then directing the teachers to conduct themselves in a particular way relative to these specific situations. Rather, teacher education can involve the examination, analysis, and adaptation of some broad principles which at some unknown point in the future and in some unanticipated circumstances may provide a guide to judgment and wise action.

Scientific Curriculum-Making in Teacher Education

Bode's astute criticism of the scientific curriculum makers notwithstanding it should be clear to anyone familiar with the current state of the art in the curriculum world that the scientific curriculum-making movement, with few adaptations and modifications, has been triumphant. It is true that behaviorism has provided a few refinements of language in stating objectives, and certain so-called academic subjects such as mathematics and science have more respectability than in the days of Bobbitt and Charters. But the key ingredients and analogies remain the same. While this modern version of scientific curriculum-making is well established in virtually all sectors of the curriculum world, it exists, not surprisingly, in its most virulent form in the area of teacher education. The vogue movements which go under the names of competency-based teacher education (CBTE) and performance-based teacher education (PBTE) are prime examples of what has evolved from the basic principles enunciated by Bobbitt and Charters. Charters himself helped direct a major study begun in 1925 which had all the earmarks of the PBTE (or CBTE) ideology.

As is the case with the current programs, the *Commonwealth Teacher-Training Study* was to be based on scientific research into the teaching process, as opposed to mere speculation and tradition. As a first step, Charters and Waples "ascertained the traits that characterize excellent teachers."[27] Adapting the consensus approach, the investigators used two methods: analyzing the professional literature and interviewing "expert judges." Working from a list of eighty-three traits, ranging alphabetically from Accuracy through Foresight and Magnetism all the way to Wittiness,[28] "translators" were given the task of interpreting statements made in writing or in the interviews. Thus, "knows how to meet people" could become translated into the traits, "adaptability" or "approachability." Reliability among the translators was determined by applying the Spearman prophecy formula. Finally, after some of the original traits of teachers were telescoped, scientifically determined lists were prepared indicating that senior high school teachers should be characterized by twenty-six traits including Good Taste and Propriety, junior high school teachers by Conventionality (morality) and Open-mindedness, and so on.

Next, in an adaptation of the job analysis technique, the investigators collected a master list of 1,001 teacher activities. Perhaps one of these activities is worth quoting in its entirety:

788, *Securing cordial relations with superintendent*

Maintaining cordial relations with superintendent. This involves being loyal to and respecting the superintendent. Becoming acquainted with superintendent and working in harmony with him. Performing friendly acts for superintendent; remembering superintendent at Christmas; making designs and drawings for superintendent; making lamp shades for superintendent's wife.[29]

Thus, after three years of research by trained investigators and a munificent grant of $42,000 from the Commonwealth Fund, was a blow dealt to fuzzy thinking in teacher education and a major stride taken in the direction of a scientifically determined teacher-education curriculum.

The Contemporary Aftermath

One of the most persistent and puzzling questions in this, the aftermath of the scientific curriculum-making movement, is why we retain, even revere, the techniques and assumptions we have inherited from Bobbitt and Charters, at the same time as we reject, implicitly at least, the actual outcomes of their research. Few people have read Bobbitt's famous study, *Curriculum Making in Los Angeles*, or his magnum opus, *How to Make a Curriculum*, or have even heard of Charters and Waples's *Commonwealth Teacher-Training Study*. If they did read these works, the most likely reaction would be one of amusement. And yet we pursue with somber dedication the techniques on which these works are based. Admittedly, performance-based teacher education may just be a slogan system resting only on a foundation of high-sounding rhetoric and pious promises and covered with a gloss of false novelty; but if it means anything, it surely implies that one can identify the particular components of teaching activity that make for good teachers and that these characteristics (Charters would call them traits) or behaviors (Charters would call them activities) can form the basis of a program of teacher training. Research takes the form of identifying the particular components of teaching that will ensure success. While its proponents seem cautious in stating the characteristics and behaviors with the same degree of conviction as Bobbitt and Charters did, an abiding faith in the efficacy of the approach remains. The persistence of this faith in the face of a record of over a half century of failure is a mystery that probably even Bode could not fathom.

At the heart of some of our most fundamental problems in the field of curriculum and of teacher education is the question of whether teaching is a technology by which carefully fashioned products in the form of learning or behavior are made. These products would have to be designed with the exactitude and specificity that Bobbitt and Charters called for. Teaching would be the application of standardized means by which predictable results would be achieved, and curriculum development would be the specification of the end-products and the rules for their efficient manufacture. Teacher education, in turn, would be the process by which persons are transformed into efficient manufacturers. The research evidence that presumably would support such an analogy between the teaching and the manufacturing process, however, has been disappointing to the proponents. For example a recent thorough examination of the research basis for performance-based teacher education led to the conclusion that eleven process variables previously identified as "promising"—such as "clarity," "variability," and "enthusiasm"—were indeed notably unpromising, leading the authors to conclude that "an empirical basis for performance-based teacher education does not exist."[30] Moreover, pessimism about the ultimate success of the approach was not based simply on flaws in statistical analysis or research design. The more fundamental problem was the framework in which such research was cast—a framework which, by the way, has held sway since the days of Bobbitt, Charters, and the scientific curriculum-making movement.

The point of all this is not simply that Bobbitt, Charters, and their like-minded contemporaries were mistaken in their faith in a given approach: the age in which they lived was one where optimism about the power of science to solve a multitude of human and social problems was near its peak. If they were naive or mistaken, one can hardly blame them. What is almost unforgivable, however, is that the half century since the zenith of their influence has produced little more by way of sophistication and refinement. With few exceptions, Bode's criticism of 1927 would carry as much force today were it directed against the present-day heirs of scientific curriculum making.

Particularly disappointing are the precipitous efforts to convert highly tentative and limited research findings into immediate prescriptions. This may be a function of the large constituency of teachers and school administrators who want immediate and concrete answers to such global questions as, What is a good teacher? and, What is a good curriculum? Part of the problem, undoubtedly, with the era of the scientific curriculum makers and with ours is the failure to recognize the complexity of the phenomena with which we deal. There is the same confusion between science and desert empiricism, the same naiveté about the nature of the teaching process, the same neglect of conceptual analysis. To be critical of scientific curriculum-making, as Bode was, is not to be critical of science or even the importance of scientific inquiry into educational processes; it is to be critical of a simplistic and vulgar scientism. Its persistence is a source of embarrassment.

Notes

1. Boyd H. Bode, *Modern Educational Theories* (New York: Macmillan, 1927).

2. Franklin Bobbitt, "Some General Principles of Management Applied to the Problems of City-school Systems," in *The Supervision of City Schools*, Twelfth Yearbook of the National Society for the Study of Education, Part 1 (Bloomington, IL: Public School Publishing Co., 1913), pp. 7–96.

3. Franklin Bobbitt, *The Curriculum* (Boston: Houghton Mifflin, 1918). *How to Make a Curriculum* (Boston: Houghton Mifflin, 1924).

4. Werrett W. Charters, *Methods of Teaching: Developed from a Functional Standpoint* (Chicago: Row, Peterson & Co., 1909). *Teaching the Common Branches* (Boston: Houghton Mifflin, 1913).

5. Werrett W. Charters, *Curriculum Construction* (New York: Macmillan, 1923).

6. Werrett W. Charters and Douglas Waples, *The Commonwealth Teacher-Training Study* (Chicago: University of Chicago Press, 1929).

7. Werrett W. Charters, "The Reorganization of Women's Education," *Educational Review* 62 (October 1921), pp. 224–31. "Curriculum for Women," in *Proceedings of the High School Conference* (Urbana, IL: University of Illinois, 1925).

8. Bobbitt, *How to Make a Curriculum*, p. 8.

9. John Dewey, "My Pedagogic Creed," *Journal of the National Education Association* 18 (December 1929), p. 292.

10. John Dewey, *Democracy and Education: An Introduction to the Philosophy of Education* (New York: Macmillan, 1916), p. 63.

11. Franklin Bobbitt, "The Orientation of the Curriculum-maker," in *The Foundations and Technique of Curriculum Construction*, Twenty-Sixth Yearbook of the National Society for the Study of Education, Part 2 (Bloomington, IL: Public School Publishing Co., 1926), p. 43.

12. Franklin Bobbitt, "A Summary Theory of the Curriculum," *Society for Curriculum Study News Bulletin* 5 (January 12, 1934), p. 4.

13. Bobbitt, *How to Make a Curriculum*, p. 32.

14. Ibid., p. 25.

15. Ibid., p. 2.

16. Ibid., p. 12.

17. Ibid., p. 14.

18. Edward L. Thorndike and R. S. Woodworth, "The Influence of Improvement in One Mental Function upon the Efficiency of the other Functions," Part 1, *Psychological Review* 8 (May 1901), p. 249.

19. Bobbitt, *How to Make a Curriculum*, p. 10.

20. Franklin Bobbitt, *Curriculum-making in Los Angeles*, Supplementary Educational Monographs, No. 20 (Chicago: University of Chicago Press, 1922), p. 21.

21. Ibid., p. 26.

22. Bobbitt, *The Curriculum*, p. 45.

23. Ibid., p. 50.

24. "Survival Test," in *Newsweek* (January 25, 1975), p. 69.

25. National Education Association Commission on the Reorganization of Secondary Education, *Cardinal Principles of Secondary Education: A Report* (Washington, DC: Government Printing Office, 1918).

26. Bode, *Modern Educational Theories*, p. 109.

27. Charters and Waples, *The Commonwealth Teacher-Training Study*, p. 4.

28. Ibid., pp. 56–61.

29. Ibid., p. 423.

30. Robert W. Heath and Mark A. Nielson, "The Research Basis for Performance-based Teacher Education," *Review of Educational Research* 44 (Fall 1974), p. 475.

6

Success and Failure in Educational Reform: Are There Historical 'Lessons'?[1]

Even early in this century when enthusiasm for reform was at its height, and reputations were being made by proposals of all sorts to modify and in many instances replace common practice in education, there already existed a pale cast of pessimism as to whether the proposed innovative practices would actually make their way into schools and, if they did, whether they would endure. In 1922, for example, W. W. Charters, one of the leading educational reformers of the twentieth century and a man who practically set the style for contemporary studies of curriculum referred to the history of education as "a chronicle of fads."[2] Since then, the terms "fads and frills" and "pendulum swings" have become commonplace characterizations of the efforts to reform school practice. While present efforts to improve school practice continue unabated and at a time when we hear calls from every side about the mediocrity of American schooling, there remains not just a pessimism but almost a cynicism about the chances for success in changing pedagogical practice. Two of the nagging questions, then, are whether this pessimism about educational reform is warranted and, if it is, why are at least some common educational practices so resistant to change. Beyond those questions is the related phenomenon of "pendulum swings" and whether and in what sense that rather cynical view of educational reform may or may not have any substance. And finally, there is the question of whether there are any lessons to be derived from previous efforts at reform.

First appeared in *Peabody Journal of Education* 65, number 2 (1988).

Three Instances of Reform Efforts

Let me begin by alluding to three historically familiar examples of educational reforms: in the first instance, there are what might be called grand reforms of the sort we associate with that revered educational reformer, Horace Mann, to create a system of common schools at public expense, as well as the later expansion of that system into the domain of secondary education during the early part of the twentieth century. Such a reform attempts to restructure a whole national system of education. There are also reform movements such as the effort in the early part of the twentieth century to make education more child-centered through a campaign that called into question certain fundamental assumptions about the educational process. In this second kind of reform, we are asked to restructure patterns of teaching and learning that have been practiced for as long as we have records of formal schooling. Finally, there is the specific change usually based on real or alleged research findings, such as the urging on the part of various educational experts in recent times that teachers organize their teaching by beginning with definite and explicitly stated educational objectives variously called behavioral objectives, performance objectives, and the like.

If we ask whether these reforms succeeded or failed, we are forced (as usual) to qualify our answer, but in different ways. Indisputably, we now have a well-nigh universal system of common schools supported by public taxation. There is hardly a child in America today between, say, six and fourteen who is not enrolled in school. The question, however, is whether that reform succeeded because Horace Mann adduced persuasive arguments on behalf of the common school, or because of his accession to a position of such power that he could personally implement that reform. When examined in those terms, it appears more likely that Mann's reform, if we can even call it his, succeeded because there were favorable social conditions that made that reform seem plausible and set the stage for its implementation. To take one example of such conditions, Carl Kaestle has interpreted the rise of the common school as the consequence of the ascendancy of middle-class, capitalist Protestants who were able to maintain their privileges against a fragmented array of political and religious minorities.[3] In this sense, the work of Horace Mann as educational reformer leaves little room for optimism about deliberate educational reform since his work can at best be regarded as a catalyst for a change that would have occurred anyway.

Along the same lines, the further question is whether universal education was successfully extended to the secondary level. It is true that the percentage of fourteen- to seventeen-year-olds attending school grew from something under seven percent in 1890 to a majority of that age group in four short decades. However, if we judge from recent critical examinations of what goes on in secondary schools, such as Theodore Sizer's *Horace's Compromise*,[4] Arthur Powell, Eleanor Farrar and David Cohen's *The Shopping Mall High School*,[5] Philip Cusick's *The Egalitarian Ideal and the American High School*,[6] and Linda McNeil's *Contradictions of Control*,[7] the issue of whether universal secondary education has succeeded becomes less clear. Each of these serious studies of what high schools are like point to the conclusion that the extension of popular education to the secondary level has been, if not a complete failure, at least a mixed success. The extension of universal education to adolescents may be regarded as an administrative success in that practically all adolescents in the United States spend a considerable amount of time in an institution called high school, but the reform is something less than a success in pedagogical terms.

The child-centered movement to reform classroom practices also succeeded in some sense, but only within a limited sphere. In 1894, the acknowledged leader of the child-study movement, G. Stanley Hall, was able to announce to the annual meeting of the National Education Association that "unto you is born this day a new Department of Child-Study."[8] At least twenty states founded child-study associations, and their meetings by all accounts were very well attended. But the question of whether teachers actually adopted the practices that the leaders of this movement were advocating is more difficult to answer. In *How Teachers Taught*, Larry Cuban estimates that perhaps as much as twenty-five percent of teachers concentrated in elementary schools tried out a few ideas associated with what became known as progressive education, with the result that a kind of hybrid developed between traditional and newer practices, and a smaller percentage, estimated to be between five and ten percent (also overwhelmingly elementary teachers), were actively trying to implement the reforms in a substantial way.[9] Even in its heyday, then, something like two-thirds of all classrooms in the United States were left untouched by the tenets of the child-centered movement, and in any case, the modest steps actually taken in that direction led to little by way of a lasting effect.

It is true that, compared to sixty or seventy years ago, schools have acquired an air of informality which is mainly expressed in the attire of both teachers and students and the easy banter that now characterizes their interactions; but these outward appearances of informality should not be confused with any significant change in authority relationships in the classroom or even in the percentage of teacher talk as compared with pupil talk, a percentage that has remained remarkably stable at least since the turn of this century. Classes are taught in pretty much the same way, with what is commonly called the recitation as the predominant mode.

Now to the third reform. Have classroom practices changed to conform to the injunction on the part of such leaders in the educational world as James Popham and Robert Mager that the stating of precise objectives is the indispensable first step in undertaking to teach a class? This reform is somewhat different from either of the first two in that research findings are usually adduced to show that this approach to organizing teaching is scientifically valid and that superior results in terms of student achievement (sometimes called output) are forthcoming. (I might add parenthetically, however, that the research compass in this case, as in other cases of research driven reforms, actually points both North and South simultaneously.) In this case, I know of no formal study of its implementation, so I must rely on my own observations as well as the experience of the many teachers who attend my courses year after year. There are, I know, certain elementary schools where a week's worth of lesson plans are required to be deposited in the principal's office on Monday morning, and these lesson plans almost invariably call for the stating of objectives right at the outset. My informants tell me almost without exception, however, that these lesson plans and the objectives that go with them are strictly *pro forma* and that once inside the safe confines of their individual classrooms, teachers carry on their activities in happy disregard of what has been safely embalmed in the file in the principal's office.

In this case, therefore, we get a modest appearance of success insofar as the innovation is concerned, but the success is more apparent that real. I should acknowledge, however, that conformity with this practice may differ by state or region. In a state like Florida, I understand, the practice of teaching has been much more bureaucratically formalized so that there may be at least outward conformity to the practice.

Unlike the other two examples of educational reform I have cited, this last reform, I believe, fails primarily because it misconstrues the relationship between social scientific research and educational practice. The problem lies mainly in its failure to take into account the supremely contextual nature of educational practice. Reform, we are told on every side, can be achieved by attending to research findings that tell us what the best practices are and provide us with the best rules for running schools as well as for how we should all behave as teachers. This is a position, by the way, that Dewey, that ardent champion of educational reform, rejected.[10] He argued that laws and facts simply do not yield rules of practice. Instead, their value lies in what he called *"intellectual instrumentalities."*[11] These are not to be regarded as specific guidelines for how to act under given circumstances, but as intellectual tools by which we can fashion our own pathways. "If we retain the word 'rule' at all," Dewey argued, "we must say that scientific results furnish a rule for the conduct of *observations and inquiries*, not a rule for overt action."[12] Science, in other words, does not tell us what to do; it offers us the opportunity to reexamine our practices in the light of certain findings.

Apart from the rather tenuous research findings that are used to justify the practice, then, the explicit stating of educational objectives failed as a reform because it was simplistically derived from these findings, and because its proponents undertook to bludgeon teachers (figuratively speaking, of course) into accepting a practice regardless of the teacher's own sense of how teaching goes forward in individual classrooms. It superimposed rules of action on the invaluable lore that teachers possess about how education actually goes forward, and, therefore, was thwarted at the point where so-called scientific results collided with the craft of teaching.

With these examples in mind, we can turn back to the question of whether educational innovations succeed or fail, but we can also begin to look at the question of what sorts of innovations tend to succeed or fail and under what circumstances. My point is that if we look at educational reform in general, we cannot give a very precise answer to the question of whether reforms succeed or fail, but if we look at the type of reform and ask ourselves with some specificity as to how and in what respects and under what circumstances these reforms succeeded or failed, we may begin to get some insights into the popular conception that educational reform is a rather futile undertaking.

What Fails? Why?

When looked at in this way, it appears, first, that successful reforms are not simply someone's good idea; they are supported by or are at least consistent with broad social and political forces in which schools are situated. For some kinds of reform, as in the case of the drive for a universal system of common schools, a favorable climate makes it possible to issue regulations or even change laws consistent with the reform. In effect, this type of reform requires something like an edict from a law-making body, a school board, a superintendent of schools, or simply a building principal in order to be implemented, providing, of course, that favorable social conditions are present. Modern counterparts to this type of reform would include new state requirements for testing of teachers or new regulations governing high school graduation. But in contrast to that kind of reform, there are those reforms that involve what teachers actually do once they are safely ensconced inside the confines of their isolated classrooms. Whether this kind of reform is prompted by a fundamental shift in assumptions about what education is all about, as in the case of child-centered education, or whether a change is proposed as a consequence of real or alleged research findings, as in the case of behavioral objectives, there seems to be an identifiable resistance to anything approaching major alterations when it comes to classroom practices in particular. Even the standard-raising kind of reform, while it often has the appearance of success in terms of implementation, tends to fail once it crosses the threshold of the classroom door.

A number of hypotheses regarding this persistent phenomenon have been offered. Some despairing reformers appear to have accepted the idea that teachers simply teach the way they have been taught and not the way they are supposed to. Others think teachers are just a recalcitrant, timid, lazy, or ungrateful lot. One frustrated reformer, for example, expounding on the reluctance of teachers to embrace instructional television with sufficient alacrity, attributed it to teachers' "failure to recognize the need for improvement, fear of experimentation, unwillingness to give time, and disillusion or frustration with past experiences,"[13] as well as to a tradition of conservatism. The problem with that answer to the question of why educational innovations fail is that it is no explanation at all. It gives us no indication as to why teachers allegedly have these attributes.

My own hypothesis about the phenomenon of teacher resistance to change in classroom practices begins with some insights John Dewey had into this matter just around the turn of this century. Essentially, Dewey argued that the reason why many educational reforms fail is that there is a conflict between the purposes and standards that are inherent in the innovative practice on one hand and what he called "external conditions" on the other. In other words, there is an unappreciated and, for that reason, fatal mismatch between what we are trying to accomplish with our reform and the actual structure of schooling. As Dewey put it:

> It is easy to fall into the habit of regarding the mechanics of school organization and administration as something comparatively external and indifferent to educational purposes and ideals. We think of the grouping of children in classes, the arrangement of grades, the machinery by which the course of study is made out and laid down, the method by which it is carried into effect, the system of selecting teachers and of assigning them to their work, of paying and promoting them, as, in a way, matters of mere practical convenience and expediency. We forget that it is precisely such things as these that really control the whole system, even on its distinctively educational side. No matter what is the accepted precept and theory, no matter what the legislation of the school board or the mandate of the school superintendent, the reality of education is found in the personal and face-to-face contact of teacher and child. The conditions that underlie and regulate this contact dominate the educational situation.[14]

If we are going to understand why educational reform fails specifically at the classroom level, then, we need to know what it is about the particular structure of schools and of classrooms that causes this disgorging of even the most noble efforts to reform pedagogical practice.

Since Dewey made that observation in 1901, there have been some indications as to where those disabling factors lie. At the heart of the conflict between what Dewey called "external factors" and enlightened pedagogical reform, it seems to me, is the antagonism between two seemingly compatible functions that teachers are asked to perform: the keeping order function and the teaching function. On the surface, it makes perfectly good sense to maintain that one cannot really get down to teaching unless there is a modicum of order; hardly anyone would dispute that. But in practice, the injunction to keep order has become so supreme that it simply swamps the teaching function.[15] The conditions of schooling are such that one can be counted as a good or at least acceptable teacher if the classroom is orderly. Yet this keeping order function is threatened by certain reforms such as those advocated by leaders of the child-centered movement. The most persuasive single reason I can adduce for the persistence of recitation as the predominant mode of teaching is that it is a reasonably effective way of keeping order. We are even told in methods classes that we should spread the questions around so that students are kept guessing as to who will get the next question from the teacher. The teacher as question asker and the student as responder is a way of insuring teacher dominance in the classroom situation. If students asked the questions, or if they addressed one another rather than the teacher, or if they engaged independently in discovery practices, the risk of disorder would be introduced, and the structure of school organization will not tolerate that kind of risk. The prevalence of worksheets, for example, is simply a more extreme although still familiar example of the same phenomenon. Worksheets are damnable pedagogically, but they persist because they are reliable instruments of control.

The short answer, then, as to why certain reforms fail—especially those that require a change in the locus of control—is that such a change threatens a loss of order, and the climate of the classroom as well as the larger work environment of teachers is not conducive to that kind of risk-taking. Educational reforms involving changes in teaching practice fail with such monotonous regularity because enlightened reform rhetoric and the generosity of spirit that impels people to attempt to change things for the better come into direct conflict with institutional realities. Good intentions and even competence notwithstanding, teachers are absolutely required to maintain a precarious order, and only the very courageous are willing to risk its loss.

The 'Pendulum Swing' Phenomenon

Related to the question of what kinds of reform succeed and which fail is another historical phenomenon to which many interested observers have alluded, the phenomenon of recurring cycles of reform. Like the belief that educational reforms are doomed to failure, concern about recurring cycles or pendulum swings may be justified in some sense but is at least overstated. I have never been a believer in the dictum, for example, that history actually repeats itself. In one of his lectures to future secondary school teachers, Émile Durkheim argued that the value of the study of history must be found elsewhere:[16] "At most [history] could put us on guard against repeating old mistakes; but then again, since the realm of errors knows no bounds, error itself can appear in an infinite variety of forms; a knowledge of old mistakes made in the past will enable us neither to foresee nor to avert those which will be made in the future."[17] To be sure, certain familiar problems may recur from time to time, but they always occur in different settings and with different actors, so whatever it is we can learn from the past must be reinterpreted in the light of those differences.

The example of a pendulum swing that comes to mind occurred roughly between the end of World War II and the mid-seventies. At a White House Conference held on June 1, 1945, Charles Prosser, a veteran of the old vocational education struggles and a hero in the victorious battle over the Smith-Hughes Act of 1917, was asked to summarize the recommendations of the conference. I do not suppose we will ever know whether he actually summarized the proceedings accurately; but he did report the participants as holding the view that twenty percent of the high school population was receiving an appropriate college-entrance education and that another twenty percent was being well served by vocational programs but that the remaining sixty percent was not receiving the life adjustment education they really needed.[18] (I have a feeling that these percentages were made up on the spot.)

In any case, what was launched by this declaration was that dismal chapter in the history of educational reform, life adjustment education. Like other reform movements, life adjustment education was in large measure a slogan system rather than a concrete agenda for reform, but two life adjustment conferences were held under the auspices of the Commissioner of Education, and we have at least a general idea of what that movement was about. Essentially, it was a revival of the old social efficiency idea that the principal function of schooling should be the adjustment (preferably the happy adjustment) of individuals to the social world in which they find themselves. In fact, the percentages of the high school population that Prosser originally used were soon forgotten in the enthusiasm for the idea, and in short order life adjustment education was being proposed for everyone. As one leading proponent of life adjustment put it, "If the products of our schools turn out to be good husbands, good wives, good fathers, good mothers, wise spenders of income, wholesome users of leisure time, and so forth, we know that our schools are good."[19] As in the case of child-centered education, we can only estimate how much of life adjustment ideology actually found itself into the classrooms of the country. There are some indications that it did here and there,[20] but what evidence we have suggests that it was less successful as a movement in that regard than was the earlier child-centered movement.

The pendulum began to swing back rather slowly. Contrary to popular belief, an adverse reaction to the anti-academic and even anti-intellectual formulations of the leaders of the life adjustment movement was already under way before Sputnik was launched on October 5, 1957. Two books sharply critical of American education were published as early as 1949: *Crisis in Education* and *And Madly Teach*.[21] A vitriolic attack on the anti-intellectualism of the American education establishment was published by a professor of botany in *Scientific Monthly* in 1951,[22] an article that drew 248 favorable responses. And in 1953, the historian, Arthur Bestor capped a number of effective attacks on life adjustment education with his book, *Educational Wastelands*.[23] (Incidentally, the re-publication of *Educational Wastelands* in 1988 was a signal to many of a return to an earlier reform era.) Apart from these attacks, however, people like Max Beberman at the University of Illinois and Jerrold Zaccharias at the Massachusetts Institute of Technology were already working on programs of reform that were practically antithetical to life adjustment education. When Sputnik was launched, it served mainly to put education in the media spotlight and to make it more of a national issue than it already was. In concrete terms, it undoubtedly was a vital factor in the passage of the National Defense Education Act which was passed in less than a year after the launching. The publication of Jerome Bruner's report of the Wood's Hole Conference under the title *The Process of Education* gave the new movement focus and its own slogan of sorts, "structure of the disciplines."[24]

The new movement was almost a polar opposite to life adjustment education in terms of what it saw as the proper role for schools in American society (hence its characterization as a pendulum swing), and it benefitted from millions of dollars made available by Congress through the National Science Foundation (NSF) for curriculum reform. (Life adjustment education received only moral support from the Federal government.) Along the lines of the Physical Sciences Study Committee, first formed in 1956, other projects in chemistry, biology, social studies and other subjects were initiated. With much media fanfare, the term "new math" came into vogue. Consistent with some of Bruner's recommendations, these new programs sought departures from traditional modes of teaching, especially rote teaching, and tried to substitute inquiry-based exploratory work. Perhaps mindful of past difficulties in getting teachers actually to change their familiar practices, administrators of these curriculum reform projects spent a large percentage of NSF funds on teacher training. By 1977, for example, approximately forty five percent of science teachers around the country had attended at least one workshop sponsored by NSF, and over thirty percent of high school mathematics teachers were involved in such workshops.[25] One survey conducted in 1976–77 found that sixty percent of secondary schools and thirty percent of elementary schools were actually using science materials emanating from NSF projects.[26]

One reason, however, for this apparent success was the strategy on the part of several of the NSF-sponsored curriculum reform projects to concentrate on creating new textbooks. Other more flexible types of materials that were also part of the proposed reforms were not nearly as widely adopted. In effect, then, the structure of the disciplines movement did succeed moderately in changing portions of the content of courses, particularly at the high school level, but it did not shift the locus of instruction away from teachers and textbooks in the direction, say, of what was widely called discovery practices. In fact, one analysis of the effects of the movement concluded that "Teachers were influenced by external factors only to the extent that it suited them and their circumstances allowed it."[27] Once again, even in the case of a moderately successful reform (at least in its time), we find the degree of success limited by the seeming impenetrability of certain familiar teaching practices such as recitation and teaching directly from the textbook.

How can we interpret this cycle of reform as distinct from the individual instances of reform I alluded to earlier? In my judgment, no single-factor explanation, such as the orbiting of Sputnik, seems plausible. Life adjustment held out the promise of a stable, smoothly running society by revivifying the longstanding doctrine that the secondary school curriculum in particular was unduly academic, a holdover from elitist schooling of the nineteenth century, and needed to be replaced with a program of studies directly tied to the everyday duties of life. That professional educators, such as the National Association of Secondary-School Principals, were in the forefront of this movement was probably prompted by the fact that the New Deal administration in the 1930s had taken some initiatives, such as the Civilian Conservation Corps and the National Youth Administration, which threatened the preeminence of the public secondary school as *the* institution where youth belonged.

The demise of life adjustment was not only the result of heroic efforts by people like Bestor or of the public clamor that attended the launching of Sputnik, but also, and perhaps primarily, a distinct decline of the yearning for a return to normalcy after World War II, a change in the national mood that quickly gave way to the Cold War. The real or perceived threat of external aggression made normalcy an outmoded doctrine. While the major figures in the structure of the disciplines movement were, to my knowledge, not cold warriors, popular and political support for an academic curriculum rather than a life adjustment one came from the notion spread not only by the likes of Admiral Hyman Rickover but by the very language of the *National Defense* Education Act. Over time, how to do mathematics and physics became a more urgent national priority than how to bake a cherry pie (to use Bestor's favorite example of life adjustment ideals). A changed social and political climate, in other words, made the ideas of life adjustment education appear obsolete, even an anathema.

Unlike the life adjustment movement, much of the leadership of the structure of the disciplines movement came from outside the education establishment. Edward G. Begle, Bentley Glass and Jerrold Zacharias, I assume, never had an education course in their lives. If nothing else, this new reform movement brought one highly significant aspect of educational reform into focus. While selected teachers were involved in some of the planning of the reforms, the large body of teachers who were supposed to bring about those reforms were, by and large, treated as consumers of external initiatives rather than actual partners in the change process. The change was essentially externally imposed. It should come as no surprise, then, that teachers used NSF-sponsored materials primarily to the extent that they felt it would fit their time-honored pattern of instruction, and left out what may have been the most important thrust of the reforms. Two factors, then, were primarily responsible for setting limits on the success of the movement. First, large numbers of teachers simply did not share the visions of how to do physics or how to do mathematics that were emanating from the various sites of the reform projects. Secondly, as in the case of other reforms, willingness to undertake new practices extended only to the point where the risk of a loss of order began.

Finally, it should be said that neither the life adjustment movement nor the structure of the disciplines movement that succeeded it was a return to something that had in any literal sense gone before. In gross terms, the change can be characterized as a switch from soft pedagogy to hard pedagogy; but although the doctrine of life adjustment education contained within it certain elements of earlier ideologies, especially social efficiency, its anti-academic and virulent anti-intellectual tenets had not been expressed in such bald and vehement terms in earlier periods. Likewise, the structure of the disciplines movement may in a very crude way have been foreshadowed by the work of the Committee of Ten,[28] and its leading spokesperson, Charles W. Eliot, but in no sense were the reforms of the 1960s infused with a mental discipline orientation as were the reforms proposed by Eliot and his contemporaries. To be sure, there was a distinct shift in pedagogical reform orientation in the later 1950s and early 1960s, but that change reflected social and political as well as pedagogical trends that were for all practical purposes unique to that period.

The Historical 'Lesson'

Let me conclude by returning to the question of what, if anything, may be learned from historical examples of the sort I cited earlier or from the lone example of what is commonly regarded as a pendulum swing. Historical lessons carry a quite different message from the implicit and even sometimes explicit lesson that a traditional social science orientation brings to educational practice. The message conveyed by the traditional research orientation, which I regard as misleading, is that the study of education can yield generalized rules of action.

That orientation undergirds many programs of teacher education. Prospective teachers enroll in programs leading to certification with the understandable expectation that, quite simply, they will be told how to teach. It is very difficult for the faculty teaching those courses to challenge such a widespread expectation, so they work valiantly in what often turns out to be a futile effort to fulfill it. They try mightily to use educational research in order to convey the rules of good teaching that their students demand. What is much more difficult to convey is that teaching is supremely contextual, and what it is reasonable to expect from teacher education under those circumstances are not recipes for what to do under particular circumstances; rather it is the ability to use whatever "intellectual instrumentalities" we are able to acquire in the course of our education as teachers in order to make wise judgments and sophisticated choices in those unique contexts.

It is precisely this kind of 'lesson' that the study of history can provide. In contrast to the widespread acceptance, even reverence, accorded to scientific research, history holds a rather peculiar place in the educational world. It is not exactly ignored; in fact, there is a kind of ritualistic obeisance paid to it. Many textbooks and yearbooks on various themes in education, for example, begin with an obligatory historical chapter on the subject. But if history does not repeat itself and we cannot use it as a reliable guide to avoiding mistakes, as Durkheim suggests, then what really can it offer by way of illumination on problems such as those I have alluded to here? In my view, if there is something that can be legitimately be called a lesson, it derives not from the substance of the issues but from the way they are treated. Reforms that entail pedagogical practice require all those involved, researchers and practitioners alike, as Dewey implied, to reinterpret the data for themselves in the light of the particular circumstances in which the problem is imbedded. This means that teachers are not simply the compliant beneficiaries of research findings passed on to them by others; they are compelled by the nature of their work as teachers to reinterpret those findings in the light of situationally determined characteristics.

Just as we are all obliged to be historians by virtue of the vagaries of memory and by the universal human impulse to create order out of raw experience, so are we all obliged to be interpreters of the way in which research findings in education resonate with our own unique mix of students, subject matter, setting, and teacher characteristics. The central lesson that educational reformers can derive from historical antecedents is that pedagogical practice is highly contextual, making the success of every reform contingent on the extent to which it can be interpreted and adapted in the light of particular conditions. In this respect, the lessons of history are not very different from lessons that are derived and properly interpreted from avowedly scientific investigations of the teaching process.

Notes

1. Paper prepared for delivery at the Holmes Group Conference, January 27–29, 1989, Atlanta, Georgia.

2. Werrett W. Charters, "Regulating the Project," *Journal of Educational Research* 5 (March 1922): 245–246.

3. Carl W. Kaestle, *Pillars of the Republic: Common Schools and American Society, 1880–1980* (New York: Hill and Wang, 1983).

4. Theodore R. Sizer, *Horace's Compromise: The Dilemma of the American High School* (Boston: Houghton Mifflin, 1984).

5. Arthur G. Powell, Eleanor Farrar and David K. Cohen, *The Shopping Mall High School: Winners and Losers in the Educational Marketplace* (Boston, Houghton Mifflin, 1985).

6. Philip A. Cusick, *The Egalitarian Ideal and the American High School: Studies of Three Schools* (New York: Longman, 1983).

7. Linda McNeil, *Contradictions of Control: School Structure and School Knowledge* (New York: Routledge & Kegan Paul, 1986).

8. G. Stanley Hall, "Child Study," *Journal of Proceedings and Addresses of the National Education Association, Session of the Year 1894* (1895): 173.

9. Larry Cuban, *How Teachers Taught: Constancy and Change in American Classroom, 1890–1980* (New York: Longman, 1984).

10. John Dewey, *The Sources of a Science of Education* (New York: Horace Liveright, 1929).

11. Ibid., p. 28.

12. Ibid., p. 30.

13. Quoted in Cuban, *How Teacher Taught: Constancy and Change in American Classroom, 1890–1980*, p. 51.

14. John Dewey, "The Situation as Regards the Course of Study," *Journal of the Proceedings and Addresses of the Fortieth Annual Meeting of the National Education Association* (1901): 337–338.

15. See, for example, Cusick, *The Egalitarian Ideal and the American High School: Studies of Three Schools.*

16. Émile Durkheim, *The Evolution of Educational Thought: Lectures on the Formation and Development of Secondary Education in France*, trans. by P. Collins (London: Routledge & Kegen Paul, 1977 [1904–5]).

17. Ibid., p. 9.

18. US Office of Education, *Vocational Education in the Years Ahead: A Report of a Committee to Study Postwar Problems in Vocational Education* (Washington, DC: US Government Printing Office, 1945).

19. Vernon L. Nickell, "How can We Develop an Effective Program of Education for Life Adjustment?" *Bulletin* 33 (National Association of Secondary-School Principals, 1949), p. 154.

20. Dorothy E. Broder, *Life Adjustment Education: An Historical Study of a Program of the United States Office of Education, 1945–1954,* unpublished doctoral dissertation, Teachers College, Columbia University, 1977.

21. Bernard I. Bell, *Crisis in Education: A Challenge to American Complacency* (New York: Whittesey House, 1949). M. B. Smith, *And Madly Teach: A Layman Looks at Public School Education* (Chicago: Henry Regnery, 1949).

22. Harold J. Fuller, "Time Emperer's New Clothes, or *Prius Dementat,*" *Scientific Monthly* 72, (January 1951), pp. 32–41.

23. Arthur E. Bestor, *Educational Wastelands: The Retreat from Learning in Our Public Schools* (Urbana, IL: University of Illinois Press, 1953).

24. Jerome Bruner, *The Process of Education* (Cambridge, MA: Harvard University Press, 1958).

25. Richard F. Elmore and Milbrey W. McLaughlin, *Steady Work: Policy Practice, and the Reform of American Education,* Report prepared for the National Institute of Education (Santa Monica, CA: RAND Corporation, 1988), pp. 15–16.

26. Ibid., p. 16.

27. J. Myron Atkin and Ernest R. House, "The Federal Role in Curriculum Development, 1950–80," *Educational Evaluation and Policy Analysis* 3 (September–October 1981), p. 13.

28. National Education Association, *Report of the Committee on Secondary School Studies* (Washington, DC: United States Government Printer Office, 1893).

Part II

Essays in Curriculum Theory

7

Bureaucracy and Curriculum Theory

Historians of education agree that American education went through a kind of metamorphosis after the turn of this century, but the nature and effect of the changes are in dispute. In the popular mind, the reforms that were wrought during that period—indeed the whole first half of the twentieth century—have become associated with a broad and loosely defined "progressive education" movement. John Dewey is seen as the dominant force in American educational practice with an undisciplined child-centered pedagogy dubiously ascribed to him. Even a cursory examination of the work of educational reformers during this period, however, indicates that influential leaders differed widely in the doctrines they espoused and in the pedagogical reforms they advocated. Clearly, the educational ideas of a David Snedden or a Franklin Bobbitt differed enormously from those of a John Dewey or a Stanwood Cobb. There is no doubt that this was a period of ferment in education, with new ideas filling the void being created by the steadily declining theory of mental discipline.

The picture that emerges from the apparently frenetic educational activity during the first few decades of this century seems to be one of growing acceptance of a powerful and restrictive bureaucratic model for education which looked toward the management techniques of industry as its ideal of excellence and source of inspiration. The dominant metaphor for educational theory in the early twentieth century was drawn not from the educational philosophy of John Dewey or even from romantic notions of child-

First appeared in *Freedom, Bureaucracy and Schooling*, edited by Vernon Haubrich, 1971 Yearbook of the Association for Supervision and Curriculum Development. Copyright 1971 Association for Supervision and Curriculum Development. Reprinted with permission. All rights reserved.

hood, but from corporate management. As Ellwood P. Cubberley explicated that model in 1916,

> Every manufacturing establishment that turns out a standard product or a series of products of any kind maintains a force of efficiency experts to study methods of procedure and to measure and test the output of its works. Such men ultimately bring the manufacturing establishment large returns, by introducing improvements in processes and procedure, and in training the workmen to produce larger and better output. Our schools are, in a sense, factories in which the raw products (children) are to be shaped and fashioned into products to meet the various demands of life. The specifications for manufacturing come from the demands of twentieth-century civilization, and it is the business of the school to build its pupils according to the specifications laid down. This demands good tools, specialized machinery, continuous measurement of production to see it is according to specifications, the elimination of waste in manufacture, and a large variety in the output.[1]

Children, in other words, were to become the "standard products" which would be fashioned according to the design specifications set forth by the social world. The institution of schooling was simply that vast bureaucratic machinery which transforms the crude raw material of childhood into a socially useful product. A redesigned curriculum, stripped of the playful and wasteful, was to be the chief instrument in effecting the change.

The Impact of Scientific Management

The context for the bureaucratization of the school curriculum that was to take place in the twentieth century was manifest in the general social and intellectual climate of American society at the turn of the century. The late nineteenth century saw the breakdown of a community-centered society and with it the ideal of the individual as the unit element in social life. The press of corporate expansion and urbanization made the individual merely a cog in a great machine. Whereas the individual retained a measure of recognition in a community-centered society, the vast new social and economic units robbed him of his identity. Responses to this fundamental change in American society ranged from the economic radicalism of Henry George to the utopian socialism of Edward Bellamy. But "the ideas that filtered through and eventually took the fort," according to Wiebe, "were the bureaucratic ones peculiarly suited to the fluidity and impersonality of an urban-industrial world."[2]

The particular response that captured the imagination of Americans at the turn of the century was a form of idealized bureaucracy known widely as scientific management. Its principal spokesperson was Frederick W. Taylor, and its watchword was efficiency. Taylorism differs from classical conceptions of bureaucracy (for example, Weber) in its emphasis on sheer practical efficiency rather than analysis of complex lines of power and influence within organizations. Under Taylor's concept of scientific management, productivity is central, and the individual is simply an element in the production system. Basic to Taylor's conception of scientific management was the assumption that human beings are motivated by economic gain and would sacrifice much in the way of job satisfaction and physical ease in order to achieve such gain. Yet scientific principles had to be applied to the worker as well as to the work, and this involved careful study of the worker's "own special abilities and limitations" in an effort "to develop each individual man to his highest state of efficiency and prosperity"[3] (anticipating, in a way, the modern guidance movement in schools).

One of Taylor's proudest accomplishments was to inveigle a man he called Schmidt into increasing his handling of pig iron at a Bethlehem Steel plant from twelve and a half tons a day to forty-seven tons. Schmidt was selected after careful observation and study of seventy-five men, partly because he was observed to trot home in the evening about as fresh as when he trotted in to work in the morning and partly because inquiries revealed that he was "close with a dollar." Taylor even gives an extended verbatim account of his discussion with Schmidt:

"Schmidt, are you a high-priced man?"

"Vell, I don't know vat you mean."

"Oh, yes you do. What I want to know is whether you are a high-priced man or not."

"Vell, I don't know vat you mean."

"Oh, come now, you answer my questions. What I want to find out is whether you are a high-priced man or one of these cheap fellows here. What I want to find out is whether you want to earn $1.85 a day or whether you are satisfied with $1.15, just the same as all those cheap fellows are getting."

"Did I vant $1.85 a day? Vas dot a high-priced man? Vell, yes, I vas a high-priced man."

"Oh, you're aggravating me. Of course you want $1.85 a day—everyone wants it! You know perfectly well that that has very little to do with your being a high-priced man. For goodness' sake answer my questions, and don't waste any more of my time. Now come over here. You see that pile of pig iron?"[4]

Using this economic motivation, Taylor proceeded to instruct Schmidt in the efficient performance of every stage of the operation. Schmidt's step must have been a little heavier as he trotted home that night.

Thus, the individual under Taylorism was not ignored; on the contrary, he was made the subject of intense investigation, but only within the context of increasing product output. Through time and motion studies, the worker's movements were broken down into minute operations, and then standards of efficiency were developed for each of the operations. The rules of scientific management and psychological principles were than applied to the worker to bring him up to the appropriate level of efficiency. As Mouzelis summarizes the individual's role under Taylorism; "The organization member was conceived as an instrument of production which can be handled as easily as any other tool (provided that one knows the laws of scientific management)."[5] The essence of scientific management was the fragmentation and analysis of work and its reordering into the most efficient arrangement possible.

One of the attractions of Taylorism was that it carried with it an ethical dimension which bore a superficial resemblance to some of the tried and true virtues of the nineteenth century. One of Taylor's first professional papers, for example, delivered in 1895 at a meeting of the American Society of Mechanical Engineers, made the case for a "piece-rate system" partly on moral grounds. The minimum time for each operation would be computed and the worker would be paid for his performance relative to that fixed performance level. In this way, the worker's interest would coincide with that of his employer and "soldiering" (loafing on the job) would be eliminated. Once the work load was broken down into elementary operations, an "honest day's work" could be scientifically computed.[6] "If a man won't do what is right," Taylor argued, "*make* him."[7] Since scientific rate-fixing could be used to outline the dimensions of virtuous activity, industry could be rewarded and sloth punished.

The appeal of Taylor's doctrine of scientific efficiency was not limited to an elite corps of business leaders. The rising cost of living in the early twentieth century was a matter of great concern to the broad American middle class, and scientific management promised lower prices through increased efficiency. The wide publicity given to the Eastern Rate Case of 1910–11 also drew much popular attention to the cause of efficiency. Railroads were asking for an increase in freight rates, and, arguing against their position, Louis Brandeis claimed that scientific management could save the railroads a million dollars a day. In support of his contention, he brought forward a series of witnesses in the form of efficiency experts. As Haber summarized the effect of their testimony: "The Eastern Rate Case was transformed into a morality play for up-to-date middle-class reformers"[8] which eventually culminated in an orgy of efficiency affecting millions of Americans. The effect on the schools was not long in coming.

Bureaucratic Efficiency in Curriculum Theory

The bureaucratic model for curriculum design had a rather unremarkable birth. School administrators simply reacted to the influence of the scientific management movement in industry by interpolating those methods to the management of schools. Managers of schools patterned themselves after their counterparts in industry and took pride in adapting the vocabulary and techniques of industry to school administration.[9] Cost accounting and maximum utilization of school plants were among their paramount concerns. The period, in fact, may be regarded as one in which the "transition of the superintendent of schools from an educator to a business manager" took place.[10]

The efficiency movement, however, was to affect more than just the administration of schools. Its most profound effect was on curriculum theory itself. Among the early prophets of the new efficiency in school administration was the man who later was to become the preeminent force in curriculum reform, and, indeed, the man who gave shape and direction to the curriculum field, John Franklin Bobbitt.

Bobbitt's early work essentially followed the main line of adapting business techniques for use in schools. In 1912, for example, Bobbitt took as his model of efficiency the operation of the Gary, Indiana schools. "The first principle of scientific management," he announced, "is to use all the plant all the available time."[11] Although the typical school plant operates at fifty percent efficiency, the "educational engineer" in Gary set as his task the development of a plan to operate at one hundred percent efficiency during school hours. Although a relatively high level of efficiency of school plant operation was achieved by creating regular and special periods of activity, perfect efficiency was thwarted by the fact that the school plant was used only five days a week. "That an expensive plant should lie idle during all of Saturday and Sunday while 'street and alley time' is undoing the good work of the schools," Bobbitt complained, "is a further thorn in the flesh of the clear-sighted educational engineer."[12] He also mourned the closing of the school plant during the summer, "a loss of some 16 percent, no small item in the calculations of the efficiency engineer."[13]

Bobbitt's second principle of scientific management, "to reduce the number of workers to a minimum by keeping each at the maximum of his working efficiency,"[14] reflected the need for division of labor and job specialization in the school. His third principle simply involved the elimination of waste. Here, Bobbitt commented on the wasteful concomitant of "ill-health and lowered vitality" and commended Superintendent Wirt's efforts to provide appropriate recreational facilities for the students in the Gary schools.

Bobbitt's fourth principle of general scientific management made the leap from the areas of simple plant and worker efficiency into the realm of educational theory:

> Work up the raw material into that finished product for which it is best adapted. Applied to education this means: Educate the individual according to his capabilities. This requires that the materials of the curriculum be sufficiently various to meet the needs of every class of individuals in the community; and the course of training and study be sufficiently flexible that the individual can be given just the things he needs.[15]

This extrapolation of the principles of scientific management to the area of curriculum made the child the object on which the bureaucratic machinery of the school operates. The student became the raw material from which the school-factory must fashion a product drawn to the specifications of social convention. What was at first simply a direct application of general management principles to the management of schools became the central metaphor on which modern curriculum theory rests.

"Educate the individual according to his capabilities" has an innocent and plausible ring; but what this meant in practice was that dubious judgments about the innate capacities of children became the basis for differentiating the curriculum along the lines of probable destination for the child. Dominated by the criterion of social utility, these judgments became self-fulfilling prophecies in the sense that they predetermined which slots in the social order would be filled by which "class of individuals." Just as Taylor decided that: "one of the first requirements for a man who is fit to handle pig iron as a regular occupation is that he shall be so stupid and phlegmatic that he more nearly resembles in his mental makeup the ox than any other type,"[16] so it was the schools that now were to determine (scientifically, of course) what biographical, psychological, or social factors in human beings fit them to be the hewers of wood and the drawers of water in our society. Although still in undeveloped form, this conception of the work of the school in relation to the child and his studies became a central element in Bobbitt's influential curriculum research and theory a decade or so later. The ramifications of this central production metaphor in educational theory are now widely felt.

Through the first quarter of the twentieth century, Bobbitt continued to take the lead in reforming the administration of public schools along the lines of scientific management advocated by Taylor. One such recommendation, for example, took the Harriman railroad system as the model of efficiency. Bobbitt pointed out how that massive enterprise had been divided into 30 autonomous divisions, each with its own specialized staff, resulting in a high rate of efficiency. Extrapolating from this and other examples, Bobbitt went on to comment on the functions of specialized supervisors in schools in determining "proper methods" and "the determination of more or less definite qualifications for the various aspects of the teaching personality."[17] The supervisor of instruction occupied that middle-management function roughly comparable to the foreman in industry.

Increasingly, however, Bobbitt was moving from the mere translation of general principles of scientific management to the management of schools into the domain of curriculum theory. As a kind of quality control, Bobbitt advocated that "definite qualitative and quantitative standards be determined for the product."[18] In the railroad industry, he pointed out, each rail "must be thirty feet in length, and weigh eighty pounds to the yard. It must be seven and three-eighths inches in height, with a head two and one-sixty-fourth of an inch in thickness and five inches deep, and a base five inches wide."[19]

Based on studies by S. A. Courtis and others and using standard scores, Bobbitt concluded that:

> The third-grade teacher should bring her pupils up to an average
> of 26 correct [arithmetic] combinations per minute. The fourth-
> grade teacher has the task, during the year that the same pupils
> are under her care, of increasing their addition speed from an
> average of 26 combinations per minute to an average of 34 com-
> binations per minute. If she does not bring them up to the stan-
> dard 34, she has failed to perform her duty in proportion to the
> deficit; and there is no responsibility upon her for carrying them
> beyond the standard 34.[20]

Two years later, Bobbitt was to apply principles of cost accounting in business organizations to school subjects. This brought
the heart of the school curriculum, the subjects, into the orbit of
bureaucratic efficiency. Bobbitt continued to be impressed by standardization in relation to efficiency in railroad administration. He
pointed out, for example, that railroad companies know that: "lo-
comotive repair-cost should average about six cents per mile-run"
and that "lubricating oils should cost about eighteen cents per
hundred miles for passenger locomotives, and about twenty-five
cents for freight locomotives."[21] Using cost per 1,000 student-hours
as his basic unit, Bobbitt was able to report, in terms comparable
to those of industry, that the cost of instruction in mathematics in
his sample of twenty-five high schools ranged from $30 to $169
and that Latin instruction was, on the average, twenty percent more
expensive than mathematics instruction. The implications of such
an accounting procedure were developed later by Bobbitt, his colleagues, and his present-day intellectual heirs.

Standardization and the Worker

The great bane of bureaucracy is uncertainty. The inevitable course
of the bureaucratization of the curriculum, therefore, was in the
direction of predictability. As in industry, this was accomplished
mainly through the standardization of activity or work units and
of the products themselves. In the curriculum field, vague conceptions of the purposes of schooling became intolerable, and "particularization" of educational objectives became a byword. "An
age of science is demanding exactness and particularity," announced Bobbitt in the first modern book on curriculum.[22] The
curriculum became something to be discovered progressively through
the scientific analysis of the activities that human beings actually
performed. Just as scientific management became associated with
virtue, so the incipient field of curriculum looked to scientific

curriculum-making as the source of answers to the great value questions that govern the purposes of education.

The process had a commonsensical appeal. "The curriculum-discoverer will first be an analyst of human nature and human affairs."[23] This involved going out into the world of affairs and discovering the particular "abilities, attitudes, habits, appreciations, and forms of knowledge" that human beings need. These would become the objectives of the curriculum. When these multitudinous needs are not filled by "undirected experiences," then "directed experiences" would be provided through the curriculum. Bobbitt set forth the basic principle: *"The curriculum of the directed training is to be discovered in the shortcomings of individuals after they have had all that can be given by undirected training."*[24] The curriculum was the mechanism for remedying the haphazard effects of ordinary living, for achieving the standard product which undirected socialization achieved so imperfectly.

One major concomitant of such a conception of the curriculum was the broadening of its scope into the boundless domain of human activity. Instead of being merely the repository of the human race's intellectual inheritance, the curriculum now embraced the gamut of human experience, "the total range of habits, skills, abilities, forms of thought, valuations, ambitions, etc., that its members need for the effective performance of their vocational labors; likewise, the total range needed for their civic activities; their health activities; their recreational activities; their language; their parental, religious, and general social activities."[25] The standard product would be designed and particularized in every detail.

A lonely voice of opposition to the "blight of standardization" was that of the president emeritus of Harvard University and the chief architect of the Committee of Ten report, Charles W. Eliot. Eliot, then 89 years old, pointed out that while standardization of the worker's movements in industry may have resulted in increased productivity, "the inevitable result was the destruction of the interest of the workman in his work." Standardization, he argued, was also having the same effect in education. What is more, it was antithetical to the true process of education as he saw it. "The true educational goal," he said, "is the utmost development of the individual's capacity or power, not in childhood and adolescence alone, but all through life. Fixed standards in labor, in study, in modes of family life, are downright enemies of progress for the body, mind, and soul of man."[26] Clearly, the temper of the time would not support such an anachronistic conception of education.

Standardization and Product Diversification

Apart from its implications for the individual as producer, the production metaphor in curriculum theory carries with it important implications for the individual as product. By the 1920s, a massive effort was under way to reform the curriculum through product standardization and predetermination. As usual, Bobbitt set the tone:

> In the world of economic production, a major secret of success is predetermination. The management predetermines with great exactness the nature of the products to be turned out, and in relation to the other factors, the quality of the output. They standardize and thus predetermine the processes to be employed, the quantity and quality of raw material to be used for each type and unit of product, the character and amount of labor to be employed, and the character of the conditions under which the work should be done. . . . The business world is institutionalizing foresight and developing an appropriate and effective technique.
>
> There is a growing realization within the educational profession that we must particularize the objectives of education. We, too, must institutionalize foresight, and, so far as conditions of our work will permit, develop a technique of predetermination of the particularized results to be obtained.[27]

The technique that Bobbitt referred to, the analysis of human activity into particular and specialized units of behavior, came to be known as activity analysis.

By the 1920s, Bobbitt had been joined in his campaign to reform the curriculum along the lines of the bureaucratic model by such extraordinarily influential education leaders as W. W. Charters and David Snedden. In the main, the reform in the 1920s took the form of using activity analysis to strip away the nonfunctional, the "dead wood" in the curriculum. Increasingly this was being done with reference to particular groups in the school. "The curriculum situation has become acute," Charters declared in 1921. "The masses who send their children to school are growing restive under what they consider to be the useless material taught in the grades."[28]

Besides his concern for the masses, Charters went on to show how a curriculum could be developed for another identifiable group, women. He developed a curriculum particularly for women as part of the famous study he conducted for Stephens College of Columbia, Missouri. Charters's task was to develop a program which would provide "specific training for the specific job of being a woman."[29] What constitutes being a woman, of course, was determined through activity analysis. Women all over the country were asked to write a complete statement of what they did for a week, and 95,000 replies were received. The replies were then analyzed into about 7,300 categories such as food, clothing, and health. Using these activities as his base, Charters developed the curriculum for Stephens College.

Just as Taylor found it necessary to identify discrete units of work, so were the educational leaders of the period embarking on the task of identifying the units of all human activity as the first step in curriculum planning. As Charters expressed it, the job is one of "finding out what people have to do and showing them how to do it."[30] The possibilities were limitless. Once women were identified and trained to be women, so could almost any other identifiable group in our society be trained for its role. To be sure, all persons would be trained to perform some activities in common, such as some of those involved in maintaining physical efficiency, but their differentiated roles in society could be programmed as well. As in current proposals, such programs could be advertised under the slogans of curriculum flexibility and individualized instruction.

Paradoxically, the effort to diversify the product along the lines of probable destination called for an even greater effort to standardize the units of work than before. Product diversification was not to be accomplished by diversifying work and creating variety in school activity, but by arranging the standard units of work into the most efficient arrangement for manufacturing the particular products. The man who took the lead in this aspect of the social efficiency movement was David Snedden. In 1921, Snedden had written that: "By 1925, it can confidently be hoped, the minds which direct education will have detached from the entanglements of our contemporary situation a thousand definite educational objectives, the realization of which will have demonstrable worth to our society."[31] Snedden devoted the next few years to the realization of that prediction, and also to differentiating the curriculum so that the right objectives were applied to the right "case groups."

Case groups were defined as "any considerable group of persons who in large degree resemble each other in the common possession of qualities significant to their school education."[32] Objectives, therefore, would not be applied indiscriminately, but only with reference to the raw material. This was a particular problem, according to Snedden, in the junior high school where "differences of abilities, of extra-school conditions, and of prospects will acutely manifest themselves, forcing us to differentiate curricula in more ways, probably, than as yet suspected."[33] Such a division of the school population into appropriate case groups, in Snedden's mind at least, required sustained attention to the standardization and atomizing of the curriculum. His smallest curriculum unit, the "peth," is probably best illustrated by a single spelling word.[34]

Peths, however, had to be assembled in relation to "strands," classifications of "adult life performance practices" such as "health conservation through habitual safeguarding practices" for which Snedden estimated fifty to one hundred peths, and "moral (including fellowship) behaviors" for which the same number was estimated. The vocational participation strand, however, necessitated differentiated numbers of peths, a streetcar motorman requiring only ten to twenty while a farmer or a homemaker would call for two hundred to five hundred peths. A "lotment," in turn, was "the amount of work that can be accomplished, or ground covered, by learners of modal characteristics (as related to the activity considered) in 60 clock hours."[35] Thus, as in Taylorism, standards of efficiency were set for individual units of work in line with idealized performance levels. Actually, much of Snedden's work parallels the work of one of Taylor's major disciples, Frank Gilbreth, who identified 18 units of motion which he called "therbligs," thereby immortalizing his name in reverse.[36]

Yet the quaint obscurity of the educational terminology of the period tends to mask the underlying serious implications of the bureaucratic model applied to curriculum theory. The schoolchild became something to be molded and manipulated on his or her way to filling a predetermined social role. Guidance departments probed the child's inner resources in order to determine which of his or her potentialities were worth mining. Usually, these policies were followed in the name of bringing the outmoded academic curriculum into line with the new high school population, now dominated by the great unwashed. The curriculum was simply being made more democratic; but as Ellul has pointed out, the individual potentialities that were identified tended to coincide, as if by magic, with the needs of modern industrial society.[37] As the raw material was processed through the curriculum on its way to its ultimate state, simple efficiency dictated a differentiated curriculum in order to achieve the diversification of human labor that a modern industrial society demanded.

Snedden's ideal curriculum, composed of minute standardized work units and organized into the most efficient combinations for distinctive case groups, was of course never achieved. The influence of such a conception of the curriculum was, nevertheless, widely felt. As early as 1923–24, when George S. Counts was conducting his classic study of the high school curriculum, the multiplication of different types of curricula designed for different population groups within the schools was evident. Of the fifteen city school systems studied, only two, Detroit and Kansas City, used a system of constants and electives in their high school programs rather than a series of labeled curricula. Los Angeles, where Bobbitt's influence was undoubtedly strong in this period, maintained eighteen different curricula in its high schools. Newton, Massachusetts listed the following fifteen differentiated curricula:[38] Classical, Scientific, General, Business, Stenographic, Clerical, Household Arts, Agriculture, Printing, Electricity, Machine Work, Cabinet and Pattern-Making, Drafting, Automobile, and Carpentry. The principle of predetermination was in this way applied to differentiated vocational roles in addition to one's role as a citizen, parent, church member, and so on.

In the 1923–24 school year, also, the Lynds found in Middletown a "manifest concern . . . to dictate the social attitudes of its young citizens."[39] This was in part reflected in a host of required courses in civic training designed to support "community solidarity against sundry divisive tendencies."[40] The inculcation of appropriate civic attitudes was second only in emphasis to vocational preparation. Upon entering high school, the Middletown student chose among twelve courses of study, eight of which were distinctly vocational. Education in Middletown was clearly becoming specific preparation for certain community-sanctioned adult roles.

By the mid-1920s signs began to appear of a decline in efficiency as the predominant educational ideal and social control as a major function of the schools. Bobbitt's contribution to the influential Twenty-Sixth Yearbook of the National Society for the Study of Education represents a curious denial of some of the basic curriculum tenets he had proposed in his most popular book, published only two years before. In *How to Make a Curriculum*, Bobbitt set forth as one of his major premises that, "Education is primarily for adult life, not for child life. Its fundamental responsibility is to prepare for the fifty years of adulthood, not for the twenty years of childhood and youth.[41] It was on this fundamental assumption that Bobbitt based his case for the analysis of adult activities as the source of curriculum objectives. The efficient performance of adult activities of all kinds was the ideal toward which the whole curriculum was directed. In 1926, however, Bobbitt was to declare:

> Education is not primarily to prepare for life at some future time. Quite the reverse; it proposes to hold high the current living, making it intense, abundant, fruitful, and fitting it firmly in the grooves of habit . . .. In a very true sense, life cannot be "prepared for." It can only be lived.[42]

Such a declaration can only mean a rejection of the production model of curriculum theory, since it denies such central concepts as predetermination and predictability. When, in 1934, Bobbitt was asked to prepare a statement summarizing his curriculum theory, his rejection of his former work was clearly evident and nearly complete.[43] In the 1930s, the ideal of social efficiency in education and the production metaphor as the basis for curriculum theory were obviously in a period of decline, a decline which, however, proved to be only temporary.

The Contemporary Revival

Just as the first great drive toward standardization, predetermination, and fragmentation in the school curriculum came about in the aftermath of the first industrial revolution, so the renewal of those curriculum tendencies has come about in the aftermath of the second one—what is sometimes called the electronic or technological revolution. To be sure, some differences are evident. In the first place, the theory of behaviorism has been raised to the status of canon law in the social sciences, and so we are admonished to state the design specifications which set forth how a student will turn out in terms of observable behaviors. Second, the 1920s doctrine of social efficiency has been overlaid with a thin veneer of academic respectability, and so the modern design specifications tend to call for a student to identify certain points on a map or to reel off the valences of a set of chemical elements instead of emphasizing practical, nonacademic activities.

Given these qualifications, Snedden's bureaucratic ideal of a thousand educational objectives to be used as a blueprint for shaping the educational product is now closer to realization than ever before. Teachers may now order from a catalog 96 objectives in language arts 7–9 for $3.00, or 158 objectives in social science (geography) K–9 for $4.00, or 25 objectives in English literature 10–12 for $3.00.[44] Snedden would have considered this a bargain at twice the price. These new objectives, furthermore, are evidently being formulated with such precision and wisdom that one major proponent of the new bureaucracy was led to observe of the period preceding the present millennium: "American educators have generally engaged in the same level of discourse regarding the specification of educational goals that one might derive from the grunts of a Neanderthal."[45] "One can only sympathize," he reflected, "with thousands of learners who had to obtain an education from an instructional system built on a muddle-minded conception of educational goals."[46]

One can avoid muddle-mindedness, apparently, by overcoming a preoccupation with means or process in favor of a focus on outcomes.[47] Current curriculum practice seems to take the form of drawing up endless lists of minute design specifications in behavioral terms and then finding the right "media mix" by which the product can be most efficiently manufactured. "Judgments about the success of an instructional procedure," we are told, "are made exclusively on the basis of results, that is, the changes in learner behavior which emerge as a consequence of instruction. Only if the hoped-for changes in learner behavior have been attained is the instructional process considered successful."[48] The efficient achievement of the end product becomes the criterion by which the means are selected.

Such a sharp dichotomy between ends and means is precisely what resulted from the introduction of the assembly line in the first industrial revolution. Work became important only insofar as it was instrumental in achieving the desired product. The success of the assembly line depends on the fact that it reduces the process of production to units so simple that the predicted outcome is assured. The worker's movements are made so elementary and routine that the product inevitably emerges independent of the will or conscious desire of the worker. John McDermott has observed about the assembly line effect: ". . . since each operation uses only a small fraction of a worker's skill, there is a very great likelihood that the operation will be performed in a minimally acceptable way. Alternately, if each operation taxed the worker's skill there would be frequent errors in the operation, frequent disturbance in work flow, and a thoroughly unpredictable quality to the end product."[49] To ensure predictability and efficiency in education, the techniques of industry are introduced with the same effect. Work loses any organic relationship with the end product.

Take, for example, the much publicized program, Individually Prescribed Instruction. Teachers prepare prescriptions—directions for what the child must accomplish. The child, after receiving his or her prescription, places a recorded disk on some playback equipment, and a disembodied voice asks: "Hello, how are you today?" (Pause for response.) "Today we are going to learn the sounds of the letters. Do you have a pencil?" The child responds and then is directed in the performance of certain tasks. If the child is able to perform these tasks with eighty-five percent accuracy, he or she is rewarded with a new prescription. If the child fails, he or she is given remedial training until the performance standard is met.[50] Progress is carefully plotted by a computer as the child passes through the standard work units. Individuality, here, refers to the speed by which one makes his or her way through the standard work units. Of course, just as corporate management can make the tedium of the assembly line tolerable by scheduling a scientifically determined number of coffee breaks, so can the modern technologist make school work bearable by building into his system an appropriate schedule of other activities. But this would go about as far to create delight in intellectual activity as coffee breaks have in restoring the dignity of work.

In education, as in industry, the standardization of the product also means the standardization of work. Educational activity which may have an organic wholeness and vital meaning takes on significance only in terms of its contribution to the efficient manufacture of the finished product. As in industry, the price of worship at the altar of efficiency is the alienation of the worker from his or her work—where the continuity and wholeness of the enterprise are destroyed for those who engage in it. Here, then, is one great threat that the production metaphor governing modern curriculum theory poses for American education.

The bureaucratic model, along with its behavioristic and technological refinements, threatens to destroy, in the name of efficiency, the satisfaction that one may find in intellectual activity. The sense of delight in intellectual activity is replaced by a sense of urgency. The thrill of the hunt is converted into an efficient kill. The wonder of the journey is superseded by the relentless pursuit of the destination. And to condition the victim to enjoy being conditioned is certainly less humane than open coercion or bribery.

The tragic paradox of the production metaphor applied to curriculum is that the dehumanization of education, the alienation of means from ends, the stifling of intellectual curiosity carry with them very few compensations. In the corporate structure, the worker who has become a cog in a vast bureaucracy is at least rewarded with an improved financial status and opportunity for leisure. The megamachine in ancient Egypt, where the autonomy of human beings was sacrificed in the great cause of the building of the pyramids, at least produced some measure of increased agricultural production and flood control.[51] What comparable benefits accrue from a corresponding regimentation in education? The particularization of the *educational* product, it turns out, is tantamount to its trivialization. A case in point is what happens to history as it is particularized in the highly regarded and liberally financed ES '70s project. One of the more than fifty pilot schools lists among its educational products the following typical examples in the form of items on a computer-printed Individual Student Progress Report (formerly known as a report card):

> Given a list which includes Sibley, Colonel Snelling, Father Galtier, J.J. Hill, Ramsey, Fur Traders, missionaries, soldiers, and settlers of Minnesota and several true statements about their contributions, the student is able to match the listed people with the proper true statements.
>
> Given several statements describing early and present day lumbering in Minnesota, the student is able to identify lumbering in Minnesota by writing E —early lumbering—, P —present day lumbering—, or B —both— in front of the applicable statements.

Educational products manufactured at such a level of particularity, even if multiplied a millionfold, could only be trivial. History (assuming that history is the discipline represented by these performance outcomes) simply is not the accurate recitation of bits and pieces of information. Nor is any discipline a specific finite assemblage of facts and skills. So to define it *is* to trivialize it.

This is not to say that instructional objectives, in and of themselves, are useless. They can add a dimension to educational activity; but they have no meaning outside the context of the means toward their achievement. There are, certainly, a variety of ways to consider the complex interrelationships between means and ends.[52] But the creation of a sharp dichotomy between means and ends or the consideration of means only in the context of efficiency is, pedagogically speaking, a travesty. From an educational point of view, behavior, *in and of itself*, is of little significance. It is, on the other hand, critically important to know how one comes to behave as one does; whether, for example, a given act derives from mere conditioning or from rational decision-making processes.

Modern curriculum theory, currently being influenced by systems analysis, tends to regard the child simply as input inserted into one end of a great machine from which he or she eventually emerges at the other end as output replete with all the behaviors, the "competencies," and the skills for which that child has been programmed. Even when the output is differentiated, such a mechanistic conception of education contributes only to regimentation and dehumanization, rather than to autonomy.

The mechanistic conception of human life, the technology-systems analysis approach to human affairs, the production metaphor for curriculum design, all share a common perspective. They represent a deterministic outlook on human behavior. The behavior of human beings is controlled in an effort to make people do the particular things that someone wants them to do. This may take the form of getting people to vote every election day, to buy the latest miracle detergent, or to recite on cue the valences of thirty out of thirty-five chemical elements. As Von Bertalanffy put it, "Stimulus-response, input-output, producer-consumer are all the same concepts, only expressed in different terms . . . people are manipulated as they deserve, that is, as overgrown Skinner rats."[53]

Notes

1. Ellwood P. Cubberley, *Public School Administration* (Boston: Houghton Mifflin Company, 1916), p. 338.

2. Robert H. Wiebe, *The Search for Order 1877–1920* (New York: Hill and Wang, 1967), p. 145.

3. Frederick Winslow Taylor, *The Principles of Scientific Management* (New York: Harper & Brothers, 1911), p. 43.

4. Ibid., pp. 44–45.

5. Nicos P. Mouzelis, *Organization and Bureaucracy: An Analysis of*

Modern Theories (Chicago: Aldine Publishing Company, 1967), p. 85.

6. Cited in Samuel Haber, *Efficiency and Uplift: Scientific Management in the Progressive Era 1890–1920* (Chicago: University of Chicago Press, 1964), pp. 1–3.

7. Frank Barkley Copley, *Frederick Winslow Taylor: Father of Scientific Management* (New York: Harper & Brothers, 1923). Quoted in Haber, ibid., pp. 2–3.

8. Haber, *Efficiency and Uplift: Scientific Management in the Progress Era 1890–1920*, p. 54.

9. The administration aspect of the bureaucratization of the schools has been ably interpreted by: Raymond E. Callahan, *Education and the Cult of Efficiency: A Study of the Social Forces That Have Shaped the Administration of the Public Schools* (Chicago: University of Chicago Press, 1962).

10. Ibid., p. 148.

11. John Franklin Bobbitt, "The Elimination of Waste in Education," *The Elementary School Teacher* 12 (February 1912), p. 260.

12. Ibid., p. 263.

13. Ibid., p. 264.

14. Ibid.

15. Ibid., p. 269.

16. Taylor, *The Principles of Scientific Management*, p. 59.

17. Franklin Bobbitt, "Some General Principles of Management Applied to the Problems of City-School Systems" in *Twelfth Yearbook of the National Society for the Study of Education*, Part 1 (Chicago: University of Chicago Press, 1913), p. 62.

18. Ibid., p. 11.

19. Ibid.

20. Ibid., pp. 21–22.

21. John Franklin Bobbitt, "High-School Costs," *School Review* 23 (October 1915), p. 505.

22. Franklin Bobbitt, *The Curriculum* (Boston: Houghton Mifflin Company, 1918), p. 41.

23. Ibid., p. 43.

24. Ibid., p. 45. (Original italics.)

25. Ibid., p. 43.

26. Charles W. Eliot, Letter to *The New York Times* 72 (23,946), p. 12; August 17, 1923. Copyright—1923 by The New York Times Company. Reprinted by permission.

27. Franklin Bobbitt, "The Objectives of Secondary Education," *School Review* 28 (December 1920), p. 738.

28. Werrett W. Charters, "The Reorganization of Women's Education," *Educational Review* 62 (October 1921), p. 224.

29. Werrett W. Charters, "Curriculum for Women," *University of Illinois Bulletin* 23 (March 8, 1926), p. 327.

30. Ibid., p. 328.

31. David Snedden, *Sociological Determination of Objectives in Education* (Philadelphia: J.B. Lippincott Company, 1921), p. 79.

32. David Snedden, " 'Case Group' Methods of Determining Flexibility of General Curricula in High Schools," *School and Society* 17 (March 17, 1923), p. 290.

33. David Snedden, "Junior High School Offerings," *School and Society* 20 (December 13, 1924), p. 740.

34. David Snedden, "Planning Curriculum Research, I," *School and Society* 22 (August 29, 1925), pp. 259–65.

35. Snedden, "Junior High School Offerings," p. 741.

36. Gilbreth's other brush with immortality was Clifton Webb's portrayal of him as the super-efficient father in the film, "Cheaper by the Dozen."

37. Jacques Ellul, *The Technological Society* (New York: Vintage Books, 1964), pp. 358–63.

38. George S. Counts, *The Senior High School Curriculum* (Chicago: University of Chicago Press, 1926), pp. 12–14.

39. Robert S. Lynd and Helen Merrell Lynd, *Middletown* (New York: Harcourt, Brace & company, Inc., 1929), p. 197.

40. Ibid., p. 196.

41. Franklin Bobbitt, *How To Make A Curriculum* (Boston: Houghton Mifflin Company, 1924), p. 8.

42. Franklin Bobbitt, "The Orientation of the Curriculum-Maker," in *The Foundations of Curriculum-Making*, Twenty-Sixth Yearbook of the National Society for the Study of Education, Part 2 (Bloomington, IL: Public School Publishing Company, 1926), p. 43.

43. Franklin Bobbitt, "A Summary Theory of the Curriculum," *Society for Curriculum Study News Bulletin* 5 (January 12, 1934), pp. 2–4.

44. Instructional Objectives Exchange, W. James Popham, Director, Center for the Study of Evaluation, University of California, Los Angeles.

45. W. James Popham, "Objectives and Instruction," American Educational Research Association Monograph on Curriculum Evalua-

tion (Chicago: Rand McNally & Company, 1969), pp. 32–33.

46. Ibid.

47. W. James Popham, "Focus on Outcomes: A Guiding Theme for ES '70 Schools," *Phi Delta Kappan* 51 (December 1969), pp. 208–10.

48. Ibid., p. 208.

49. John McDermott, "Technology: The Opiate of the Intellectuals," *New York Review of Books* 13 (July 31, 1969), p. 34.

50. "Individually Prescribed Instruction," in *Education U.S.A.*, Special Report (Washington, DC: National School Public Relations Association, 1968).

51. Lewis Mumford, *The Myth of the Machine* (London: Secker & Warburg, 1967), p. 12.

52. See, for example, D. S. Shwayder, *The Stratification of Behavior* (New York: Humanities Press, 1965), pp. 144–64.

53. Ludwig Von Bertalanffy, *Robots, Men, and Minds: Psychology in the Modern World* (New York: George Braziller, Inc., 1967), p. 12.

8

What Is the Question in
Teacher Education?

As she lay dying, Gertrude Stein is reputed to have uttered one last memorable line: "What *is* the answer? . . . . In that case, what is the question?"[1] The question of the question is not only one of the most elusive in a broad philosophical sense, but also probably the most critical in the development and definition of a field study. "A question," writes Susanne K. Langer, "is really an ambiguous proposition; the answer is its determination. There can be only a certain number of alternatives that will complete its sense. In this way the intellectual treatment of any datum, any experience, any subject, is determined by the nature of our questions and only carried out in the answers."[2] The question sets limits on and creates the framework for the kinds of answers that are sought.

Unfortunately, the fundamental questions that characterize a field of study are frequently so submerged that they are rarely raised to the level of self-conscious examination and are sometimes only vaguely known at all. This is probably because the members of any scholarly community undergo professional socialization into their fields, which makes the fundamental questions seem entirely normal and natural. Possible alternative questions simply do not arise very readily. In one sense, the function of the question in guiding research is similar to what Thomas Kuhn associates with the paradigm: "One of the things a scientific community acquires with a paradigm is a criterion for choosing problems that, while the paradigm is taken for granted, can be assumed to have solutions."[3]

First appeared in *New Perspectives on Teacher Education,* Donald McCarty and Associates, under the title "The Question in Teacher Education." Copyright 1973 Jossey-Bass, Inc. Reprinted with permission. All rights reserved.

Where can the question (paradigm) in teacher education be found? To locate its hiding place, we need to review the kinds of questions posed by research on teaching as well as consider the historical evolution of the field of teacher education.

Early Formulations

Teaching is such a natural and spontaneous form of human activity that its origins are lost in prehistory. A "science" of teaching, however, begins in the late nineteenth century. Probably the first scientific studies of teaching to have a major impact on public consciousness were those conducted by Joseph Mayer Rice, whose exposés of American educational practice created a national furor. His early articles in *The Forum* reflected a growing concern about waste, not only in education but also in other aspects of American life. Rice felt that two fundamental questions in education had been subjected to a "mass of philosophical opinion" and had become "waterlogged in a sea of opinions."[4] "How much time shall be devoted to a subject?" and "What results shall be accomplished?" were questions that should be subjected to scientific inquiry. His "plan of application" lay "in subjecting children taught under different systems to one and the same test . . . and comparing the results."[5] Science would provide not only the appropriate standard of achievement to be reached but also the best way to achieve it. Rice estimated, for example, that some schools devoted approximately seventy percent of their instructional time to the three R's. Would a reduction to, say, fifty percent result in a comparable reduction in achievement? Or does the additional twenty percent represent a waste of instructional time and effort? In the outline of this research procedure lie the roots of the development of the scientific study of teaching and of the attempt to build a program of teacher education on that foundation.

Beginning early in 1895, Rice arranged for the testing of approximately 33,000 children using a standard spelling test that he had devised. Since the early results indicated a range of accuracy of from 33 to 95.3 percent, he at first believed "that the spelling problem had already been solved and that nothing was needed to put all our teachers on the right path beyond a careful study of the methods employed where the highest standards had been secured, and then by carrying the message to those whose results had been less favorable."[6] Upon visiting the classes involved, however, Rice discovered that the favorable results were achieved not by any particular methodology or special technique for teaching spelling, but by the teachers' careful enunciation during testing, which provided obvious clues to the correct spelling of the words.

Undaunted, Rice undertook a second round of testing, this time under his personal supervision. The new results, however, were puzzling. The ranges in achievement were extremely narrow, which made it difficult to attribute success or failure to "mechanical schools" as opposed to "progressive schools" or even "to distinguish the schools attended by the children of cultured parents from those representing the foreign laboring element."[7] Rice finally concluded that there was no relation between the then identifiable methods of teaching spelling and that the results were attributable to "the ability of those who use them."[8] Neither could any relationship be found between the amount of time spent in spelling instruction and achievement in spelling. "Our efforts," he recommended, "should be primarily directed toward supplying our schools with competent teachers."[9] Since not enough teachers are "born to the profession," however, the "only course lies in developing the requisite powers, as well as we can, where they are naturally weak."[10] This could be accomplished by first establishing with precision the job to be done and the time needed to do it and then making the teacher's job dependent on his or her success in doing it.

Apart from the overtones in Rice's conclusions of what is now called accountability, his recommendations contain the seeds of what has become the major effort insofar as teacher education was concerned. Since the number of "born" teachers was obviously too small to staff our burgeoning school systems, research in teaching would have to be directed toward identifying those qualities, characteristics, and behaviors that constituted good teaching; and teacher education, in turn, would be directed toward using that research in order to provide a competent corps of teachers for the schools.

What constitutes good teaching? On the basis of this deceptively complex question, a massive research effort was undertaken, with the ultimate practical aim of developing teacher education programs that would instill the techniques of good teaching into tomorrow's teachers. In general, bad teaching came to be associated with *waste*, a term Rice anticipated, and for a time *economy* enjoyed a vogue as the great enemy of waste; but ultimately, *efficiency* became the term most educators accepted as synonymous with good. A good teacher achieved a prespecified task with maximum efficiency. Given this conception, only two problems remained to be resolved: first, stipulating the specifications or standards of success that define good teaching; and second, discovering the means by which such success could be most efficiently achieved.

Educational leaders and teacher educators were in virtual agreement as to the task before them. Franklin Bobbitt, an extraordinarily prolific writer and influential reformer who was particularly active during the first quarter of this century, set the tone. The new era in education would be governed by Science—scientific management in the administration of schools, scientific curriculum-making, and the scientific discovery of the qualities of a good teacher. "Efficient *methods*," Bobbitt declared, "are dependent on definite standards."[11] Notable success had already been achieved in the area of standards by such researchers as S. A. Courtis, Leonard P. Ayers, and Edward Thorndike. The number of correct arithmetic combinations per minute for each grade level, for example, could already be accurately determined, and teachers' success could be gauged in terms of rate of efficiency in raising achievement to prescribed levels of speed and accuracy. Ultimately, differentiated criteria of success for different categories of students—future accountants, musicians, bricklayers—could be set, thus accomplishing even greater efficiency and scientific accuracy.

Here also would lie the key to teacher education. The personal qualities that were closely linked with success in achieving the predetermined achievement rates could then be isolated. If it could be known that a stoker or a ditch digger "would better be of sluggish mentality," and that a lawyer or a banker should be possessed of a "keen and ever-alert intelligence,"[12] then the particular qualities that make for success in teaching could be identified. Citing Frederick Winslow Taylor, the efficiency engineer, and his study of women working in a bicycle factory, Bobbitt, like Rice, felt that the technique for the identification and training of good teachers was already within our grasp. It consisted essentially of two tasks: The first was "to locate a fairly large sample of the best 5 percent of teachers in the profession, those who in their original nature probably possess the native elements, rightly proportioned, of the so-called 'born teacher,'" and the second, "to analyze out and to define in reasonably definite terms the characteristics of personality which this group of teachers exhibits."[13]

By the 1920s, little doubt existed as to the appropriate course of action for developing a scientifically based teacher education. Essentially, it was to follow the lines that Taylor had developed in industry and took the form of job analysis. Comparisons were constantly being made with technological and industrial jobs, and concern was frequently expressed that precise lists of abilities in teaching had not yet been formulated. "The teacher-training institution is a vocational school," declared Bobbitt.[14] If we can discover the 165 jobs that a plumber has to perform, why are we unable to accomplish the same with the admittedly more complex job of teaching? "To discover the objectives of teacher training, therefore, the investigator will go where teachers are performing all their tasks as they ought to be performed. He will than list the 200 or 500 or 5000 tasks which the competent teacher accomplishes in his work. The *abilities* to perform these tasks, then, are the fundamental teacher-training objectives—the abilities to do the jobs are the objectives. There are no others."[15]

W. W. Charters, another exceptionally influential reformer of the 1920s endorsed the same general framework. If, for example, a teacher performs three activities between 8:40 a.m. and 9:00 a.m.—correcting papers, planning a lesson, and greeting students—these activities should be duly noted, and the abilities involved in performing these activities successfully would become the objectives of teacher education programs.[16]

Charters, along with Douglas Waples, conducted one of the most massive inquiries into the activities of teachers ever undertaken. The Commonwealth Teacher Training Study, as it was called, was initiated in 1925 as the latest in a series of scientific inquiries into teaching sponsored by the Commonwealth Fund. Apart from Charters and Waples, an impressive staff of scientifically minded investigators was assembled (including Ralph Tyler of the University of North Carolina, as supervisor of statistical operations) to discover scientifically the traits and activities that define good teaching. Once discovered, these would become the elements of a new teacher education curriculum.

Instead of assuming that certain activities and traits of teachers were desirable, the study was designed to extract from teachers and supervisors the positive components of the activity of teaching. By polling "competent critics" of teachers, for example, the twenty-five most important traits of teachers were isolated and then broken down into behavioral components. Thus, adaptability could be seen in a teacher who "does not dance nor play cards if the community objects," animation in a teacher who "expresses enthusiasm in eyes," attractive personal appearance in one who "does not wear shoes that are run over at the heels," and cleanliness in one who "washes faces when they need washing."[17]

This neutrality now exists.

To secure a comprehensive list of the activities of teachers, 22,000 questionnaires were sent to experienced teachers in forty-two states. Over 6000 usable replies were obtained indicating some 211,890 activities. In addition, various studies of the activities of teachers were analyzed, each yielding roughly three hundred more. Finally, after elimination of duplication and some telescoping, a master check list of the 1001 activities of teaching was developed. The teacher-training institutions had only to use the lists of traits and activities thus formulated to develop a teacher education program that reflected the world of the classroom.

Yet teacher education institutions, for a while at least, remained curiously intractable to Charters's recommendations. Although sporadic efforts were made to inject the products of this research into programs of teacher education, and thousands of check lists were reproduced for use by supervisors, the Commonwealth Teacher Training Study is largely forgotten today.

The major intent of the study, however, is still recognized, and the search for the correct set of teacher behaviors and personality traits (or competencies) continues undiminished. Perhaps the most influential person identified with the movement to isolate the characteristics of good teachers is A. S. Barr. Although his best-known study was published in 1929, his search continued for many years afterward and probably involved hundreds of studies. In his 1929 book, Barr compared forty-seven good social studies teachers with forty-seven poor ones as identified by city and county superintendents in the State of Wisconsin, carrying the scientific study of teaching one step further than the Commonwealth study by deriving his data from observation of classroom performance rather than through questionnaires or opinions of supervisors.

The range of behaviors Barr observed was enormous. They included verbal behavior, such as characteristic expressions, posture, assignments made, and even the physical conditions in the classrooms. Barr reported, for example, a virtual tie (42 to 44) in the use by good and poor teachers of the most frequently used expression, "all right." For "yes," the expression next in frequency, there was a flat tie (34 to 34).[18] The data on posture were not much more illuminating. Although the category of "folds hands" was won by the good teachers by a score of 7 to 4, most other scores were close, such as the 3 to 3 tie in the category "puts hands to chin or cheek."[19] Although Barr's behavior categories may seem naive by modern standards, he was carrying forward, in broad outline at least, the central line of inquiry in research on teaching.

The Limitations of Teaching Technology

In at least some important respects, the scientific study of teaching currently being supported by the U.S. Office of Education (USOE) and other prestigious agencies under the banner of teacher competencies follows the same path that Rice trod some eighty years ago, one that is by now well worn. Attired in new rhetorical finery, performance-based or competency-based teacher education not only has captured the imagination of many leading teacher educators but also has become the essential condition for the granting of many federal and even some state funds. State departments of education from Florida to Oregon either have announced their intention to or have begun to implement teacher certification and teacher rating plans involving the specific performance or competence of teachers.

Identifying any precise meaning for the terms and catchwords that are used is difficult however. Even the statement issued by the Committee on Performance-Based Teacher Education of the American Association of Colleges for Teacher Education admits that "no entirely satisfactory description of performance-based teacher education has been framed to date."[20] The statement refers to one observer's description of performance-based teacher education as "a multifaceted concept in search of practitioners."[21] A more accurate description at this stage would probably be that it is a slogan system in search of followers. Much has gone on under the rubric of competency-based teacher education, but the key notion seems to be that identifiable behaviors, competencies, and characteristics of teaching, once isolated, can form the basis of teacher education and teacher certification. Those who believe in competency-based teacher education, like Rice before them, are directing a major portion of their efforts and expenditures (which are considerable in many cases) toward cutting through the logjam in the "sea of opinions" that surrounds the performance of teachers, and toward identifying scientifically demonstrated behaviors that define good or at least competent teaching. As Charters and Barr discovered, the process of isolating those specific behaviors is more complex than appears at first. In fact, it would be difficult to name even a single specific behavior that has been shown to be consistently correlated with a reasonable definition of competent teaching. Why is this?

J. M. Stephens, one of the few professional students of education to strike out in an alternate direction in trying to explain the persistent failures to isolate critical teacher behaviors, raises the possibility that although teaching is usually considered to be a highly deliberate process, there may be blind, spontaneous (that is, nondeliberative) factors at work that have much to do with the effects and effectiveness of schooling.[22] In fact, these nondeliberative, sometimes even unconscious, tendencies may have more to do with what the schools accomplish than do the deliberate particular behaviors that teachers exhibit in the classroom. Engaging in intellectual play, talking to others about what we find interesting and exciting, and expressing approval or disapproval of the performance of others, particularly children: these widely distributed, perhaps even universal, human characteristics are all examples of spontaneous, natural behaviors that may account for what schools do. Norman Wallen and Robert Travers express a similar position.[23]

If this position has merit, it may, Stephens points out,[24] explain the persistent phenomenon in educational research of *no significant differences*, a problem that in a wide range of studies comparing one educational technique with another (that is, lecture versus discussion, homogeneous versus heterogeneous grouping) is rarely given serious consideration. One answer to this problem, according to Stephens, is that the spontaneous tendencies of human beings, along with what might be called the culture of the school, account in such large measure for the impact of schooling that the particular modifications we introduce are not sufficient to show up in statistical measures of school achievement.

At the heart of the difference between Stephens's position and the dominant tradition, from Rice to USOE'S performance-based teacher education programs, is the most fundamental question that faces us as teacher educators: Is teaching a *technical* process? When one learns to be a teacher, is one learning a technique? (The term, *technique* is being used here in Jacques Ellul's sense as a standardized way to achieve a predetermined end.)[25] When one teaches teachers or future teachers, does one teach the single right way to accomplish some particular thing? Certainly, this assumption is basic to the concept of what we thought was a science of teaching. It is also the impetus for the expenditure of millions of dollars by the USOE. The sheer intensity of the effort to convince or, in some instances, to compel teachers to express in minute terms the exact behavioral outcomes of their instruction is one crucial manifestation of this assumption. Without this manifestation, a *technique* of teaching can not exist.

Research reported by one of the leading proponents of specific performance objectives and performance-based teacher education is an interesting case in point. Teaching Performance Tests were developed at University of California, Los Angeles to assess the proficiency with which pre-specified achievement objectives are achieved. "By holding the instructional goals constant," it was asserted, "it becomes possible to contrast teachers with respect to their skill in accomplishing identical goals."[26] This is, of course, the same fundamental assumption that prompted Rice to construct and administer his tests of spelling achievement. The results were the same. Experienced teachers performed no better than college students in teaching social science, and tradesmen did about as well as experienced teachers in teaching auto mechanics and electronics. Again, there were *no significant differences.* James Popham, in explaining his conclusion that "experienced teachers are not particularly skilled at bringing about specified behavior changes in learners,"[27] lays the blame squarely on teacher-training institutions. The reason experienced teachers fail to win the race against their untutored and presumably flabby opponents is that the right techniques for achieving prespecified objectives have not been correctly instilled in them during their pre-service or in-service training. Although the investigator declares this to be "*a totally unacceptable* state of affairs," he does not reveal the particular techniques that would have enabled the experienced teachers to win the race.

It is easy to understand the reason for the omission: no one knows what these techniques are—if indeed there are any. Our basic presuppositions make this difficult to admit. Many professors of education prefer to pretend, either to themselves or to others, that they do know what these techniques are. Certainly, a great many students come to their classes expecting professors of education to release the secrets of efficient instruction that in the past have been so closely guarded. No wonder they often leave these courses disappointed. Even the relative effectiveness of the so-called lecture and discussion techniques, one of the most intensely investigated problems in all of research on teaching, is completely unknown. In a remarkable study undertaken at the Center for the Advanced Study of Educational Administration, for example, ninety-one comparative studies in college instruction conducted between 1924 and 1965 were reviewed and re-analyzed. The stark conclusion was: "These data demonstrate clearly and unequivocally that there is no measurable difference among truly distinctive methods of college instruction when evaluated by student performance on final examinations."[28] Even that old chestnut has not been pulled from the fire.

The issue is not the reluctance of teacher-training institutions to emphasize a technology of teaching or even the strength of their commitment to the notion that finding and disseminating a technology of teaching as their central task. It goes far beyond the issue of whether Stephens's theory of spontaneous schooling has any explanatory power. In view of an unbroken record of failure to answer the question of how to achieve educational aims most effectively, the decision before us is whether we should pursue that question now with increased vigor and determination or whether we should reformulate the question itself.

Certainly, the USOE has committed itself largely to the first alternative, and it seems fair to say that most professional students of teaching prefer to rededicate themselves periodically to the pursuit of their traditional question. N. L. Gage, for example, a leading exponent and practitioner of a science of teaching, sees some reason for optimism. He notes four process variables that promise a significant correlation with desirable outcome variables, such as student achievement and positive reactions on the part of students. The four are warmth, indirectness, cognitive organization, and enthusiasm. An examination of the last one may illustrate some problems associated with these tentative signs of optimism. Gage describes two studies in which a positive outcome (student achievement) seems to be related to the teacher's enthusiasm. In the first, two investigators asked teachers to present lessons "in a static, or unenthusiastic fashion (read from a manuscript, with no gestures, eye contact, or inflections), and also in a dynamic, or enthusiastic, fashion (delivered from memory, with much inflection, eye contact, gesturing, and animation."[29] After the ten-minute lessons, test results indicated more learning on the part of the latter class. In a second study, twenty teachers were asked to lecture in an "indifferent" manner one week and "enthusiastically" the next. In all but one of the classes, mean achievement scores were higher for the enthusiastic lessons. It appears that students are able to remember more of their dynamic lessons than they are of their boring lessons.

Whatever the strength of the statistical relationships may be, it is difficult to derive great optimism about a science of teaching from findings such as these. For example, if teachers are asked to teach in a static or indifferent way, they will with good reason probably interpret the instructions as an injunction to teach poorly. They are, in effect, being asked to make their lessons as dull as they can. When they are told to teach enthusiastically, the effect is to ask them to give their teaching abilities full rein. As reported, then, the experiments could be said to indicate that the teachers involved were reasonably successful in following the instructions of the investigators. In most instances, compared with their efforts to teach well/enthusiastically, their efforts to teach poorly/unenthusiastically were rewarded by poor results on achievement tests. Another important question to consider in examining the findings is whether the relationship between the independent and the dependent variables is linear. Would success, however defined, continue to rise with the level of enthusiasm? Does the research indicate that the best teacher is one who conducts his or her classes in an absolute frenzy of enthusiasm? Or is anything above the level of a zombie-like stupor sufficient to achieve success?

These objections aside, what if a truly independent variable were found to be consistently related by reliable statistical measures to a desirable outcome variable, say, client satisfaction? Suppose that there is strong relationship between the teacher's use of a high percentage of vertical hand gestures, Harry Truman style, and positive student attitudes as opposed to the use of horizontal hand gestures or no gestures at all. Would it be reasonable to assume in view of indisputable statistical evidence that vertical hand gestures are a sure road to popularity as a teacher? The task of teacher-training institutions would then be to ensure that up and down movements of the arm became an integral part of the repertoire of every certified teacher.

The question is not a facetious one. It is related to the wellmeaning efforts of some teacher-training institutions to teach indirectness, for example, in the Flanders interaction sense, as one of the ingredients in good teaching. Would prospective teachers who master the technique of "accepts or uses ideas of student: clarifying, building, or developing ideas suggested by a student" then be on the high road to success as teachers? The key problem would be whether vertical hand gestures (or indirectness) themselves cause client satisfaction or whether a previously undiscovered cause somehow manifests itself both in the tendency toward the vertical hand gestures and the client satisfaction. In that case, teacher-training institutions that were successful in inculcating the appropriate hand movements would be no better insofar as developing popular teachers than would be institutions that systematically ignored this important statistical relationship.

Guidelines to Restating the Question

What has gone on in the name of the scientific study of teaching has been, in large measure, raw empiricism, a blind and almost necessarily futile groping for statistically significant relationships. Even if a persistent statistical relationship were somehow found, the absence of analytical clarification of the concepts involved and the lack of a theoretical framework for the research would preclude the development of any scientific understanding of the relationship and, for that matter, would probably rule out any useful purpose to which the research could be put. Lee Cronbach's description of the typical research in this area is as accurate as any:

> John Doe contends that programed presentation of college geology is better than conventional lectures. He assembles a writing team and spends two years drafting material, editing every sentence, trying it on pilot classes, and revising. Then Doe runs a grand experiment in which ten classes are taught with his material, while ten classes take the regular lecture course. Unless his writers were painfully inept, the test scores favor the new method, and unless Doe is a very saint of an experimenter, he concludes that programed instruction is more effective than the lecture method. Doe has shown that his programs give better results than the lectures in their casual, unedited, tired old form, but the outcome would very likely to have been reversed if he had put the same two-year effort into tuning up the lectures. Nothing of explanatory value has been learned from his study.[30]

One other feature of typical research on teaching is worth noting. One of the reasons there can be nothing of explanatory value in Doe's results is that he has not conceptualized the problem. There is no theoretical framework in which the research is set. The typical research on teaching is essentially a horse race. Sometimes one horse wins, sometimes the other; often, it is a tie. In any case, the outcome of the race adds nothing to our understanding of the complex processes that are involved in teaching. As David Hawkins puts it; "To call something an independent variable is not to use a name but to claim an achievement."[31] Certainly, the case for warmth or indirectness or enthusiasm as truly important variables related to success in teaching can never rest on statistical corre-lations alone.

A second guideline for reformulating the question in teacher ed-ucation involves the naivete or, perhaps, the pretentiousness of the research we have been doing. The main research effort of the past eighty years has been built on the assumption that one can skip over all the little intermediate questions that may lie in the path of any given line of inquiry and answer the ultimate question at once. It is as if biologists set as their single-minded purpose the discovery of the secret of life. We might as well admit that the secrets of success in teaching, if they are knowable at all, are a long way from being revealed and are particularly impregnable to a direct assault. The big question is too formidable, too imposing, too cosmic to ask directly. We have to sneak up on it.

The way to do this is to be more modest in the research task we set for ourselves. We have to engage in the slow and sometimes unrewarding process of trying to understand the phenomena with which we are dealing. As B. O. Smith expresses it: "The first task of research is to build a body of pedagogical knowledge."[32] Al-though, on the face of it, this is not a startling pronouncement, at least some research on teaching is designed to improve the process of teaching in the absence of any understanding of what it is.

An important step toward pedagogical knowledge may involve nothing more spectacular than natural history research. Essen-tially, this involves making observations "in the wild" and seeing what goes on.[33] This has been, generally, a neglected phase of the inquiry process in research on teaching and only in recent years have there been any concerted efforts to study classroom processes as they go forward, independent of any judgments about good and poor teaching. The natural history stage in the inquiry process should not be lightly disregarded. Northrup makes this point clearly:

> Nothing is more important . . . for a clarification of scientific method, empirical logic, and philosophy than a clear recognition of the different stages of inquiry. Once this is appreciated the natural history type of scientific knowledge gains the importance which is its due. In no empirical inquiry will anything ever take the place of looking and seeing.[34]

Natural history research is not simply an alternative to the fa-miliar research effort directed toward isolating the components of good teaching. It is a necessary stage in the development of a field of inquiry. "The great point," observes George Homans, "is to climb down from the big words of social science, at least as far as common-sense observation. Then, if we wish, we can start climbing up again, but this time with a ladder we can depend on."[35] Curbing our overwhelming sense of urgency and scaling down our grandiose ambition by taking on modest tasks may in the long run bring us rewarding returns on our research efforts in teaching.

The third guideline for the development of a new question in teacher education has already been alluded to. It calls into question one of the basic assumptions that has guided research in teacher education from the time of Rice's refreshingly naive crusade for educational reform to at least some of the recent frenetic efforts of the USOE to discover the behavior and skills—the much-heralded competencies—that presumably hold the key to good teaching. The assumption is that teaching, like typing or bricklaying, consists of a set of standard ways to do a particular thing. The notion appeals to a common human impulse. In approaching any complex activity, we like to think that there must be a trick to it which, once discovered, makes one a skilled practitioner. But we might as well face the likelihood that teaching may not consist of standard best ways to do particular things. Being a good teacher, like being a good statesman or a good mother, may involve infinite possible human excellences and appropriate behaviors, no one much more a guarantor of success than the other. As we attempt to observe and understand teaching, we may discover that teaching, after all, does not involve the exercise of a technical skill.

The technological framework as applied to teaching involves both precise pre-specification of outcomes and progressively efficient means toward their achievement. For years, teachers have been invited to accept this framework, then cajoled and even threatened; yet they seem to be perversely resistant to it. Teachers want their students to learn, but getting them to state learning outcomes or "terminal behaviors" in a particularized form has turned out to be a more formidable task than first imagined (although, under pressure, teachers may go through the motions). Perhaps their resistance is not due to any natural recalcitrance; perhaps their instincts and their experience tell them that the process of teaching cannot be made to fit the technological mold. This may have something to do with the interactive setting in which the activity of teaching goes on. "In the interactive setting," Philip Jackson observes, "the teacher commonly encourages his students to do what he thinks will be good for them without giving too much thought to the precise outcome of his instructional efforts."[36] Teachers, in other words, like to engage in worthwhile activities, activities that they think are good for their students. When Jackson interviewed a specially selected group of outstanding teachers, he found that they derived their greatest professional satisfaction not from high scores on achievement tests in their classes, but from the interest and involvement of their students. The technological framework places its highest value on the educational *product*, on predictability and precision; the teachers in Jackson's study valued *process*, an educationally worthwhile activity from which will flow something desirable.[37] Studies such as his are illuminating because if one wishes to understand the process of teaching or even to improve it, one cannot afford to ignore teaching as it goes forward in its most familiar setting, the classroom.

Efforts to impose an artificial technological framework on the activities of teaching and learning provide the backdrop for the search for the secrets of good teaching, because if teaching means a particular way to accomplish a particular thing, the secret may ultimately be revealed. But once the technological framework is discarded, the search for the best way becomes meaningless, and new, perhaps more fruitful, questions in teacher education may emerge.

The dream of educational reformers, like Rice, Charters, Barr and even the current performance-oriented teacher educators, is not an ignoble one. Omar Khayyam, too, was intrigued by "the sovereign Alchemist that in a trice, Life's leaden metal into Gold transmute[s]," but like the alchemist's ambition, the teacher educator's dream of unlocking the secrets of success in teaching has been, in large measure, misconstrued and misdirected. The long and widely recognized record of failure does not suggest an extensive and frenzied search for the magic formula. Instead, it points toward a radical reformulation of the question in teacher education in modest terms and a critical exploration of the directions of *new* paths.

Notes

1. Donald Sutherland, *Gertrude Stein* (New Haven: Yale University Press, 1951), p. 203.
2. Susanne Langer, *Philosophy in a New Key* (New York: New American Library, 1948), pp. 15–16.
3. Thomas Kuhn, *The Structure of Scientific Revolutions* (Chicago: University of Chicago Press, 1964), p. 37.

4. Joseph Mayer Rice, *Scientific Management in Education* (New York: Hinds, Noble, & Eldredge, 1913), p. 5.

5. Ibid., p. 7.

6. Ibid., p. 68.

7. Ibid., p. 77.

8. Ibid., p. 90.

9. Ibid., p. 99.

10. Ibid.

11. Franklin Bobbitt, "Some General Principles of Management Applied to the Problems of City-School Systems," in *Twelfth Yearbook of the National Society for the Study of Education, Part I* (Chicago: University of Chicago Press, 1913), p. 45.

12. Ibid., p. 63.

13. Ibid., p. 64.

14. Franklin Bobbitt, "Discovering and Formulating the Objectives of Teacher-Training Institutions," *Journal of Educational Research* 10 (October 1924), p. 187.

15. Ibid., p. 188.

16. Werrett W. Charters, "The Objectives of Teacher-Training," *Educational Administration and Supervision* 6 (September 1920), pp. 305–306.

17. Werrett W. Charters and Douglas Waples, *The Commonwealth Teacher-Training Study* (Chicago: University of Chicago Press, 1929), pp. 223–244.

18. Arvil S. Barr, *Characteristic Differences in the Teaching Performance of Good and Poor Teachers of the Social Studies* (Bloomington, IL: Public School Publishing, 1929), p. 39.

19. Ibid., p. 64.

20. Stanley Elam, *A Resume of Performance-Based Teacher Education* (Washington, DC: American Association of Colleges for Teacher Education, 1972), p. 1.

21. Ibid.

22. J. M. Stephens, "The Residual Theory Again: An Analytical Study," *Educational Theory* 5 (July 1955), pp. 158–166. "Nondeliberative Factors in Teaching," *Journal of Educational Psychology* 47 (January 1956), pp. 11–24. "Nondeliberative Factors Underlying the Phenomenon of Schooling," *Educational Theory* 6 (January 1956), pp. 26–34. *The Process of Schooling* (New York: Holt, Rinehart, and Winston, 1967).

23. Norman E. Wallen and Robert M. W. Travers, "Analysis and Investigation of Teaching Methods," in *Handbook of Research on*

Teaching, ed. Nathaniel L. Gage (Chicago: Rand McNally, 1963), pp. 448–505.

24. Stephens, *The Process of Schooling*, pp. 71–90.

25. Jacques Ellul, *The Technological Society* (New York: Vintage Books, 1964.)

26. W. James Popham, "Teaching Skill Under Scrutiny," *Phi Delta Kappan* 52 (June 1971), p. 600.

27. Ibid., p. 601.

28. Robert Dubin and Thomas C. Taveggia, *The Teaching-Learning Paradox* (Eugene, OR: Center for the Advanced Study of Educational Administration, 1968), p. 35.

29. N. L. Gage, *Teacher Effectiveness and Teacher Education: The Search for a Scientific Basis* (Palo Alto, CA: Pacific Books, 1972), p. 38.

30. Lee J. Cronbach, "The Logic of Experiments on Discovery," in *Learning by Discovery*, eds. Lee S. Shulman and Evan R. Keisler (Chicago: Rand McNally, 1966), p. 80.

31. David Hawkins, "Learning for the Unteachable," in *Learning by Discovery*, eds. Lee S. Shulman and Evan R. Keisler (Chicago: Rand McNally, 1966), p. 6.

32. B. Othanel Smith, "Teaching: Conditions of Its Evaluation," in *The Evaluation of Teaching* (Washington, D.C.: Pi Lambda Theta, 1967), p. 71.

33. Hawkins, "Learning for the Unteachable," p. 6.

34. F. S. C. Northrup, *The Logic of the Sciences and Humanities* (New York: Meridian, 1959), p. 39.

35. George G. Homans, *The Human Group* (New York: Harcourt Brace Jovanovich, 1950), p. 13.

36. Philip W. Jackson, *Life in Classrooms* (New York: Holt, Reinhart, and Winston, 1968), p. 162.

37. Ibid., pp. 115–155.

9

The Tyler Rationale

One of the disturbing characteristics of the curriculum field is its lack of historical perspective. New breakthroughs are solemnly proclaimed when in fact they represent minor modifications of early proposals, and, conversely, anachronistic dogmas and doctrines maintain a currency and uncritical acceptance far beyond their present merit. The most persistent theoretical formulation in the field of curriculum has been Ralph Tyler's syllabus for Education 360 at the University of Chicago, *Basic Principles of Curriculum and Instruction*, or, as it is widely known, the Tyler rationale.[1] Tyler's claims for his rationale are modest, but over time his proposal for rationally developing a curriculum has been raised almost to the status of revealed doctrine. In an issue of the *Review of Educational Research* devoted to curriculum, John Goodlad, commenting on the state of the field, reports that "as far as the major questions to be answered in developing a curriculum are concerned, most of the authors in [the] 1960 and 1969 [curriculum issues of the *Review*] assume those set forth in 1950 by Ralph Tyler." Later, he concludes with obvious disappointment, "General theory and conceptualization in curriculum appear to have advanced very little during the last decade."[2] Perhaps the twentieth anniversary of the publication of the Tyler rationale is an appropriate time to reexamine and reevaluate some of its central features.

Tyler's rationale revolves around four central questions which Tyler feels need answers if the process of curriculum development is to proceed:

First appeared in *School Review* 78, number 2 (1970). Copyright 1970 by University of Chicago Press. Reprinted by permission.

1. What educational purposes should the school seek to attain?
2. What educational experiences can be provided that are likely to attain these purposes?
3. How can these educational experiences be effectively organized?
4. How can we determine whether these purposes are being attained?[3]

These questions may be reformulated into the familiar four-step process by which a curriculum is developed: stating objectives, selecting "experiences," organizing "experiences," and evaluating.[4] The Tyler rationale is essentially an elaboration and explication of these steps. The most crucial step in this doctrine is obviously the first, since all the others proceed from and wait upon the statement of objectives. As Tyler puts it, "If we are to study an educational program systematically and intelligently we must first be sure as to the educational objectives aimed at."[5]

The Selection of Educational Objectives

Tyler's section on educational objectives is a description of the three sources of objectives: studies of learners, studies of contemporary life, and suggestions from subject-matter specialists, as well as an account of how data derived from these "sources" are to be "filtered" through philosophical and psychological "screens." The three sources of educational objectives encapsulate several traditional doctrines in the curriculum field over which much ideological blood had been spilled in the previous several decades. The doctrines proceeded from different theoretical assumptions, and each of them had its own spokespeople, its own adherents, and its own rhetoric. Tyler's proposal accepts them all, which probably accounts in part for its wide popularity.

While we are aware that compromise is the recourse frequently taken in the fields of diplomatic or labor negotiation, simple eclecticism may not be the most efficacious way to proceed in theorizing. When Dewey, for example, identified the fundamental factors in the educative process as the child and the "values incarnate in the matured experience of the adult," the psychological and the logical, his solution was not to accept them both but "to discover a reality to which each belongs."[6] In other words, when faced with essentially the same problem of warring educational doctrines,

Dewey's approach is to reformulate the problem; Tyler's is to lay them all out side by side.

Of the three "sources"—studies of the learners themselves, studies of contemporary life, and suggestions about objectives from subject-matter specialists—the last one seems curiously distorted and out of place. Perhaps this is because Tyler begins the section by profoundly misconceiving the role and function of the Committee of Ten. He attributes to the Committee of Ten a set of objectives which, he claims, has subsequently been followed by thousands of secondary schools. In point of fact, the notion of objectives in the sense that Tyler defines the term was not used and probably had not even occurred to the members of the Committee of Ten. What they proposed were not objectives, but "four programmes": Classical, Latin-Scientific, Modern Languages, and English. Under each of these rubrics is a listing of the subjects that constitute each of the four courses of study. This recommendation is followed by the reports of the various individual committees on what content should be included and what methods should be used in the various subject fields. Unless Tyler is using the term "objective" as being synonymous with "content" (in which case it would lose all its importance as a concept), then the belief that the use of the term "objective" is applicable to the Committee of Ten is erroneous. Probably the only sense in which the term "objective" is applicable to the Committee of Ten report is in connection with the broad objective of mental training to which it subscribes.

An even more serious error follows: "It seems clear that the Committee of Ten thought it was answering the question: What should be the elementary instruction for students who are later to carry on much more advanced work in the field? Hence, the report in History, for example, seems to present objectives [*sic*] for the beginning courses for persons who are training to be historians. Similarly the report in Mathematics outlines objectives [*sic*] for the beginning courses in the training of a mathematician."[7]

As a matter of fact, one of the central questions that the Committee of Ten considered was; "Should the subject be treated differently for pupils who are going to college, for those who are going to a scientific school, and for those, who, presumably, are going to neither?"[8] The Committee decided unanimously in the negative. The subcommittee on history, civil government, and political economy, for example, reported that it was "unanimously against making such a distinction"[9] and passed a resolution that "instruction in history and related subjects ought to be precisely the same for pupils on their way to college or the scientific school, as for those who expect to stop at the end of grammar school, or at the end of the high school."[10] Evidently, the Committee of Ten was acutely aware of the question of a differentiated curriculum based on probable destination. It simply rejected the doctrine that makes a prediction about one's future status or occupation a valid basis for the curriculum in general education. The objective of mental training, apparently, was conceived to be of such importance as to apply to all, regardless of destination.

Tyler's interpretation of the Committee of Ten report is more than a trivial historical misconception. It illustrates one of his fundamental presuppositions about the subjects in the curriculum. Tyler conceives of subjects as performing certain "functions." These functions may take the form of a kind of definition of the field of study itself, such as when he sees a function of science to be enabling the student to obtain a "clearer understanding of the world as it is viewed by the scientist and man's relation to it, and the place of the world in the larger universe." Alternatively, the subject may perform external functions such as the contribution of science to the improvement of individual or public health or to the conservation of natural resources. The first sense of function is essentially a way of characterizing a field of study; in the second sense of function, the subject field serves as an instrument for achieving objectives drawn from Tyler's other two sources. Tyler's apparent predisposition to the latter sense of function seems to be at the heart of his misreading of the Committee of Ten report. To Tyler, studying history or algebra (as was universally recommended by the Committee of Ten), if they are not meeting an obvious individual or social need, is a way of fulfilling the vocational needs of a budding historian or mathematician. Otherwise, how can one justify the existence of mathematics *qua* mathematics in the curriculum? As such, "suggestions from subject-matter specialists" are really not a source in the sense that the other two are. Subject matter is mainly one of several means by which one fulfills individual needs, such as vocational aspirations, or meets social expectations.

Needs of the Learner as a Source of Objectives

The section on the "learners themselves as a source of educational objectives," although it is less strained and more analytical than the one on subject matter, is nevertheless elliptical. Tyler pro-

ceeds from the assumption that "education is a process of changing behavior patterns of people."[11] This notion, of course, is now
widely popular in this country, but, even if one were to accept such
a view, it would be important to know the ways in which education would be different from other means of changing behavior,
such as hypnosis, shock treatment, brainwashing, sensitivity training, indoctrination, drug therapy, and torture. Given such a definition, the differences between education and these other ways of
changing behavior are not obvious or simple.

Tyler proceeds from his basic definition of education to a consideration of the reason for wanting to study the learner: "A study
of the learners themselves would seek to identify needed changes
in behavior patterns of the students which the educational institution should seek to produce."[12] There follows an extended discussion of "needs," how they are determined, and how they contribute to the determination of educational objectives. The notion
of needs as a basis for curriculum development was not a new one
when Tyler used it in 1950. It had been a stable element in the
curriculum literature for about three decades.[13] When tied to the
biological concept of homeostasis, the term "needs" seems to have
a clear-cut meaning. Hunger, for example, may be conveniently
translated into a need for food when one has in mind a physiological state of equilibrium. Need becomes a much trickier concept
when one speaks of the "need of a haircut" or the "need for a
good spanking." These needs involve rather complex social norms
on which people of good will may differ sharply. Tyler astutely
recognized that the concept of need has no meaning without a set
of norms, and he described the kind of study he envisioned essentially as a two-step process: "first, finding the present status of the
students, and second, comparing this status to acceptable norms
in order to identify the gaps or needs."[14] This formulation is virtually identical to what Bobbitt referred to as "shortcomings" in
the first book written exclusively on the curriculum, published in
1918.[15] The key term, in Tyler's version, of course, is "acceptable
norms." They are neither self-evident nor easy to formulate.

One of Tyler's illustrations of the process he advocates is a case
in point: A "discovery" is made that sixty percent of ninth-grade
boys read only comic strips. The "unimaginative" teacher, Tyler
says, might interpret this as suggesting the need for more attention
to comic strips in the classroom; the imaginative teacher uses the
data as a justification "for setting up objectives gradually to broaden
and deepen these reading interests."[16] What is the acceptable norm

implicit in Tyler's illustration? Apparently, it is not a statistical norm since this could imply that the forty percent minority of boys should be encouraged to emulate the sixty percent majority. The norm seems to be the simple conviction that having broader and deeper reading interests is better than limiting oneself to the reading of comic strips. The question is what does the sixty percent figure contribute to the process of stating education objectives? What difference would it have made if the figure had been eighty percent or forty percent? The key factor seems to be the nature and strength of the teacher's conviction as the acceptable norm, toward which the status study contributes very little.

The whole notion of need has no meaning without an established norm, and, therefore, it is impossible even to identify "needs" without it. As Archambault put it, "An objective need can be discovered, but only within a completely defined context in which the normal level of attainment can be clarified."[17] Furthermore, even when a genuine need is identified, the role of the school as an institution for the remediation of that or other needs would have to be considered. Even the course that remediation should take once the need and the responsibility have been established is an open question. These serious value questions associated with the identification and remediation of needs make the concept a deceptively complex one whose advantages are more apparent than real. Komisar, for example, has described this double use of need, "one to report deficiencies and another to prescribe for their alleviation," as so vague and elusive as to constitute a "linguistic luxury."[18]

As already mentioned, Tyler is acutely aware of the difficulties of "deriving" educational objectives from studies of the child. His last word on the subject in this section is to suggest to his students that they compile some data and then try using those data as the basis for formulating objectives. He suggests this exercise in part to illustrate the difficulty of the process. Given the almost impossible complexity of the procedure and the crucial but perhaps arbitrary role of the interpreter's value structure or "philosophy of life and of education," one wonders whether the concept of need deserves any place in the process of formulating objectives. Certainly, the concept of need turns out to be of no help insofar as avoiding central value decisions as the basis for the selection of educational objectives, and without that feature much of its appeal seems to disappear. As Dearden concluded in his analysis of the term:

The concept of "need" is an attractive one in education because it seems to offer an escape from arguments about value by means of a straightforward appeal to the facts empirically determined by the expert. But . . . it is false to suppose that judgments of value can thus be escaped. Such judgments may be assumed without any awareness that assumptions are being made, but they are not escaped.[19]

Studies of Contemporary Life as a Source of Objectives

Tyler's section on studies of contemporary life as a source of curricular objectives follows the pattern set by the section on the learner. His conception of the role that such studies play in determining objectives is also similar in many respects to that of his spiritual ancestor, Franklin Bobbitt, who stimulated the practice of activity analysis in the curriculum field. Like Bobbitt, Tyler urges that one "divide life" into a set of manageable categories and then collect data of various kinds which may be fitted into these categories. One of Tyler's illustrations is especially reminiscent of Bobbitt:

> Students in the school obtain[ed] from their parents for several days the problems they were having to solve that involved arithmetic. The collection and analysis of this set of problems suggested the arithmetic operations and the kinds of mathematical problems which are commonly encountered by adults, and became the basis of the arithmetic curriculum.[20]

Tyler tends to be more explicitly aware than Bobbitt of the traditional criticisms that have been directed against this approach. Bode, for example, once pointed out that "no scientific analysis known to man can determine the desirability or the need of anything." The question of whether a community with a given burglary rate needs a larger police force or more burglars is entirely a question of what the community wants.[21] Tyler's implicit response to this and other traditional criticism of this approach is to argue that in his rationale studies of contemporary life do not constitute the sole basis for deriving objectives, and, of course, that such studies have to be checked against "an acceptable educational philosophy."[22] In this sense, the contemporary life source is just as dependent on the philosophical screen as is the learner source.

The Philosophical Screen

Tyler's treatments of the learner and of contemporary life as sources of educational objectives are roughly parallel. In each case, Tyler is aware of the serious shortcomings of the source but assumes that they can be overcome, first, by not relying exclusively on any one of them—in a sense counting on his eclecticism to blunt the criticism. And secondly (and probably more importantly), he appeals to philosophy as the means for covering any deficiencies. This suggests that it is philosophy after all that is the source of Tyler's objectives and that the stipulated three sources are mere window dressing. It is Tyler's use of the concept of a philosophical screen, then, that is most crucial in understanding his rationale, at least insofar as stating the objectives is concerned.

Even if we were to grant that people go through life with some kind of primitive value structure spinning around in their heads, to say that educational objectives somehow flow out of such a value structure is to say practically nothing at all. Tyler's proposal that educational objectives be filtered through a philosophical screen is not so much demonstrably false as it is trivial, almost vacuous. It simply does not address itself in any significant sense to the question of which objectives we leave in and which we throw out once we have committed ourselves to the task of stating them. Filtering educational objectives through a philosophical screen is simply another way of saying that one is forced to make choices from among the thousands or perhaps millions of objectives that one can draw from the sources that Tyler cites. (The number of objectives is a function of the level of specificity.) Bobbitt was faced with the same predicament when he was engaged in his massive curriculum project in Los Angeles in 1921–23. Bobbitt's solution was to seek "the common judgment of thoughtful men and women,"[23] an appeal to consensus. Tyler's appeal is to divine philosophy, but the effect is equally arbitrary as long as we are still in the dark as to how one arrives at a philosophy and how one engages in the screening process.

Take, for example, one of Tyler's own illustrations of how a philosophy operates:

> If the school believes that its primary function is to teach people
> to adjust to society it will strongly emphasize obedience to pres-
> ent authorities, loyalty to the present forms and traditions, skills
> in carrying on the present techniques of life; whereas if it em-
> phasizes the revolutionary function of the school it will be more

concerned with critical analysis, ability to meet new problems, independence and self-direction, freedom, and self-discipline. Again, it is clear that the nature of the philosophy of the school can affect the selection of educational objectives.[24]

Although Tyler appears elsewhere to have a personal predilection for the latter philosophy, we really have no criterion to appeal to in making a choice. We are urged only to make our educational objectives consistent with our educational philosophy, and this makes the choice of objectives precisely as arbitrary as the choice of philosophy. One may, therefore, express a philosophy that conceives of human beings as instruments of the state and the function of the schools as programming the youth of the nation to react in a fixed manner when appropriate stimuli are presented. As long as we derive a set of objectives consistent with this philosophy (and perhaps make a brief pass at the three sources), we have developed our objectives in line with the Tyler rationale. The point is that, given the notion of educational objectives and the necessity of stating them explicitly and consistently with a philosophy, it makes all the difference in the world *what* one's guiding philosophy is, since that consistency can be as much a sin as a virtue. The rationale offers little by way of a guide for curriculum-making because it excludes so little. Karl Popper's dictum holds not only for science, but all intellectual endeavor:

> *Science does not aim, primarily, at high probabilities. It aims at high informative content, well backed by experience. But a hypothesis may be very probable simply because it tells us nothing or very little.* A high degree of probability is therefore not an indication of "goodness"—it may be merely a symptom of low informative content.[25]

Tyler's central hypothesis that a statement of objectives derives in some manner from a philosophy, while highly probable, tells us very little indeed.

Selection and Organization of Learning Experiences

Once the crucial first step of stating objectives is accomplished, the rationale proceeds relentlessly through the steps of the selection and organization of learning experiences as the means for achieving the ends and, finally, evaluating in terms of those ends. Typically, Tyler recognizes a crucial problem in connection with the concept of a learning experience but passes quickly over it: The problem is how learning experiences can be *selected* by a teacher or a curriculum maker when they are defined as the *interaction* between a student and his or her environment. By definition, then, the learning experience is in some part a function of the perceptions, interests, and previous experience of the student. At least this part of the learning experience is not within the power of the teacher to select. While Tyler is explicitly aware of this, he nevertheless maintains that the teacher can control the learning experience through the "manipulation of the environment in such a way as to set up stimulating situations—situations that will evoke the kind of behavior desired."[26] The Pavlovian overtones of such a solution are not discussed.

[margin handwritten note: Thorndike; Stin-response]

Evaluation

"The process of evaluation," according to Tyler, "is essentially the process of determining to what extent the educational objectives are actually being realized by the program of curriculum and instruction."[27] In other words, the statement of objectives not only serves as the basis for the selection and organization of learning experiences, but the standard against which the program is assessed. To Tyler, then, evaluation is a process by which one matches initial expectations, in the form of behavioral objectives, with outcomes. Such a conception has a certain commonsensical appeal, and, especially when fortified with models from industry and systems analysis, it seems like a supremely wise and practical way to appraise the success of a venture. Actually, curriculum evaluation as a kind of product control was set forth by Bobbitt as early as 1922,[28] but product control when applied to curriculum presents certain difficulties.

One of the difficulties lies in the nature of an aim or objective and whether it serves as the terminus for activity in the sense that the Tyler rationale implies. In other words, is an objective an end point or a turning point? Dewey argued for the latter:

> Ends arise and function within action. They are not, as current theories too often imply, things lying outside activity as which the latter is directed. They are not ends or termini of action at all. They are terminals of deliberation, and so turning points *in* activity.[29]

If ends arise only *within* activity it is not clear how one can state objectives before the activity (learning experience) begins. Dewey's position, then, has important consequences not just for Tyler's process of evaluation but for the rationale as a whole. It would mean, for example, that the starting point for a model of curriculum and instruction is not the statement of objectives but the activity (learning experience), and whatever objectives do appear will arise within that activity as a way of adding a new dimension to it. Under these circumstances, the process of evaluation would not be seen as one of matching anticipated consequences with actual outcomes, but as one of describing and of applying criteria of excellence to the activity itself. This view would recognize Dewey's claim that "even the most important among all the consequences of an act is not necessarily its aim,"[30] and it would be consistent with Robert Merton's important distinction between manifest and latent functions.[31]

The importance of description as a key element in the process of evaluation has also been emphasized by Lee Cronbach:

> *When evaluation is carried out in the service of course improvement, the chief aim is to ascertain what effects the course has.* . . . This is not to inquire merely whether the course is effective or ineffective. Outcomes of instruction are multidimensional, and a satisfactory investigation will map out the effects of the course along these dimensions separately.[32]

The most significant dimensions of an educational activity, or any other activity, may be those that are completely unplanned and wholly unanticipated. An evaluation procedure that ignores this fact is plainly unsatisfactory.

Summary and Conclusion

The crucial first step in the Tyler rationale on which all else hinges is the statement of objectives. The objectives are to be drawn from three sources: studies of the learner, studies of society, and suggestions from subject-matter specialists. Data drawn from these sources are to be filtered through philosophical and psychological screens. Upon examination, the last of the three sources turns out to be no source at all but a means of achieving objectives drawn from the other two. Studies of the learner and of society depend so heavily for their standing as sources on the philosophical screen that it is actually the philosophical screen that determines the nature and scope of the objectives. To say that educational objectives are drawn from one's philosophy, in turn, is only to say that one must make choices about educational objectives in some way related to one's value structure. This is to say so little about the process of selecting objectives as to be virtually meaningless. One wonders whether the long-standing insistence by curriculum theorists that the first step in making a curriculum be the specification of objectives has any merit whatsoever. It is even questionable whether stating objectives at all, when they represent external goals allegedly reached through the manipulation of learning experiences, is a fruitful way to conceive of the process of curriculum planning. Certainly, the whole concept of a learning experience requires much more analysis than it has been given. Finally, the simplistic notion that evaluation is a process of matching objectives with outcomes leaves much to be desired. It ignores what may be the more significant latent outcomes in favor of the manifest and anticipated ones, and it minimizes the vital relationship between ends and means.

One reason for the success of the Tyler rationale is its very rationality. It is an eminently reasonable framework for developing a curriculum; it duly compromises between warring extremes and skirts the pitfalls to which the doctrinaire are subject. In one sense, the Tyler rationale is imperishable. In some form, it will always stand as the model of curriculum development for those who conceive of the curriculum as a complex machinery for transforming the crude raw material that children bring with them to school into a finished and useful product. By definition, the production model of curriculum and instruction begins with a blueprint for how the student will turn out once we are done. Tyler's version of the model avoids the patent absurdity of, let us say, Robert Mager's by drawing that blueprint in broad outline rather than in minute detail.[33]

For his moderation and his wisdom as well as his impact, Ralph Tyler deserves to be enshrined in whatever hall of fame the field of curriculum may wish to establish. But the field of curriculum in its turn, must recognize the Tyler rationale for what it is: Ralph Tyler's version of how a curriculum should be developed—not *the* universal model of curriculum development. Goodlad once claimed that "Tyler put the capstone on one epoch of curriculum inquiry."[34] The new epoch is long overdue.

Notes

1. Ralph W. Tyler, *Basic Principles of Curriculum and Instruction* (Chicago: University of Chicago Press, 1950). Note differences in pagination in 1969 printing.

2. John I. Goodlad, "Curriculum: State of the Field," *Review of Educational Research* 39 (June 1969), p. 374.

3. Tyler, pp. 1–2.

4. I have argued elsewhere that the characteristic mode of thought associated with the field of curriculum frequently manifests itself in enumeration and particularization as a response to highly complex questions. Herbert M. Kliebard, "The Curriculum Field in Retrospect," in *Technology and the Curriculum*, ed. Paul W. F. Witt (New York: Teachers College Press, 1968), pp. 69–84.

5. Tyler, p. 3.

6. John Dewey, "The Child and the Curriculum," in *John Dewey on Education*, ed. Reginald D. Archambault (New York: Random House, 1964), pp. 339–40. (Originally published by University of Chicago Press in 1902.)

7. Tyler, p. 17.

8. National Education Association, *Report of the Committee on Secondary School Studies* (Washington, DC: Government Printing Office, 1893), p. 6.

9. Ibid., p. 203.

10. Ibid., p. 165.

11. Tyler, p. 4.

12. Ibid., pp. 4–5.

13. *See, e.g.,* H. H. Giles, S. P. McCutchen and A. N. Zechiel, *Exploring the Curriculum* (New York: Harper & Bros., 1942); V. T. Thayer, Caroline B. Zachry and Ruth Kotinsky, *Reorganizing Secondary Education* (New York: Appleton Century, 1939). The former work was one of the volumes to come out of the Progressive Education Association's Eight-Year Study. Tyler was closely associated with that research. The latter volume was published under the auspices of the Progressive Education Association's Commission on Secondary School Curriculum. Tyler was also a member of the committee that prepared the NSSE yearbook on needs. Nelson B. Henry, ed., *Adapting the Secondary School Program to the Needs of Youth*, Fifty-Second Yearbook of the National Society for the Study of Education, Part 1 (Chicago: University of Chicago Press, 1953). An early statement of needs in relation to curriculum organization ap-

peared in *The Development of the High-School Curriculum*, Sixth
Yearbook of the Department of Superintendence (Washington, D.C.;
Department of Superintendence, 1928). Needs as the basis for the
curriculum in English was mentioned by E. L. Miller as early as
1922. North Central Association of Colleges and Secondary Schools,
*Proceedings of the Twenty-seventh Annual Meeting of the North
Central Association of Colleges and Secondary Schools* (Cedar Rapids, Iowa: Torch Press, 1922), p. 103.

14. Tyler, p. 6.

15. Franklin Bobbitt, *The Curriculum* (Boston: Houghton Mifflin Co., 1918), p. 45 ff.

16. Tyler, p. 10.

17. Reginald D. Archambault, "The Concept of Need and Its Relation to Certain Aspects of Educational Theory," *Harvard Educational Review* 27 (Winter 1957), p. 51.

18. B. Paul Komisar, " 'Need' and the Needs Curriculum," in *Language and Concepts in Education*, eds. B. O. Smith and Robert H. Ennis (Chicago: Rand McNally & Co., 1961), p. 37.

19. R. F. Dearden, " 'Needs' in Education," *British Journal of Educational Studies* 14 (November 1966), p. 17.

20. Tyler, pp. 16–17.

21. Boyd H. Bode, *Modern Educational Theories* (New York: Macmillan Co., 1927), pp. 80–81.

22. Tyler, p. 13.

23. Franklin Bobbitt, *Curriculum-Making in Los Angeles*, Supplementary Educational Monographs No. 20 (Chicago: University of Chicago, 1922), p. 7.

24. Tyler, p. 23.

25. Karl R. Popper, "Degree of Confirmation," *British Journal for the Philosophy of Science* 6 (August 1954), p. 146 (original italics).

26. Tyler, p. 42.

27. Ibid., p. 69.

28. Franklin Bobbitt, "The Objectives of Secondary Education," *School Review* 28 (December 1920), pp. 738–49.

29. John Dewey, *Human Nature and Conduct* (New York: Random House, 1922), p. 223. (Originally published by Henry Holt & Co.)

30. Ibid., p. 227.

31. Robert K. Merton, "Manifest and Latent Functions," in *Social Theory and Social Structure* (Glencoe, IL: Free Press, 1957), pp. 19–84.

32. Lee J. Cronbach, "Evaluation for Course Improvement," in *New Curricula*, ed. Robert W. Heath (New York: Harper & Row, 1964), p. 235 (original italics).

33. Robert F. Mager, *Preparing Instructional Objectives* (Palo Alto, Calif.: Fearon Publishers, 1962).

34. John I. Goodlad, "The Development of a Conceptual System for Dealing with Problems of Curriculum and Instruction," U.S. Department of Health, Education, and Welfare, Office of Education Cooperative Research Project No. 454 (Los Angeles: Institute for the Development of Educational Activities, UCLA, 1966), p. 5.

10

Curriculum Theory: Give Me a 'For Instance'[1]

Introduction

Often, in our attempts to make sense out of social and intellectual movements, we use guideposts to set off the route our subject has taken. The publication of *On the Origin of Species* in 1859 is frequently taken as the starting point for a massive intellectual upheaval that went far beyond the realm of scientific inquiry alone. There is, of course, nothing in the curriculum field comparable to Darwin's revolutionary theory. Nevertheless, we do have a few modest guideposts which help us make our way in the development of curriculum as a field of study. One is the publication in 1918 of Franklin Bobbitt's *The Curriculum*, which set off curriculum as a field of professional specialization in its own right and not simply, as had been considered earlier, an offshoot of general educational considerations. The publication of Bobbitt's book cannot be said to have actually initiated the movement toward a distinctive field of study called curriculum; it is, however, reflective of that movement as it developed in the early part of this century. It embodied the particular assumptions and predispositions that were to dominate the thinking of those who were identified with the curriculum field for at least half a century and extending to the present. The publication of *The Curriculum* may be taken as the starting point of the era of so-called scientific curriculum-making, with all that implied for how the curriculum was to be conceived, how the development of the curriculum was to take place, and what constituted the criteria of success by which the curriculum was to be judged.

First appeared in *Curriculum Inquiry*, number 3 (1979).

A second milestone in the development of the field was the publication, in 1927, of the Twenty-Sixth Yearbook of the National Society for the Study of Education. Both volumes, *Curriculum-Making: Past and Present* and *The Foundations of Curriculum-Making*, were devoted to a review of the state of the art as it had developed to that point, as well as, in the second volume particularly, an attempt to resolve some of the controversies that had evolved in the curriculum field in the previous decade. Under the vigorous leadership of a rising young star in the curriculum field, Harold Rugg, major figures associated specifically with the curriculum field, such as Bobbitt, W. W. Charters, and George S. Counts, as well as those who were identified primarily with other aspects of education, such as William Heard Kilpatrick and Charles H. Judd, were invited to direct their very considerable energies and talents to the problems of curriculum. Specifically in the second volume, an attempt was made to resolve the growing cleavage between those, like Judd, Counts, and William C. Bagley, who saw social needs and issues as the principal basis of curriculum-making, and on the other hand, those like Frederick Bonser, Kilpatrick, and, in a surprising reversal, Bobbitt, who saw the individual needs and interests of children as the primary curriculum focus. While the attempt to resolve the differences between the divergent ideologies left something to be desired,[2] the Yearbook stands as a symbol of the curriculum field having "arrived." Major academic institutions were represented, such as Teachers College, Columbia University, and the University of Chicago, as were some of the leading superintendents and school administrators of the country, such as Jesse Newlon of Denver and Carleton Washburne of Winnetka. The curriculum had emerged not only as a field of study, but also as an urgent and recognized concern of practical schooling.

A third milestone—in a sense, the one we are celebrating here today—was a conference on curriculum theory held at the University of Chicago in October, 1947. Two-and-a-half years later, in March 1950, a volume comprising the papers delivered at that conference, compiled and edited by Virgil E. Herrick and Ralph W. Tyler, was published as a Supplementary Educational Monograph by the University of Chicago Press. Entitled *Toward Improved Curriculum Theory*, the monograph addressed itself most particularly, as the title implies, to a much-neglected aspect of curriculum development: theory building. The preface to the volume went so far as to say that "curriculum development without curriculum theory is tragic and that curriculum theory without curriculum development denies the essential purpose of the theory."[3] If the development of theory is taken to be the crowning accomplishment within a field of study generally, then certainly the attention to curriculum theory which was an outgrowth of the 1947 conference marked another significant stage in the evolution of curriculum as a field of study. Like the Twenty-Sixth Yearbook, this volume, although much more modest in size, also included many of the established and emerging leaders in the curriculum field. B. Othanel Smith opened the volume with a perceptive social analysis, pointing to what he called a "disintegrating culture" and arguing that the curriculum should be oriented toward certain collective social goals, social reconstruction, and moral commitment. Subsequent papers were devoted to a call for a theory that would indicate how objectives may be derived, an attempt to reconcile the long-standing controversy between individual and social aspects of curriculum, a discussion of the concept of curriculum design by Virgil Herrick, an effort to spell out the organizing elements of the curriculum by Gordon Mackenzie, and an analysis of the principal topics that would be included in a theory of curriculum organization by Ralph Tyler. But beyond the merits or deficiencies of the individual articles contained in the monograph, it no doubt contributed as a whole to the identification and legitimation of an entity called curriculum theory.

What is Curriculum Theory?

At least since the publication of the volume, the notion of curriculum theory has occupied a major place in the thinking of those concerned with curriculum generally. Since that time, many articles on curriculum theory have been written by able scholars, doctoral degrees have been awarded, and even a journal established which is dedicated to curriculum theory. In these respects, at least, the organization of the conference and the monograph that emerged from it was a distinct success. And yet, one curious and disturbing fact emerges from the work in the area of curriculum theory that has gone on in the thirty years since that conference. Although much has been done in the name of curriculum theory, there remains a great deal of confusion as to what a curriculum theory is, and we might even have some difficulty in actually providing a concrete and generally accepted example of what we are talking about when we use the term.

One of the problems here, undoubtedly, is that, like the word "philosophy," "curriculum theory" is used in a variety of commonsensical ways that have been accepted into general usage. Football coaches tell us they have a philosophy of coaching, stockbrokers speak of their philosophy of investment, and people generally speak of having a philosophy of life. But if challenged to state them, their philosophies would, in all likelihood, turn out to be beliefs about how football players should train, the tricks of buying or selling in the stock market, or practical maxims drawn from something like *Poor Richard's Almanac*. Likewise, what passes for a curriculum theory may take the form of a list of the "tricks of the trade," a series of steps for "how to do it," or a set of bald assertions about what schools are supposed to be doing.

It would seem to me that there are at least three ways that one can address oneself to this state of affairs. First, we might try to be reasonably clear as to what domain a curriculum theory would cover. Second, we should have some idea of what form a curriculum theory would take. Theories come in all sorts of shapes and sizes. What kind of theory do we mean when we refer to a curriculum theory? Finally, and for me most important, we could set forth an exemplar—a "for instance"—however incomplete; we could try to establish whether, in all the years that have been devoted to the central problems of curriculum, anything has emerged that, in the light of our previous considerations, could stand as an example of a curriculum theory. If there were such a thing, it might provide the most useful guidance of all in unravelling our problem.

In considering the first issue, the question of the domain of curriculum, it may be worthwhile to remind ourselves at the outset that curriculum theory—or any theory—has its origins in human thought, human curiosity, human activity, and human problems. Theories do not spring full-blown as rarified abstractions, but evolve as a way of addressing oneself to certain situations. Theories in the natural sciences have their origins in our sense of wonder about our natural environment and, perhaps, the need to have some reliable knowledge about the seasons, the land, and the stars. Aesthetic theory probably springs from the human necessity to make aesthetic choices or the inner delight we take in forms and colors. Ethical theory addresses itself to issues of right and wrong behavior as they emerge from the very process of living. Theories in social science derive from the common inclination to make sense out of the vagaries of human behavior. One may ask, therefore, what distinctive human activity can we identify or what special problem gives rise to the idea of a curriculum theory? A simple answer is that deliberate teaching requires choice as to what to teach; hence curriculum development, at least, may be regarded as that activity which gives systematic attention to the question of what we should teach.

Such a question may provide a starting point for consideration of curriculum theory because the kind of activity it represents would dictate to some extent the issues to which a curriculum theory would be addressed. There is nothing arcane or mysterious about curriculum development. It does not require a high degree of technical skill, nor is it reserved only for the specially anointed; but it does present us with some enormously complex questions. At the very least, we must decide among competing options, and whether we naively take certain things for granted as a response to that question or whether we treat that question with intelligence and sophistication, we are still faced with a serious choice. People often innocently assume that the answer to that question lies in certain defined subject areas which are to be taken for granted. Thus, they mask any sensible answer to that question by saying simply, teach history or science, and assuming that such a response satisfies the terms of the question. Even if we were to provide lists of topics under each subject heading, the choices available to one who undertakes deliberate teaching would still be countless. Furthermore, one should not rule out the possibility that the question, at least in the form that it is commonly expressed, cannot be answered. We may not, in other words, be able to answer it in the form of a list of subjects or a series of topics. The value of the question, instead, may lie in the issues it generates rather than as a question to which a straightforward answer may be given. These issues may serve to define the scope and substance of a curriculum theory.

First, the question of what we should teach invites a justification. No reasonable person, it would seem to me, would be satisfied simply with the bald statement alone. Curriculum theory, then, addresses itself to the question of what we should teach, in part by calling for a rationale for why we should teach one thing rather than another. As the English like to say, "why poetry rather than push-pin?" Given the fact that we cannot teach everything—a limitation imposed in part by the nature of schooling, of teaching, and of human intellectual capacities—we are obliged to provide some justification for the choices we make. And if a curriculum theory is to be anything more than an intellectual exercise, it should also provide practical guidance as to what to teach.

The second consideration implied by our central question is a by-product of the ineluctable fact that we never simply teach history or science; we always teach it *to* someone. The question of who gets taught not only implies some sort of criterion that bears on the choice involved, but also raises the question of who gets taught what. In other words, we are also called upon to give attention to the question of how knowledge gets distributed both by choice and as a consequence of incidental or accidental factors. Historically, for example, a persistent point of controversy in the curriculum field has been the question of curriculum differentiation. The question of who gets what knowledge has been argued to a large extent in terms of the differing capacities or probable destinations of different groups of students, and the extent to which these differences imply fundamentally different curriculum decisions for each of the identifiable groups.

A third consideration implied by our central question lies not so much in the domain of the distribution of knowledge as a kind of commodity, but in considering what effects would accrue from the study, particularly the prolonged study, of a given domain of knowledge. Presumably, the effect of studying mathematics for a long time would not be limited to the ability to perform certain specific mathematical operations, and the study of foreign languages would not be limited to the ability to read, write, and speak a particular language, but might also affect our characteristic habits of thought, frames of reference, dispositions, and ways available to us for addressing certain kinds of problems. In other words, we not only learn facts, skills, and generalizations, but our very way of thinking becomes affected by the way in which we address ourselves to what is studied. Therefore, in developing a curriculum, we do not simply name the things to be taught and provide good reasons, but we try to enunciate rules for how those things should be taught. We have every right to assume that the *way* in which something is taught is of utmost importance in considering the question of what we should teach because it is, in fact, a determining factory in what we *do* teach.

Finally, there is the complex question of how the various components of the curriculum are interrelated. Even if we were to consider answering the question of what should we teach in terms of a list of subjects or topics, we would need some justification not only for each component as a separate entity but for the curriculum as a whole. The terms balance and integration are frequently used to express this persistent concern for the interrelationship among the component parts of the curriculum.

Out of the central question of curriculum—what should we teach?— we are confronted, then, with a series of problems which arise almost inevitably when we address ourselves to it:

(1) *Why* should we teach this rather than that?

(2) *Who* should have access to what knowledge?

(3) What *rules* should govern the teaching of what has been selected? and

(4) How should the various parts of the curriculum be inter-related in order to create a coherent whole?

The Forms of Theory

We turn now to the question of theory itself, and particularly what sense of the word theory can reasonably be applied to the central concerns of curriculum as we have identified them. Time permits only a brief examination of this enormously complex question, and I shall restrict myself to the four senses of theory that Ernest Nagel has identified. Nagel first refers to what he calls the "positive sciences" —physics, chemistry, biology—where the term "theory" is usually meant to designate a system of universal statements.[4] Generally speaking, these statements are removed from actual phenomena but are nevertheless appropriate to things that happen in the real world. Nagel has in mind such theories as New-tonian mechanics involving gravitational theory, Maxwell's elec-tromagnetic theory, and evolutionary theory. One feature of this type of theory is that it relates, to some extent at least, to empirical findings. The basic questions that control curriculum develop-ment, however, do not seem to lend themselves to anything as grand or as all-encompassing as this first sense of theory that Nagel iden-tifies.

The second sense of theory is somewhat more restrictive than the first but is generally of the same order and, like the first sense of theory, depends to a larger extent on empirical verification for acceptability. This type of theory may be more restricted in the sense that it covers a smaller domain (in the way that Boyle's law does) or it may be dependent to some extent on statistical or quasi-statistical evidence (as is the law of effect in psychology or Grimm's law in linguistics.) While offshoots of certain psychological theo-ries may find their way into educational theory generally, there is very little reason to believe that the normative questions that characterize curriculum lend themselves to empirically based, law-like generalizations such as those described. The reasons for why we should teach *this* rather than *that*, for example, depend only to a limited extent on empirical findings.

The third sense of theory that Nagel distinguishes is neither a systematically organized set of statements nor a single explicit generalization. Rather, it is an attempt to identify the factors or variables which "constitute the major determinants of the phenomena that are investigated in some given discipline."[5] Here, Nagel's principal example is Keynesian economic theory, which is, more or less, a set of variables on which the economy (presumably) depends—national income, total consumption expenditure, total investment—and which does not state exactly what the relationship among these variables is. This theory gives us certain things to look for, but essentially says nothing about the relationships among the things that are named. In the field of curriculum, we do have examples of the attempt to identify such major components of curriculum theory as society, the individual, and the disciplines of knowledge. We are sometimes told that a relationship exists between these factors and curriculum development, but the nature of this relationship has not, to my knowledge, been adequately explicated. Unlike Keynesian economic theory, we have been unable to posit and verify even the most tenuous relationships among the identified variables.

The final sense of theory to which Nagel refers is "any more or less systematic analysis of a set of related concepts."[6] It is essentially an attempt to clarify what may be initially vague concepts, and thereby to unpack the nature of the problems under consideration. Here, empirical considerations play a relatively minor role. It is this last and most vague of Nagel's senses of theory that we may find most appropriate to a consideration of the central problems of curriculum. Since the central questions of curriculum are normative ones, in the sense that they involve choices among competing value options, the question of empirical verification comes into play only in a peripheral sense. What is critically important is conceptual clarification.

Our question now is whether there exists a "more or less systematic . . . set of related concepts" in which the concepts considered are those that are central to the problems in the curriculum field. It seems to me that a rather fully articulated theory in this sense is the one enunciated by John Dewey, and it is this theory that I believe may stand as our exemplar. Unfortunately, as in the case of his theory of value, Dewey did not treat the central concepts involved in one place and at one time. Therefore, if one were to establish Dewey's curriculum theory, it would be necessary to draw from several sources and a full explication of that theory would require a far more extended treatment than is possible here. Nevertheless, there may be some benefit derived from even a cursory sketch of this theory.

The central core of Dewey's curriculum theory is nether an empirically verifiable generalization nor an experimental finding but a metaphor. It is through the lens of this metaphor that Dewey is able to scrutinize the central issues that define curriculum and so to clarify the concepts that arise from these problems. The metaphor itself was not invented by Dewey, but he characteristically give it a special meaning and significance that was only partly evident of earlier versions.

One of the early versions of this metaphor as applied to curriculum issues was expressed by an Italian Enlightenment philosopher, Giambatista Vico, who, though somewhat obscure in his own time, is now enjoying a well-deserved resurgence of interest and acclaim. Only one of Vico's works, a very early one published in 1709, deals directly with education. The series of lectures which was published under the title *On the Study Methods of Our Time* is distinguished, however, from other pedagogical treatises of that period in that its argument (at least the part of it that deals with curriculum matters) rests on a fundamental principle and was not, as was much more common, a series of practical maxims on when such and such a subject should be introduced, nor helpful hints on how one should approach the teaching of a given subject. The "law"—in effect, the metaphor—that Vico enunciated embodies the idea that the analogy between the development of the individual and the development of the human race may be pertinent to the question of what we should teach. The analogy asserts that just as the individual traverses through a series of stages from infancy to adulthood, so also has civilization reached its present state through a series of identifiable stages. What is more, this parallelism is dictated by *nature*—not nature in the sense of an uncultivated or primitive state, but nature in the sense of a natural law. The question of what to teach is presumably an outgrowth of this natural law. Vico added that each stage, both in an individual's development and in the historical development of humanity, is discernible through a characteristic use of language in that stage.

The metaphor recurs in an educational context in *Émile*. Rousseau had earlier identified five distinct stages in the history of Western civilization,[7] and, in Émile's individual development, we find those same stages represented at least in rough outline.[8] We are guided as to the question of what we should teach Émile, not simply by his own stages of psychological development, but by the historic stages that run parallel to them. The "natural law" to which Rousseau appeals, in trying to answer the question, is really one of correspondence between two sets of stages.

John Dewey's Curriculum Theory

We turn now to a direct examination of Dewey's curriculum theory. Although time permits only a broad sketch of the development of Dewey's theory of curriculum, any consideration of the evolution of Dewey's theory must begin with his own reaction to and criticism of the prevailing curriculum ideas of the day: the late nineteenth century controversy between, on the one hand, the old education—represented in part by William Torrey Harris, the powerful and articulate Commissioner of Education—and, on the other, the American disciples of Johann Friedrich Herbart, a zealous group of educational reformers. That conflict between the Herbartians and Commissioner Harris reached a furious high point at the Department of Superintendence meeting held in Cleveland in 1895, when Harris, speaking for the Committee of Fifteen, used the term "correlation" in a manner unacceptable to the Herbartians.[9] Although the Herbartians themselves were by no means agreed on how correlation should be defined, the term in general referred to the coordination of the various component parts of the curriculum, the fourth of the major considerations identified earlier as integral to systematic curriculum development. Correlation provides one example of a concept arising out of the central curriculum question which, presumably, a coherent theory of curriculum would serve to clarify. Dewey's own notion of the coordination of school subjects was forged out of the criticisms he directed both at Harris's notion of correlation and at the Herbartians (with whom he was nominally identified), as well as in reconstructing the fundamental metaphor of recapitulation as it evolved at least since the period of the Enlightenment.

Dewey by no means rejected the importance of the general notion of correlation—only the particular versions that had been expressed in turn by Harris and the Herbartians. In effect, Dewey thought that there were simply too many different subjects being taught in school and that new subjects were being incorporated into the curriculum constantly and old subjects splitting up. There appeared to be what he called a "congestion in the curriculum."[10] How, he asked, can all these subjects be integrated and made to reinforce one another? "The child starts," Dewey said, "before he goes to school at least, with a unity of experience, not with a number of different subjects or studies. The fundamental problem then is how this unity of experience has come to be broken up into this number of isolated school studies."[11] What bothered Dewey was that the notion of correlating arithmetic, science, and geography, for example, already assumed that there were different things to be correlated. Dewey tried to raise the more fundamental question: "Where do these . . . subjects come from if they have been introduced bodily from without, already cut and dried and distinct?"[12] Dewey insisted that these studies, abstract and remote as they may appear, actually were arrived at through a gradual differentiation out of and within the unity of the child's own experience. This led Dewey to ask, "What has been the course, the procedure of that gradual differentiation?"[13] He was at this point more interested in the basis for breaking up the unity of experience into a collection of school studies than he was in enunciating a principle around which the various components may be interrelated.

Specifically, Dewey criticized Harris's concept of correlation as expressed partly in the report of the Committee of Fifteen[14] as well as in Harris's *Psychologic Foundations of Education.*[15] Harris identified five coordinated groups of study, each representing a distinctive and necessary phase of experience. Harris believed that out of the five groups of study one could evolve a comprehensive definition of the whole of experience. Language studies, for example, represented in outward form the thought or intellect of mankind generally. Dewey complained, however, that there was no real principle of unity involved. Although one may posit a relationship between each of the studies or groups of study and a phase of experience, there was no principle integrating the various phases of experience. A field like mathematics, Dewey argued, "sprang up, not out of the group, not out of nature, but out of human life and human needs. . . . [The branches of mathematics] were necessary tools for doing things that had to be done, just as much as plows and harrows were. . . ."[16] Even if we were to agree that a subject like mathematics now has an independence and self-existence, it is simply the result of a process of development from mathematics as a basic tool.

When Dewey turned his attention to the Herbartian version of correlation, he was faced with another sort of problem. Unlike Harris's notion of correlation, the Herbartians did have an integrating principle—a theory, you might say—out of which their concept of correlation arose. The principle involved the aforementioned metaphor of recapitulation, but they expressed it in a much more literal form than had Vico or Rousseau. The culture epochs theory, as it was called by the Herbartians, was recognized by Dewey as the theoretical basis for the selection and organization of the components of the curriculum. Correlation rested actually, as Dewey pointed out, on two fundamental assumptions. The first was the familiar parallelism between the stages in the development of the human race generally and the stages through which the individual passes on the way to maturity. The second assumption was that the material representative of each of the historic stages was the appropriate basis on which instruction of a child should be carried forward. The appealing feature of this general notion to Dewey was that it took into account both the psychological and social aspects of experience. The culture epochs theory, however, was for Dewey a far too literal interpretation of the general notion of recapitulation. Is it worthwhile, for example, to retain a child's education at a given stage, simply because the human race has tarried a long time in the parallel stage of historical evolution?[17]

Another facet of the theory to which Dewey objected in particular was the fact that, in practice, literary works were used to represent to the children the stages of historical development and thereby coordinate the various elements of the curriculum. Thus, in the early stages of a child's education, emphasis would be placed on the "savage" stage of human development through the myths and legends that may have evolved during those periods. Any attempt to correlate instruction around the literary residue of a given stage in history was bound to be artificial and unrewarding for the child. With all that, the Herbartian theory of culture epochs did provide a rationale for what should be taught, and one of the concepts to arise from that basic theory, correlation, addressed itself to the issue of how the things were to be taught as well as how interrelated.

To Dewey, the theory was full of deficiencies but, perhaps, not worth abandoning altogether. What Dewey did essentially was to shift the basis on which the central metaphor rested. Instead of resting the case, so to speak, on the concurrence between historical and individual stages of development, Dewey made his case on *epistemological* as well as psychological grounds. The historical parallelism enunciated by the Herbartians, in effect, was immaterial. Even if there were some validity to the notion, there would be no reason to believe that appropriate materials for study would be found in each of the historical stages. What was important was the epistemological question of how knowledge came to reach its present abstract and refined form. What would be reconstructed in the curriculum, therefore, would not be the historical stages in the development of modern civilization, but the progressive evolution of human knowledge from its origins in practical social activity (what Dewey called "occupations" in the Dewey School). Through this reconstruction, we would be restoring knowledge which appears at first to be so remote and obscure back to its origins in human experience. Through the concept of experience, Dewey hoped to tie together the two elements that constitute the heart of any curriculum theory: the child, on the one hand, with its crude, unsystematized, concrete forms of experience; and on the other, the abstract, highly refined, and systematically organized experience of the human race. Out of the range of activity and experience of the child, we would select those elements that offer some promise of leading on to an ever more refined and logical grasp of experience as embodied in the disciplines of knowledge. The metaphor was thus transformed from one where we view the child's educational development through certain defined stages of human history, to one where the child in its individual development follows the same course as civilization generally *in achieving knowledge.*

Unfortunately, time has permitted only a sketchy outline of Dewey's evolving curriculum theory. But even in such a gross outline form, some features of an entity we can call curriculum theory may become clear. It may, at least, help us to understand what a curriculum theory is not. It does not provide us with an immediate printout of a new and foolproof curriculum. It is not a powerful drug that will cure the ills that plague modern programs of study. It does not relieve us of the necessity to make ad hoc decisions based on practical experience. It does provide us with a central principle. That principle addresses itself to the question of what we *ought* to do when we teach children and youth. As one example, Dewey's theory provides us with a justification for engaging children initially in the same basic occupations—cooking, growing, building—that our early ancestors followed as a way of leading them in the direction of our present state of knowledge. This is particularly important in a technological society where the relationship between knowledge and human affairs has been obscured. Specialists, not the population generally, now perform the tasks of providing heat and illumination, constructing shelter, and getting food to the table. Knowledge and the appreciation for knowledge as instrumental to human affairs can be restored, however, when activities such as these become the starting points of a deliberate reconstruction of the evolution of knowledge in the curriculum. Knowledge, for Dewey, was a social inheritance to which all of us are heirs and not something reserved for an elite few.

As a normative theory, a curriculum theory is not, essentially, verifiable through empirical evidence, particularly the sort of empirical evidence that uses the criterion of efficiency to test how quickly certain means accomplish presumably desirable ends. Dewey's curriculum theory tells us, for example, something about desirable means and ends at the same time. Certain forms of empirical research may have a bearing on the theory—such as what is teachable, particularly what is teachable at given stages of maturity—but that evidence, though pertinent, may not be regarded as definitive. Ultimately, a curriculum theory provides us with a lens through which we can view the problems we must face in curriculum development. If it is a poor lens, it will obscure more than it clarifies; or, it may magnify and thereby exaggerate certain features of our problem and throw others out of focus. But if it is a good theory, it will disclose to us much more of what is vital to curriculum than is visible to the naked eye.

Notes

1. Paper originally delivered at a conference entitled Conference on Curriculum Theorizing Since 1947: Rhetoric or Promise? State University of New York, Geneseo, October 7–8, 1976.

2. For a perceptive analysis of the Yearbook, its accomplishment and weakness, see Decker F. Walker, The Curriculum Field in Formation," *Curriculum Theory Network* 4, No. 4 (1975), pp. 23–80; "Straining to Lift Ourselves: a Critique of the Foundations of the Curriculum Field," *Curriculum Theory Network* 5, No. 1 (1975), pp. 3–25.

3. Virgil E. Herrick and Ralph W. Tyler, eds., *Toward Improved Cur-*

riculum Theory, Supplementary Educational Monograph, No. 71 (Chicago: University of Chicago Press, 1950), p. iii.

4. Ernest Nagel, "Philosophy of Science and Educational Theory," *Studies in Philosophy and Education* 7 (Fall 1969), pp. 5–27.

5. Ibid., p. 9.

6. Ibid., p. 10.

7. Arthur O. Lovejoy, "The Supposed Primitivism of Rousseau's Discourse on Inequality," in *Essays in the History of Ideas* (Baltimore: Johns Hopkins Press, 1948), pp. 14–37.

8. Jean-Jacques Rousseau, *Émile*, trans. Barbara Fox (New York: E. F. Dutton & Co., 1938).

9. For Harris's report and discussion that followed, see William Torrey Harris, "Report of the Sub-committee on the Correlation of Studies in Elementary Education," *Journal of Proceedings and Addresses* (St. Paul, MN: National Educational Association, Department of Superintendence, 1895), pp. 287–350.

10. John Dewey, *Lectures in the Philosophy of Education: 1899*, ed. Reginald D. Archambault (New York: Random House, 1966), p. 185.

11. Ibid.

12. Ibid.

13. Ibid., p. 186.

14. William Torrey Harris, "Report of the Sub-committee on the Correlation of Studies in Elementary Education," *Journal of Proceedings and Addresses* (St. Paul, MN: National Educational Association, Department of Superintendence, 1895), pp. 287–350.

15. William Torrey Harris, *Psychologic Foundations of Education* (New York: D. Appleton and Co., 1898).

16. Dewey, p. 191.

17. Ibid., p. 203

11

Vocational Education as Symbolic Action: Connecting Schooling with the Workplace

Most of us are attuned to judging policies in terms of an instrumental rationality. We deem policies of all sorts—to aid the homeless, to shore up America's nuclear capabilities, to reduce the national deficit—as good or bad, if not in terms of their announced purpose, at least in terms of demonstrable consequences. Thus, in educational policy, we may launch a program to reduce or eliminate illiteracy, to raise the level of performance in mathematics, or to display proficiency in recognizing terms on a list purported to represent American culture. The first indication of success comes when and if the policy is translated into a concrete program of action and the second when the policy is weighed in terms of the extent to which it actually succeeded in accomplishing the stated purpose. Accordingly, when a high official in the Department of Education announces a policy called "Right to Read," we would be interested first in knowing whether those words and the proposals behind them actually affect the way schools operate to implement that policy; and secondly, we would want to know if there is anything like a demonstrable reduction in the level of illiteracy emanating from those concrete programs.

Debates about the efficacy of curriculum policies according to an instrumental rationality, however, have tended to obscure another facet of educational policy-making drawn primarily from within the political sphere. It is one that goes largely unrecognized but which should occupy at least as significant a role in judging the effects and the power of curriculum policies, the arena of symbolic action. There is, of course, a widely recognized domain of

First appeared in *American Educational Research Journal*, 27, number 1, pp. 9–28. Copyright 1990 by the American Educational Research Association. Reprinted by permission of the publisher.

unintended consequences to which several observers of the educational scene have deservedly drawn attention. But the arena of symbolic action is more encompassing than if it were just an unforeseen by-product of a social or educational policy. It is primarily a way of shaping public consciousness and gives meaning and direction to an entire sphere of social relations and social institutions.

My effort to understand curriculum policy proceeds from three interrelated themes: the overarching first theme is the conception of policy as symbolic action; the second relates to the rise of professionalism, particularly professionalism linked to the notion of applied science as it grew to prominence in the late nineteenth and early twentieth centuries; and the final one is represented by the way in which certain symbols served to reconcile the traditional Protestant work ethic with a new industrial order that had transformed the nature of labor. Although these themes bear no obvious relationship to one another, each, in its own way, contributed to shaping our consciousness about the relationship between education and the workplace.

Curriculum Policy as Symbolic Action

Symbolic action is centrally concerned with the symbols that give meaning and order to our world, including social relations, and thereby shapes our beliefs and prompts us to behave in certain ways. In the political sphere, symbolic action works at least in part by giving cues to targeted social groups that they occupy a certain status in relation to other groups. When Ronald Reagan ran for re-election as President in 1984, he promised that he would appoint an Italian-American to the Supreme Court. When he appointed Antony Scalia, this did nothing in any instrumental sense to improve the standard of living or the well-being generally of Italian-Americans any more than the earlier appointment of Thurgood Marshall improved the lot of African-Americans in terms of resource allocation. These appointments as symbols, however, did serve (or at least were supposed to serve) as a signal to these groups regarding their status.

To cite another example, it is highly unlikely that proponents of school prayer as an educational policy actually believe that its implementation would be instrumental in raising the level of religiosity in this country or in increasing church attendance. What is being sought by proponents of school prayer as educational policy is symbolic sanction for a particular set of beliefs. The implementation of that policy would serve to accomplish no instrumental purpose; its effect would be to fortify the social, political, and moral superiority of those who hold those beliefs. Symbolic action, therefore, is centrally concerned with status and sanction rather than concrete means toward the accomplishment of an unambiguous goal. Success in terms of symbolic action is achieved by attracting allegiances through the ratification of certain norms and beliefs, thus enhancing the station of those who are identified with them.

Rather than serving to accomplish a defined purpose, the main function of symbolic action resides in its use of language to organize allegiances, perceptions, and attitudes. At times, this means using rhetoric to render the main intent of the policy to appear harmless or even contrary to the actual intent of the policy. In this respect, Kenneth Burke, recognized as the leading theoretician in this area, has referred to political rhetoric as taking on the form of what he calls "a secular variant of prayer."[1] When appealing to a higher authority, one acts to soften the blow by conveying consequences that may actually be at odds with the instrumental effects of the policy. "One could hardly call this hypocrisy;" says Burke, "it is the normally prayerful use of language, to sharpen up the pointless and blunt the too sharply pointed."[2] The modern concept of "spin control" is a manifestation of this process. In politics, if fears are aroused, we are told to believe that they are unfounded; if a blunder has been committed, we are told to believe that it is wisdom in disguise; if there is a failure in a given policy, we are told to think of it as a victory.

It is in these terms that the concept of symbolic action may cast light on what we regard as the success (and perhaps even the failure) of vocationalism as curriculum policy. As instrumental action, vocationalism was a policy that would bring the American curriculum in line with the requirements of a modern industrial society by providing needed job skills for certain segments of the school population and by shoring up American industry to meet the competition presented in the world marketplace. But the answer to the question of why vocational education has sustained itself so successfully, according to Daniel Rodgers and David Tyack, does not lie in its ability to work significant changes in job structures or in creating opportunities for a new population to enter the workforce: "The answer . . . ," they say, "will lie in a deeper recognition of the symbolic function education serves in American political life."[3]

The significance of this symbolic function arises from the fact that the emergence of a vigorous vocational education movement could not have been merely coincidental with the widespread perception on the part of Americans of social upheaval and deteriorating social institutions. Its triumph will not be found, however, in its role as an instrumental policy addressing a clearly defined problem; rather, its success is attributable to its expression as mythic drama in which protagonists representing competing ideologies vie for dominance. Articulated policies such as were advocated by the proponents of vocational education, in this sense, are to be viewed as the dramatization of ritualistic myths about America and its values played out on the proscenium of the public school. This is what Murray Edelman refers to as "dramaturgy" in politics,[4] and it should come as no surprise to see dramas of a similar nature being played out in terms of educational policy. In fact, if the civil rights struggle of the 1960s is any indication, it is precisely in the amphitheater of the public schools that Americans in particular give expression to deeply held moral and social values. According to David Cohen and Bella Rosenberg, for example, social expressions about the nature and value of schooling,

> are like theater, for both engage our attention with the values, feelings and ideas they express, and with the various formal structures used to shape and achieve that expression. These cultural conflicts over school can be seen in the same way as we see a play. To understand a play we need not understand what caused the play—though it helps a great deal to understand its context. But given that understanding we focus on what is expressed in the play and what it means. The play's significance—like the significance of many social phenomena—lies partly in the act, in its content, and formal qualities.[5]

Recent critical reports about American education with titles like "A Nation at Risk," containing phrases such as "rising tide of mediocrity," are striking reminders of the fact that public schooling is the theater of choice where visions of the apocalypse are enacted; and it is through the dramas enacted there that Americans derive their catharses as well as, in some cases, a sense of efficacy with respect to a troubling present and a portentous future.

Only human beings reconstruct their histories, create meanings, and develop allegiances through the use of symbols. But the ability of the symbols we create to facilitate understanding and to frame courses of action can also distort and filter our perceptions of the world. It may be humanly possible for us to choose to satisfy our wants and develop political loyalties on the basis of rational decision-making processes that involve invoking empirical evidence on one side or the other; but any satisfactory explanation of human action must also attend to the symbols that intervene between our world and our reactions to it. Once these symbols are systematized and coordinated, they become the myths by which we organize our responses to matters of moment and concern. Any attempt to explain the vocationalizing of the American curriculum would be fragmentary and incomplete without going beyond the dubious claims of instrumental success and into the realm of the symbolism of the policies that were enunciated.

The Emergence of a New Professional Class

If the vocational education movement succeeded neither in the instrumental purpose of providing advertised occupational skills to students in order to enter the job market nor in making the United States more competitive in terms of world trade, it becomes especially appropriate to inquire as to who benefited from the policy. While the answer requires a much more extended analysis than can be provided here, it seems likely that the movement's principal beneficiaries were not what G. Stanley Hall called that "great army of incapables" then inhabiting schools or what are called at-risk students today but a corps of educational experts from whom ultimately flowed considerable power and influence. One difference between the examples of policy cited earlier and the vocational education policy in question, then, is that the latter helped sanction the emergence of a new professional cadre rather than conferring status on an already established interest group.

One propitious condition for the emergence of professional classes is crisis or at least the appearance of crisis. It is in a period of real or imagined crisis that professional expertise is in high demand. With newly emerging mass circulation newspapers reporting vice and corruption in the streets of urban ghettos and with persistent reports of the failure of the standard curriculum to hold the new population of students in schools, such as the Douglas Commission Report of 1906 or even the Cardinal Principles Report of 1918, the conditions were rife for the ascendance of a new professional class of educational policy makers who could provide the expertise to resolve these problems. Whether this was actually a crisis or one that was semantically induced—or even whether a particular interpretation of the crisis was unequivocally embraced—is not as important as it may seem. As Murray Edelman puts it, "There is . . . always a sense in which the labeling of a set of events as a crisis is arbitrary and problematic. Mass acceptance of the label is necessary even if the acceptance is ambivalent."[6] In the first few decades of this century, public schooling and society generally, for that matter, may or may not have been in deep trouble; but what was more important, insofar as the emergence of a professional class was concerned, was that a widespread perception of a crisis should be present.

This perception of crisis was conducive to the emergence of a class of professionals whose persistent references to the use of applied science in the resolution of the crisis made their claims widely plausible. The atmosphere of crisis also served a vital function in terms of the increasing bureaucratization of schooling. Professionalization in the context of a state apparatus like schools is different from the professionalism of, say, physicians. Magali Larson distinguishes two types of professionalism within the context of a state apparatus. In one, professionals such as social workers and librarians use the claims of professional expertise as a way of shielding themselves against bureaucratic power. By contrast, school superintendents and their confederates used their claims of technical knowledge as a way of ascending to power themselves. "The main instrument of professional advancement, much more than the profession of altruism," says Larson, "is the capacity to claim esoteric and identifiable skill—that is, to create and control a cognitive and technical basis."[7] By laying claim to such skills, the emerging class of educational professionals became, in their own words, "educational engineers,"[8] a new breed of policy makers with the specialized and technical knowledge purportedly needed in order to avoid disasters such as the disjuncture between what was taught in school and what Americans really needed to know in order to function effectively. By virtue of their claims of expertise, educational engineers were able to establish at least a modicum of independence from bureaucratic control (*e.g.* school boards) and even some control over them despite the fact that these new professionals were often imbedded in large-scale bureaucracies.

It matters little whether the scientific authority that is claimed is authentic or not. In this respect, the emergence of an identified group of professional specialists to deal with curriculum policy and practice closely parallels the professionalization of psychology in roughly the same period. Whatever may have been the psychologists' success or failure in terms of instrumental action, such as in actually improving pedagogical practice, their success in acceding to a measure of professional dominance in certain areas of educational and even general social policy is widely recognized.[9] They became the engineers, in an important sense, of a new way of ordering society. This social-policy aspect of professionalization in the related area of applied psychology early in this century was astutely recognized by Walter Lippmann in the course of his well-known debate with Lewis Terman on mental testing in the pages of *New Republic*. Lippmann deduced that the most significant effect of the tests that Terman and other psychologists had advanced so successfully was not principally in the interest of dispassionate inquiry into the nature of human intelligence. It was primarily a way of conferring status on one interest group relative to others, particularly in terms of who should exercise power in creating a scientifically driven social order, a new society based on measuring instruments purportedly designed to tap native intelligence. Moreover, it was their scientifically designed tests that set the standards and, more importantly, defined the limits by which status and material rewards in American society would be allocated. "If," Lippmann observed, "they [the tests] constitute a sort of last judgment on the child's capacity, that would reveal 'scientifically' his predestined ability, then it would be a thousand times better if all the intelligence testers and all their questionnaires were sunk without warning in the Sargasso Sea."[10] In his caustic reply to Lippmann, Terman was clearly interested in aligning himself with the new forces of science and against the old order of fallacy and superstition. Lippmann, that poor bumbling layman, Terman suggested, had intruded onto the sacred ground reserved only for scientists, and his lack of scientific credentials clearly disqualified him from raising objections on policy questions relating to mental testing. "Does not Mr. Lippmann owe it to the world," Terman asked sarcastically, "to abandon his role of critic and to enter the enchanting field of research? He may safely assume that if he unravels the secret of turning low IQ's into high ones, or even into moderately higher ones, his fame and fortune are made."[11]

At one point, John Dewey, a regular contributor to *New Republic*, was drawn into the controversy. Referring to various classes of persons who give different meanings to what constitutes superiority and inferiority, he questioned the right of psychologists to set the terms of that debate:

Superior or inferior in *what?* Is a student inferior for the purposes of reciting lessons, or fitting into a school administration,
of influencing companions, or "student activities" or what? Is
an adult superior in money-making, in music, in chicanery and
intrigue, in being a wise parent or good neighbor, as a homemaker, a chauffeur or a librarian, a congenial companion, a confidence man, an investigator of higher mathematics, an expert
accountant, a tractable worker or a revolutionist, in writing acceptable movie scenarios or in research in the library?[12]

If the psychologists were to ascend to a position where it would
be they who define who is superior and who is not, according to
Dewey, then it they who would have the power to establish the
rules for who reaps the rewards that society has to offer.

In like manner, if curriculum policy makers could achieve access
to the temple of science, their power to shape destinies, like that
of the psychologists, would be assured. The language of applied
science, in other words, was not just a convenient but probably
an indispensable vehicle to gain political ascendancy. Edelman puts
it this way:

> The chief function of any political term is to marshall public
> support or opposition. Some terms do so overtly; but the more
> potent ones including those used by professionals, do so cov-
> ertly, portraying a power relationship as a helping one. When
> the power of professionals over other people is at stake, the lan-
> guage employed implies that the professional has ways to ascer-
> tain who are dangerous, sick, or inadequate; that he or she knows
> how to render them harmless, rehabilitate them, or both; and
> that the procedures for diagnosis and for treatment are too spe-
> cialized for the lay public to understand or judge them.[13]

Insofar as the new mass of students who were entering American
secondary schools in the first few decades of this century were
concerned, the ability of professional curriculum makers to define
their own role as helping these unfortunates put them in a very
powerful position indeed. Applied science in terms of curriculum-
making was identified with the setting of precise standards, predictability, and the elimination of waste. This required the early
identification of future social as well as occupational roles and a
curriculum that prepared children and youth directly and specifically to function efficiently in those roles.

But it would be at least an exaggeration to interpret the rise of
professional curriculum-making simply as a calculated attempt to
keep immigrants, minority groups, women, and those otherwise

relegated to low social status in their place. While a stabilized social order would not have been inconsistent with the beliefs of the vast majority of its proponents, there seems to be no reason to question the sincerity of school reformers who, in their public declarations, professed only humanitarian motives. For example, for people like that ardent champion of vocational education, Charles Prosser, the introduction of vocational education was a way of breaking the elitist barrier that academics had so long maintained within the American curriculum. Non-academic, practical, and occupationally oriented courses were principally a way of adapting American schooling to the needs of a newly emerging class of students, particularly at the secondary level. The point is that however benign their motives, these curriculum makers were also establishing a power relationship. It is in this respect that the highly successful vocational guidance movement was so crucial to the overall success of vocationalism as curriculum policy.[14] In their publicly sanctioned ability to diagnose scientifically who was to go here and who there in terms of schooling and ultimately in terms of their place in the social order lay their ability to render the target groups harmless.

Reconciling the Work Ethic with the New Industrial Order

Almost without exception, the expansion of vocationalism within the American school curriculum became a sine qua non for the new breed of scientific curriculum makers. But vocationalism as curriculum policy over the course of the twentieth century was challenged by a pivotal paradox, and it was this paradox that the new curriculum professionals as well as social leaders generally needed to resolve. At the same time that vocationalism was enjoying its greatest success in terms of installing and expanding programs in schools to develop occupational proficiency, the very skills that had in an earlier era been required for success in the workplace were becoming less and less important. One of the principal arguments by the proponents of the expansion of vocational education was (and probably still is) that the old system of apprenticeship, the traditional avenue for entering into the workforce, had practically disappeared (at least in the United States) and that a new way of passing on vital work skills was needed. The problem with that argument is that the system of apprenticeship declined for good reason. It declined because it was no longer necessary to work elbow to elbow with the master of a craft over a period of years in order to work in a modern-day factory. The modern factory was deliberately designed to require the least possible skill on the part of the worker.[15]

One monumental task facing the new class of professionals, therefore, was to preserve the fiction that years of study were still required to enter the labor force. Even beyond that, however, was the problem of reconciling potent symbols associated with the established Protestant work ethic, such as the dignity of labor, with the new reality of the degradation of labor that now characterized the modern workplace. In addition to installing programs of vocational education in schools, in other words, symbols were needed that would command allegiances and achieve an appropriate response to a new industrial order that had transformed the nature of work itself. It is in this sense that the vocationalization of American education was a far more significant development than would be represented simply by its instrumental success in installing or expanding courses of study designed to teach occupational skills or even by introducing vocational components into the traditional subjects of study. What was needed, and was at least partially accomplished by the new professionals, was a reinterpretation of how work was to be perceived and with it a redefinition of the value and function of schooling.

In the course of achieving that redefinition, some interesting, even ingenious, bypaths were taken as Americans struggled with this transformation of the workplace and, consequently, with the question of how the labor required to keep the economy going could continue to be marshalled. Imbedded in the traditional work ethic, for example, was the belief that no work was too degrading and that labor was always to be preferred to idleness. Yet, by the turn of the century, the degradation of work was already evident to millions of Americans toiling in factories. One of the early efforts to restore the dignity traditionally associated with labor was to resurrect an older form of craft labor, not as a way to earn a living, but as itself a source of satisfaction. The handicraft movement that emerged just before the turn of the century with William Morris as its acknowledged leader and Elbert Hubbard as its chief promoter is interpreted by Rodgers as just such an attempt.[16] In the long run, however, the movement, as Rodgers indicates, turned out to be primarily a reaction to what was regarded as the sterility of machine-made products rather than a reconciliation between older work values and the new industrialism. Hubbard's advocacy of handicraft wavered between an attempt to reassert the dignity

of labor and simple obedience of the worker to American business.[17] In the long run, major figures in the movement, such as
Gustav Stickley, became much more concerned with aesthetic issues than problems related to the nature of work that were created
by the mechanization and fragmentation of production. (Stickley's
mission oak furniture, by the way, is in high demand in the world
of antiques.)

A second attempt to cope with the degradation of labor is represented by the efforts of such social reformers as Jane Addams
and John Dewey to suffuse labor with a social context through
education. The reason modern labor had become mere drudgery,
according to Addams, was that the worker simply did not understand the modern industrial system:

> If a child goes into a sewing factory with a knowledge of the
> work she is doing in relation to the finished product; if she is
> informed concerning the material she is manipulating and the
> processes to which she is subjected; if she understands the design
> she is elaborating in its historic relation to art and decoration,
> her daily life is lifted from drudgery to one of self-conscious ac-
> tivity, and her pleasure and intelligence is registered in her prod-
> uct.[18]

It was this kind of message that Addams tried to deliver to the
National Society for the Promotion of Industrial Education, a group
in which she was quite active. As the movement for vocational
education progressed, however, the concept that industrial education could become a force through which a variety of studies
could be integrated and through which a fundamental understanding of modern industrial society could be achieved was abandoned
in favor of the kind of emphasis that such ardent promoters of
vocationalism as Charles Prosser and David Snedden continued to
lay on just plain occupational proficiency.

In the end, the symbols that were most successful in reconciling
the work ethic with the new industrial economy were derived not
from fanciful reactions to the mechanization of industry, such as
the arts and crafts movement, or from Addams's admirable effort
to situate the nature of work within a larger social framework.
Reconciliation, at least in large measure, came from the very heart
of the new production system itself, scientific management. One
of the fundamental assumptions that Frederick Winslow Taylor,
the acknowledged leader of scientific management, promulgated
was that strife between labor and management in the new indus-

trial order could be assuaged through a motive common to both parties, profit. One early response, for example, was to give workers a new incentive for their labors through profit sharing, and this plan enjoyed some support for a time. But the position specifically advocated by Taylor was more direct. If the creative stimulus to accomplish a task was to be a victim of the new industrialism, he argued, then a new stimulus should be provided by the economic incentive of wages tied to actual production.

One of Taylor's very early papers, delivered to the American Society for Mechanical Engineers,[19] expressed the basic rationale for this response. To be sure, his central theme was simply efficiency of production. "Each workman," Taylor claimed, "with a definite price for each job before him, contrives a way of doing it in a shorter time, either by working harder or by improving his method; and he thus makes a larger profit."[20] But there was also an implicit recognition on Taylor's part that the new industrial system had created troublesome divisions between labor and management. Taylor alluded, for example, to the fact that one of the proposed avenues toward greater cooperation had been profit-sharing. The problem with that approach as he saw it was that "the few misplaced drones, who do the loafing and share equally in the profits with the rest, under cooperation are sure to drag the better men down toward their level."[21] Under his piecework plan, however, the interests of the workers (which he described as "THE UNIVERSAL DESIRE TO RECEIVE THE LARGEST POSSIBLE RETURN FOR THEIR TIME") and the interests of the management (which he described as "THE DESIRE TO RECEIVE THE LARGEST POSSIBLE RETURN FOR THE WAGES PAID") would be reconciled.[22] As early as 1895, then, Taylor recognized that the new industrial system had created substantial changes in labor-management relations, and he was reaching for a solution to that problem by trying to identify a common interest. Piecework did indeed gain some currency, but the economic incentive that was the centerpiece of Taylor's whole system was not sufficiently potent in itself to cope with the degradation of work.

Clearly implied in Taylor's effort to reconstruct labor-management relations was the concept of teamwork, not simply as a way to reduce strife, but as a symbol to workers that the older value of individual craftsmanship had to give way to a system where the cooperation of many workers was needed to achieve a mutually desired outcome. (This is, after all, practically what we mean by an assembly line.) Teamwork as a key symbol in the new industrial society, for example, was employed by one of vocationalism's most ardent advocates as he set forth his vision of a social order in the making. In "Education for a World of Team-Players and Team-Workers,"[23] David Snedden envisioned a society in which, like the modern factory, each member would perform specialized tasks toward the accomplishment of a common goal. His opening sentence declared his theme: "The most formidable current problem of educational science is this: How far should we educate people to be alike, and how far dare we educate them to be different from each other?"[24] The obvious point was that a curriculum that was predominantly for all had run its course because what society needed in order to run smoothly was each person performing his or her designated task in the interest of a common purpose. Only two percent of the population, according to Snedden, could attain real mastery in algebra. Teamwork required not that all, or even as many as possible, learn algebra but only that handful who could contribute to the success of the common enterprise. Not simply the study of school subjects but the "great community," as Snedden envisioned it, required what he called "specialization of service."[25] Clearly, in Snedden's mind, the model for the "great community" as well as for the school curriculum had become the modern factory.

But the symbol of teamwork, powerful as it was in itself, worked in conjunction with other symbols, such as leisure. The decade of the 1890s has been cited by several historians as a critical one in American life. John Higham, for example, has noted:

> From about the middle of the nineteenth century until about 1890 Americans on the whole had submitted docilely enough to the gathering restrictions of a highly industrialized society. They learned to live in cities, to sit in rooms cluttered with bric-a-brac, to limit the size of their families, to accept the authority of professional elites, to mask their aggressions behind a thickening facade of gentility, and to comfort themselves with a faith in automatic material progress. Above all, Americans learned to conform to the discipline of machinery. The time clock, introduced into offices and factories in the early 1890's, signaled an advanced mechanization of life.[26]

What were the mechanisms, however, that led to this conformity to that discipline of machinery? One clue may be found in what Higham calls "a boom in sports and recreation,"[27] a phenomenon that was associated with outdoor life generally, as well as with physical culture. The new obsession with recreation in the 1890s was one indication that Americans (and, incidentally, Europeans as well) had turned away from work as a source of satisfaction and fulfillment and were looking toward recreation to fill that void. In the period around the 1890s, leisure was becoming not only a sanctioned but a glorified activity. The modern revival of the Olympic Games, for example, occurred in 1896.

It is no coincidence that the revered seven aims of the Cardinal Principles Report, even in its first incarnation in 1916,[28] included "wise use of leisure" (later changed to "worthy use of leisure") as one of the principal aims of secondary education. It is important to note in this regard that those immortal "seven aims" as eventually formulated in 1918[29] as well as countless aims of schooling that have been promulgated ever since do not really function as purposes to be attained. The function of such goals, as Edelman observes,

> is precisely, and only, what they actually do in the present, not what they connote for a never-attained future. They evoke political support and opposition; and their semantic ambiguity, coupled with their socially supported teleological connotations, is precisely what makes them potent condensation symbols.[30]

"Worthy use of leisure," like other broad educational aims, functions not as a goal to be achieved but as symbolic authorization for certain activities. Work was no longer infused with dignity and intrinsic satisfaction; it became something to be endured as a way of acquiring an entitlement for the enjoyment of leisure during those designated periods allocated for that purpose, and only when one has earned the right to enjoy it.

The symbol of teamwork turned attention away from individual accomplishment in the workplace and toward setting up a kind of analogy between the teamwork necessary to win in many sports and the necessity to coordinate many isolated tasks in industry in order to manufacture a given product. In the case of leisure, Americans were being told symbolically that going out and enjoying oneself after a hard day's work and on weekends was not only morally acceptable but desirable. Through such symbols as teamwork and leisure, the expectations and desires of Americans were not so much being satisfied as reshaped. As Edelman points out, political action and, by extension, policies in a wide range of human social endeavor "*chiefly arouse or satisfy people not by granting or withholding their stable substantive demands, but rather by changing the demands and expectations.*"[31] Dignity of labor and individual pride in craftsmanship gave way to imparting discrete and often minute contributions to a common production goal through teamwork. Likewise, the pursuit of personal gratification was not to be found in the workplace, but on the playing field, the sports arena, or even the neighborhood tavern.

Conclusion

Rather than seeing vocationalism as curriculum policy in terms of being actually instrumental in bringing schools in line with the demands of modern industrial society, it may be more useful to think of it as a morality play. The central theme of the drama is the intersection of fundamental American (and even general Western) values with the social transformation that flowed in the wake of the Industrial Revolution. Ever since Max Weber's pioneering interpretation of the Protestant Ethic, the importance of the Reformation has figured prominently in explaining certain characteristic tendencies in Western societies.[32] Work had dignity; idleness was wicked. What would happen, however, if the nature of work was so transmuted that the dignity of manual labor or even the promise of substantial reward through honest toil was no longer as apparent as it had been in a pre-industrial age? That theme is played out as the protagonists, the new education professionals, served to fuse traditional virtues associated with work in American society with modern industry through the use of potent symbols.

It is true that the ostensible purpose of vocational education policy was to accommodate America's school system to the needs of a modern industrial society as well as to serve an ever growing class of students new to public education. However, the incompatibility between the workplace as transformed by industrialism on one hand and the time-honored value of the dignity of labor on the other, as well as the fact that this new social order did not require prolonged training in school as preparation for work, created a major dilemma for educational policy makers. In the course of attempting to resolve this dilemma, professional educators established their standing as experts who could resolve the crisis through a transformation of values about schooling. In effect, this made them the primary beneficiaries of the new policy. Once the perception of crisis became established, then a new professionalism, buttressed by applied science and using the script of the helping professions,[33] was able to define and control the kinds of re-

rms that were to dominate educational policy for most of the
wentieth century.

By reconciling and even recasting traditional values associated
with the traditional work ethic with such symbols of virtue as
teamwork and the explicit sanctioning of leisure, emerging professionals helped create a transformation in the way Americans thought
about the value of schooling. This led *both* to vocational education's failure as a curriculum policy in an instrumental sense and
to its success in pointing American schooling decidedly away from
certain traditional conceptions of education associated with the
liberal arts and in the direction of schooling as vehicle for economic benefit in individual and in national terms. As a policy that
would bring needed job skills into the workplace and greater opportunity for the mass of the school population, vocational education can almost certainly be counted a failure. The skills taught
in vocational courses were remote from the workplace and resulted in little or no advantages for those trained, either in terms
of entry-level jobs or higher salaries.[34] But, if the vocational education movement is seen as a form of symbolic action, a moral
drama, through which certain values and ways of thinking about
schooling became imbedded in American consciousness, then vocational education can be counted as a notable, perhaps even the
most singular, success of all the proposed educational reforms that
were competing for dominance during the twentieth century.

In no sense, however, should the triumph of vocationalism as a
curriculum policy be seen as *merely* symbolic. In the first place,
educational policies of any scope include instrumental as well as
symbolic elements. At the very least, schools and courses of study
in schools changed and changed significantly as a result of the acceptance of the policy. More importantly, however, symbolic victories in the arena of educational policy have consequences of profound social as well as pedagogical significance. The victory of
vocationalism conferred status and power on one interest group
to define the role and function of education in American society.
In his excellent study of the development of vocational education
in California, Harvey Kantor concludes that vocational education
left what he calls a "divided legacy."[35] Vocationalism failed as a
policy in an instrumental sense. It succeeded very dramatically,
however, in recasting the way most Americans think about the
curriculum.

In an important respect, the battle over the curriculum and who
controls it parallels battles over status interests in the larger po-

litical arena. Just as laws confer legitimacy or illegitimacy on certain kinds of behavior, so inclusion of certain kinds of studies in the curriculum sanctifies some elements of our culture and not others. The curriculum is a manifest expression of the cultural values just as laws are manifest expressions of what a society deems to be right or wrong behavior. The symbolic victory of the vocationalists not only conferred status and even power on an emerging professional class, it made certain components of the curriculum not only more significant in terms of enrollments and sheer visibility, and, more importantly, in terms that we regard as worthwhile or rewarding. Humanistic subjects, to take one example, were not exactly delegitimized; but their standing vis-à-vis the frankly occupationally oriented subjects in the curriculum waned significantly. Even subjects commonly associated with the academic curriculum, such as mathematics and science, became sanctioned not as important ways of knowing or as invaluable repositories of knowledge but as indispensable vehicles to achieving certain high-status occupations. The anonymous president of Middletown's school board was not engaging in hyperbole when he stated, early in the 1920s, that whereas previous educational policy had been aimed at other purposes, the new function of schooling was plainly to get jobs.[36] Instead, he was giving voice to a genuine transformation in the way that the role of schooling was perceived, a transformation that had taken place within his own lifetime. The symbolic achievement on the part of vocationalists has been so complete that many of today's students and even teachers would be hard-pressed to justify the many years spent in school in other than occupational terms.

In the end, despite their failure in terms of instrumental policy, vocationalists won a much more significant victory by making economic mobility and national economic issues the centerpiece of our thinking about schools. Even beyond the success of vocationalists in materially recasting the course of study for a significant segment of the school population, vocationalism as curriculum policy reconstructed values and attitudes about the relationship between education and the workplace for nearly everyone.

Notes

1. Kenneth Burke, *A Grammar of Motives* (New York: Prentice Hall, 1952), p. 393.
2. Ibid.

3. Daniel T. Rodgers and David B. Tyack, "Work, Youth, and Schooling: Mapping Critical Research Areas," in *Work, Youth and Schooling: Historical Perspectives on Vocationalism in American Education*, eds. H. Kantor and D. Tyack (Stanford, CA: Stanford University Press, 1982), p. 293.

4. Murray Edelman, *Constructing the Political Spectacle* (Chicago: University of Chicago Press, 1988).

5. David K. Cohen and Bella H. Rosenberg, "Functions and Fantasies: Understanding Schools in Capitalist America." *History of Education Quarterly* 17 (Summer 1977), pp. 121–22.

6. Murray Edelman, *Political Language: Words that Succeed and Policies that Fail* (New York: Academic Press, 1977), p. 46.

7. Magali Sarfatti Larson, *The Rise of Professionalism: A Sociological Analysis* (Berkeley, CA: University of California Press, 1977), p. 180.

8. W. W. Charters, "Is There a Field of Educational Engineering?" *Educational Research Bulletin* 20 (November 1941), pp. 29–37, 56; Charters, W. W., "Idea Men and Engineers in Education," *Educational Forum* 74 (October 15, 1949), pp. 1577, 1617–20.

9. See, for example, Stephen Jay Gould, *The Mismeasure of Man* (New York: W. W. Norton & Co., 1981); JoAnne Brown, "The Semantics of Profession: Metaphor and Power in the History of Psychological Testing, 1890–1929" (Ph. D. diss., University of Wisconsin-Madison, 1985).

10. Walter Lippmann, "The Abuse of Tests," *New Republic* 32 (Nov. 15, 1922), p. 297.

11. Lewis Terman, "The Great Conspiracy," *New Republic* 33 (Dec. 27, 1922), p. 119.

12. John Dewey, "Individuality, Equality and Superiority," *New Republic* (Dec. 13, 1922), p. 61.

13. Edelman, *Political Language*, p. 60.

14. See, for example, Marvin Lazerson, " 'Choosing our Roles': American Youth Guidance in Historical Perspective" (Paper Prepared for Organization for Economic Co-operation and Development, Center for Educational Research and Innovation Project on *The Educational Response to the Changing Needs of Youth*, March 1981.)

15. Ivar Berg, *Education and Jobs; The Great Training Robbery* (New York: Praeger, 1970).

16. Daniel T. Rodgers, *The Work Ethic in Industrial America 1850–1920* (Chicago: University of Chicago Press, 1974).

17. Ibid., 79.

18. Jane Addams, *Democracy and Social Ethics*, quoted in Rodgers, *Work Ethic*, p. 83.

19. Frederick Winslow Taylor, "A Piece-Rate System Being a Step Toward the Partial Solution of the Labor Problem," American Society of Mechanical Engineers, *Transactions* 16 (1895), pp. 856–903.

20. Ibid., p. 863.

21. Ibid., p. 866.

22. Ibid., p. 867.

23. David Snedden, "Education for a World of Team-Players and Team-Workers," *School and Society* 20 (November 1, 1924), pp. 9–14.

24. Ibid., p. 9.

25. Ibid., p. 11.

26. John Higham, "The Reorientation of American Culture in the 1890s," in *The Origins of Modern Consciousness*, ed. John Weiss (Detroit: Wayne State University Press, 1965), p. 27.

27. Ibid.

28. Draft of Reviewing Committee on Secondary Education Appointed by the National Education Association (for consideration at July 2, 1916 meeting), undated. (Reorganization of Secondary Education, National Archives, Group 12.)

29. National Education Association, *Cardinal Principles of Secondary Education: A Report of the Commission on the Reorganization of Secondary Education* (Washington, DC: Government Printing Office, 1918).

30. Murray Edelman, *Politics as Symbolic Action: Mass Arousal & Quiescence* (New York: Academic Press, 1971), p. 16.

31. Ibid., p. 7. (original emphasis).

32. cf. Rodgers, *Work Ethic*.

33. Edelman, *Political Language*, pp. 57–75.

34. There are exceptions. Some evidence indicates that women were able to use commercial courses in order to make the transition to white-collar occupations. Harvey A. Kantor, *Learning to Earn: School, Work, and Vocational Reform in California, 1880–1930* (Madison, WI: University of Wisconsin Press, 1988).

35. Ibid., p. 168.

36. Robert S. Lynd and Helen Merrell Lynd, *Middletown* (New York: Harcourt Brace & Co., 1929), p. 129.

12

Curriculum Theory as Metaphor

One of the surest ways to kill a conversation on the subject of curriculum theory is to ask someone to name one. There appears to be so much disagreement and confusion on this subject that discussions revolve not so much around the merits of rival theories as on the question of what in the world we are talking about. My purpose here is to present one version of what a curriculum theory is and to indicate something of how it functions. In doing so, it would be futile to hold up an example of a theory drawn from the natural or social sciences and to assume that any legitimate curriculum theory must exhibit the same characteristics, although some insight into the nature of theory may accrue from comparisons. One has only to think of theories that exist in such fields as ethics, physics, political science, and psychology to realize that theories in those fields not only deal with different phenomena but also assume considerably different forms.

The general idea of theory presented here comes closest to the last and least restrictive of four senses of the term *theory* that Ernest Nagel has distinguished, namely that it refers to "any more or less systematic analysis of a set of related concepts."[1] The principal purpose of such a theory is essentially an explication or reconstruction of initially vague concepts and questions, although, as we shall see, it may serve other purposes as well. In the case of a curriculum theory, these vague concepts arise when we attempt to address the question of what we should teach, and, in general terms, a curriculum theory is a coherent attempt to make those concepts somehow more comprehensible. In this loose sense of

First appeared in *Theory into Practice*, 21, number 1, pp. 11–17. (Theme issue on "Curriculum Theory".) Copyright 1982, College of Education, The Ohio State University.

theory, it does not seem to serve any useful purpose to distinguish between what we commonly call a model and a theory, and those terms will be used more or less interchangeably.

What is a Curriculum Theory?

Perhaps an example of a curriculum theory, albeit a discredited one, will help clarify the question of what a curriculum theory is. The curriculum theory that dominated education in this country during most of the nineteenth century was known as mental discipline. For our purposes, it may be helpful to distinguish between mental discipline, or, as it was sometimes called, formal discipline, from a closely associated theory, faculty psychology. Faculty psychology was a theory of how the mind works; mental discipline as here defined was a theory about what we should teach. Faculty psychology was based on the notion that there existed at birth certain faculties or powers of the mind that could be developed through use. Thus, the faculty of memory could be strengthened by remembering, the faculty of reasoning by reasoning, and the faculty of imagination by imagining. Mental discipline was based on the notion that there were certain subjects of study, and, more particularly, certain ways of studying certain subjects, that were especially useful in developing those powers of the mind. Thus, the study of mathematics in particular was believed to have the effect of strengthening the power of reasoning.

In its more elaborated form, the theory of mental discipline addressed the questions that we commonly associate with the question that defines the field of curriculum. With respect to the central question of the field, what should we teach, it prescribed a set of subjects that were presumably more efficacious than others in carrying forward the major task of education. (The major task of education was assumed to be the development of intellectual capacities.) Not only could mental disciplinarians name some subjects that were better than others in fulfilling this function, they had a plausible-sounding way of justifying those decisions. In general, the form of a subject was considered to be of much greater significance than its content. Thus, although mental disciplinarians may have disagreed among themselves as to whether modern languages had as much disciplinary value as classical languages, they were in agreement as to the criterion on which such a judgment should be made. If French or German could demonstrate its disciplinary value, then it belonged in the curriculum alongside Greek and Latin. The natural sciences, then clamoring for a place in the curriculum, also had to justify their place in terms of their ability to train the mind. Incongruously, even Edward L. Thorndike, in making the case for psychology as a high school subject, felt called upon to allude to its disciplinary value.[2]

Not only did the theory of mental discipline provide a basis for what to teach and how to justify that decision, it also addressed the other critical questions that we commonly associate with curriculum, and addressed them in a reasonably coherent way. The question is frequently raised, for example, as to whether to differentiate the curriculum for different identifiable groups within the school population. Should, for example, one kind of curriculum be developed for those high school students who were destined to go to college and another one for those who were merely preparing for "life?" To a mental disciplinarian like Charles W. Eliot and the other mental disciplinarians who comprised the National Education Association's Committee of Ten in 1893, the answer was unequivocally no. After all, although people may differ as to the extent of their capacities, they still all had the same ones, and it was the job of the school (through the curriculum) to develop those powers of the mind as far as possible. Not only that, the Committee of Ten recommended that the subjects should be taught in the same way; that is, once the right way of teaching the various subjects was determined, those rules should be applied to teaching them for all, not just a select segment of the school population, however defined. Why should we deny to some groups in the school population the best means available for strengthening their mental powers?

Finally, the theory of mental discipline provided some guidelines for such questions as sequence and balance in the curriculum. Since there was presumed to be a natural order for the emergence of the faculties, that order could be followed in the curriculum. The subjects that were believed to strengthen the power of observation could be presented early in the school curriculum, and higher mathematics could be presented at the end, when reasoning was supposed to emerge. Balance would be achieved by attending to all the faculties of the mind. Since it was believed that faculties not developed at the proper time would atrophy or wither, it became the duty of curriculum makers to see to it that all the faculties of the mind were developed, thereby achieving intellectual harmony.

Although subscribing to mental discipline as a curriculum theory did not mean absolute agreement on all questions of substance in the curriculum field, it did imply a realm of shared meanings. Thus, though mental disciplinarians may have disagreed among themselves as to the disciplinary value of one or another subject and even on the question of how many faculties there were, they had a common language and therefore a common basis for addressing the questions that give form and substance to the curriculum field: What should we teach? Why should we teach one thing rather than another? How should knowledge be distributed through the curriculum? What rules should be applied to the teaching of school subjects? And what should be the relationship among the various things we teach?

But how did these shared meanings arise and how were they communicated? One of our most fundamental ways of creating and communicating meaning is by, consciously or unconsciously, juxtaposing our familiar world of perception and senses with the puzzling and abstract, and thereby achieving a new understanding of the latter. Nobody has ever seen a mind. It is intrinsically something beyond our ability to perceive or to sense directly. Yet, if we create an analogy between the mind and the body, we are able to "see" the mind in some sense. The arcane mysteries of memory and imagination appear somewhat more comprehensible when seen through the lens of the visible and palpable muscles of the body. Such appearances, of course, may be deceiving, but they do represent an entree into the realm of theory.

Words, as J. L. Austin once observed, never quite escape their etymologies, ("well, hardly ever," he says),[3] and the etymology of the word theory is derived from the Greek *theorein* meaning, to contemplate, but originally, looking at or seeing. A theory, therefore, in its root meaning, may be construed as a way of seeing— but, it may be argued, a particular way; it is a way of seeing one thing as if it were another. A curriculum theory, in this sense, begins in the transference of meaning metaphorically from the familiar and the comprehensible to the abstract and persistently perplexing problems that arise when we address the question of what we should teach.

Metaphor as a Process of Thought

The literature on metaphor is vast in scope and covers at least two millennia in time. It begins in the profound speculations of

Aristotle and continues to the present, in the work of distinguished linguists, literary critics, philosophers, anthropologists, and political scientists. No attempt will be made here at a comprehensive review of that literature—only an effort to acknowledge particular indebtedness and to carry forward some intriguing conceptual analyses of metaphor into the domain of curriculum theory.

Two assumptions about metaphor need to be made clear at the outset. One is that metaphor represents a fundamental vehicle of human thought. We need, in other words, to get rid of the commonsensical idea that metaphor represents a mere ornament to speech and writing irrelevant or incidental to the task of clarifying and conveying meaning. As James M. Edie put it, metaphor is not "an accidental weakness of human thought" that can somehow be transposed into literal language if only we put our minds to it.[4] Far from being mere literary devices or instances of imprecise language requiring literal translation, metaphors represent a fundamental way that human beings have evolved to express and organize their world, especially the world that lies beyond immediate perception. The origins of metaphor lie not in the effort to decorate language. "They originate in the practical need to progress from 'known' (already distinguished, already named) phenomena to what is as yet unknown and unnamed."[5] In this sense, metaphors become "primary perceptual categories"[6] by which the complex and puzzling become more familiar and more readily understood. Metaphorical language, therefore, becomes the fundamental way by which we move from the immediate and sensory into the remote and abstract, the realm of theory.

A concomitant to that first assumption is the idea that in performing their function in thought, metaphors are no more infallible routes to truth and righteousness than they are necessarily treacherous side roads that are irrelevant or impediments to straightforward and logical thought. Metaphors are, quite simply, not only universal, but inevitable. As such, it behooves us to explore how they function in language. It is not, after all, language that is the symbolic mirror of our thought; rather, language provides us with the conceptual categories by which thought and understanding are ordered.

The view of metaphor presented here is derived directly from the philosopher, Max Black.[7] Black distinguishes three theories of metaphor. The first, which he calls the substitution theory, is based on the assumption that any metaphorical statement can be translated into a literal one. According to this view, the use of metaphor in language is reduced essentially to two functions: one is a kind of *catachresis* in which there is a gap in our literal language and we must resort to metaphor in order to fill it. Thus, we refer to the "eye" of a needle simply because we have no other way of naming the hole that we find at one end. The other function of metaphor is to give pleasure. Presumably, it simply delights us to hear Richard referred to as a lion rather than to being described simply as brave.

The comparison theory of metaphor, according to Black, is actually a special case of the substitution theory. It is based on the idea that metaphor is an elliptical simile, a comparison with some details left out. Thus, if I were to say, Charley is a rat, that statement can be reconstructed into an extended simile with the missing parts supplied: Charley is like a rat in that he possesses the qualities of stealth, meanness, selfishness, etc. As in the case of the substitution theory of metaphor, the comparison theory holds that a metaphor is basically an interesting way to express something and that, at least in principle, the metaphorical statement can be translated into a literal one.

Black's objection to both these theories is based in part on the idea that implicit in them are "objectively given" similarities between the two elements in a metaphor. It is better to say, he argues, that the metaphor *creates* a similarity rather than alluding to similarities that exist antecedently. Black's own position, which he calls the interaction theory of metaphor, begins with the idea that any metaphorical statement has two subjects, a "principal" one and a "subsidiary" one, and that each of these is actually a system of things rather than one thing. The metaphor operates by transferring some implications or part of "a system of commonplaces" from the subsidiary subject to the principal one, (and sometimes even *vice versa*). We therefore begin to see the principal subject in a different way, because the subsidiary subject acts as a kind of lens through which the principal subject is perceived, say with some features suppressed and others exaggerated. Thus, when we say that Charley (principal subject) is a rat (subsidiary subject), we are setting up a system of interaction in which some "commonplaces" that we associate (rightly or wrongly) with rat-ness are transferred over to Charley in a way that makes us see Charley differently. (It is also possible that we will begin to see rats as more human.) Black's interpretation of metaphor, of course, is consistent with the idea that metaphor represents a powerful way to organize thinking rather than simply a way to dress up language.

While I know of no one who would claim that a theory is nothing but metaphor, it can be argued that metaphors and theories have in common the effort to organize thinking by setting in motion an interaction between the familiar and/or the comprehensible on one hand and the thing to be explained on the other. The metaphor acts to take those "initially vague concepts" that Nagel refers to and hold them up to scrutiny under a lens that reconstructs our perception of them. A large part of what we call theory consists of the effort to extend by analogy understandings, concepts, and explanations that exist in one domain over to another. Not all metaphor, obviously, achieves the status of theory, but much, if not all theory, has its origin in metaphor. "Theoretical science," according to Anatol Rapoport, "is essentially disciplined exploitation of metaphor."[8]

Thus, while it is true that, as meanings are transferred from the secondary system to the primary system, we begin to see the primary system (the thing to be explained) in a new way, this shift of meanings may not in itself represent a fruitful theory, even in an incipient form. For one thing, some metaphors have little, if any, explanatory power; they simply do not lead anywhere. A metaphorical explanation may easily turn out to be naive or weak. There are few, if any, ground rules for creating successful metaphors, although Aristotle's view that the implied comparison should be neither too removed nor too familiar is still a reasonable starting point. (Giambattista Vico called metaphors "credible impossibilities.") To call the curriculum a banana is simply far-fetched; to call a curriculum a route over which one travels (a metaphor consistent with its etymology) is to evoke implications of the student as traveler, the teacher as guide, and knowledge as a map.[9]

But the path from even a rich metaphor to the status of model or theory is difficult, if not impossible, to trace with any degree of exactitude, and that path almost certainly is different depending on the nature of the field of study. A commonly accepted criterion of a good model or theory, in any field, however, is its disclosure value. Scientists, for example, do not actually believe that the carbon atom is a tetrahedron. But if we conceive of the carbon atom as if it were a tetrahedron, it becomes possible to explain how that atom combines to form compounds as well as to understand the concept of valency.[10] The pretense that the carbon atom is a tetrahedron has become a conscious tool of understanding. In the natural sciences, some (but certainly not all) would claim that this metaphorical make-believe will eventually be abandoned as model or theory becomes more like a hypothetical-deductive system, but, even if this were the case, this should not blind us to the theory's metaphorical origins. As Black put it, "Perhaps every science must start with metaphor and end with algebra."[11]

Metaphors, then, as elements in models and theories, may be fruitful, leading to powerful explanations, or they may be trivial and lead nowhere. They also may be misleading or even treacherous. There are at least two reasons for this: one is that metaphors have a way of becoming literal, and if we lose sight of what is metaphorical about metaphor, we may restrict our thinking or simply deceive ourselves. Colin Murray Turbayne, for example, has distinguished three stages in the life of a metaphor.[12] At first, we simply give a name to one thing that belongs to another. At this stage, there is usually resistance to this misnaming. The body, after all, is not a machine with metal parts. In the second stage, we begin to acquiesce in the make-believe. We suspend our literal sense in order to gain some insight or explanation not otherwise available to us. Finally, there is a dangerous third stage in which the thing becomes what it has pretended to be. It is in this stage that "the human body is nothing but a machine" or the curriculum is nothing but a mechanism for producing the kinds of people that society needs. Our willing sense of make-believe is converted into a literal prison. "The victim of metaphor," according to Turbayne, "accepts one way of sorting or bundling or allocating the facts as the only way to sort, bundle, or allocate them."[13] To think of the mind as if it were a muscle may prove illuminating in some respects, but once that "as if" quality is lost, and the mind becomes quite literally a muscle, then we are in danger of falling into a metaphorical trap. The mind, whatever it is, is neither a muscle as the mental disciplinarians imagined, nor a machine, as some modern psychologists seem to believe, nor, for that matter, a ghost in the machine as Gilbert Ryle characterized the Cartesian theory of mind,[14] although each of these metaphors carries with it powerful implications for how we can make sense of a perplexing question.

Secondly, metaphors are not simply linguistic tools by which we try to understand something; once expressed, they also carry with them a hortatory dimension (comparable to what Israel Scheffler calls a programmatic definition).[15] Orators, for example, have long been aware of the power of metaphor to fashion allegiances and control attitudes. As Rapoport put it, "[M]etaphors are not only symptoms of the way events are perceived but also factors in the shaping of perception."[16] In other words, the expression of a metaphorical relationship is not merely an observation about analogous elements in dissimilar things. Once expressed, a metaphor gets projected as a form of argument. To see the school as if it were a factory and the curriculum as means of production is not merely to make an observation; that metaphor has imbedded in it an element of persuasion, and one who is not critically aware of the power of metaphor can easily become its victim. Perhaps the only defense against being victimized by metaphor is sophistication. Conscious pretense, after all, is not delusion.

Between Metaphor and Theory

Basic to the preceding discussion is the idea that curriculum metaphors provide a language or explanation which permits us to "see" things that otherwise might not be visible to the naked eye. Thus, although metaphors are not identical to theories as we know them in the curriculum field, they provide the seed from which theory may take root. Metaphors can be nurtured into theories to the extent that they serve certain functions. One would be to advance inquiry. Mary Hesse, in her treatment of the relationship between metaphor and scientific explanation, indicates that "metaphor becomes explanatory when it satisfies further conditions."[17] Essentially rejecting the orthodox deductive account of scientific explanation, Hesse takes the position that metaphors, "if they are good ones,"[18] correct or even replace the original literal descriptions. In doing so, "the original observation language will be shifted in meaning and extended in vocabulary," making certain kinds of prediction possible.[19] The metaphorical language in science, in other words, serves to generate hypotheses that may be tested by inquiry. It would be naive to assume that all the conditions relevant to inquiry in the natural sciences can be transposed to education and curriculum, but one implication of the way metaphors function in the natural sciences is that "good" curriculum metaphors make possible a form of prediction in roughly the same way that scientists can make predictions about the behavior of gas molecules by pretending they are billiard balls. The predictions, of course, may turn out to be false, but even then, the metaphorical language has served a useful purpose.

Surely, this must have been the case with William James's experiments with memory reported in 1890. One implication of the mind-body metaphor on which the theory of mental discipline rested was that the faculty of memory could be improved by exercise in roughly the same way that the muscles of the body could be developed by exercise. One could predict, in other words, that a period of practice in memorizing would strengthen the faculty of memory. But, in a crude before-and-after experiment, James and his students found that after about a month of practice in memorizing, their ability to memorize poetry had actually deteriorated slightly.[20] By the early twentieth century, the testing of hypotheses derived from the mental disciplinary metaphor had become a minor industry,[21] and the failure of that theory to hold up under empirical testing was one factor in its demise.

A contemporary example is provided by the "correspondence theory" developed by Samuel Bowles and Herbert Gintis in *Schooling in Capitalist America*.[22] Rejecting conventional explanations of the function of schooling which emphasize cognitive factors, Bowles and Gintis argue that there exists "a close correspondence between the social relationships which govern personal interaction in the workplace and the social relationships of the educational system." Specifically, the relationships of authority and control between administrators and teachers, teachers and students, students and students, and students and their work replicate the hierarchical division of labor which dominates the workplace."[23] The proposed relationship between the workplace and the school suggests several empirical propositions, some of which Michael Olneck and David Bills have undertaken to test. Would, for example, holding constant relevant non-cognitive traits reduce the apparent relationship between years of schooling and economic success? Are the non-cognitive characteristics which schools reward with higher grades the same characteristics the labor market rewards? In their research, Olneck and Bills conclude that there is "little support for the correspondence theory as it is advanced by Bowles and Gintis."[24] The conclusiveness of this finding and the details of their intriguing research are not important for our purpose. Nor does it really matter whether the correspondence theory is a theory of schooling rather than a curriculum theory in the sense of addressing the same questions that mental discipline did. What is important is that the theory that Bowles and Gintis advanced unquestionably provided the impetus for an empirical investigation.

Moreover, in interpreting their conclusions, Olneck and Bills explicitly adopt the language of the analogy between school and the workplace on which the correspondence theory rests. "Schoolwork," they say, "is largely cognitive and solitary (even when pur-

sued in a classroom), while adult work is largely physical or in-
terpersonal" and "the child's 'boss' is not accountable to the same
kind of production or profit criteria as is the worker's boss."[25] In
line with Hesse's position, the original observation language has
obviously given way to a metaphoric language suggesting empirical relationships which may be verified or falsified. Data gathered
in experiments such as these, therefore, ought not be considered
as some kind of objective verification of a metaphorical statement.
The experiments are themselves metaphorical in the way they bear
on the subject under study. As Richard Brown put it; "In each
case the data, as raw data, are unimportant, one might even say
unknowable or meaningless. But when the data are seen as an original iconic metaphor of the larger theoretical domain, they sud-
denly become significant."[26]

But verification or falsification of hypotheses is far too restricted
a way to consider the functions of curriculum theory, even when
empirical inquiry is concerned. The metaphor may serve the function of providing a conceptual language that guides research when
no particular hypothesis is involved. For example, in the research
on teaching conducted by Bellack and his colleagues ,[27] no predictions or hypotheses were formulated, but the metaphor of a
language game suggested that there were certain "rules" that were
being followed by teachers and students, and much of the research
took the form of explicating those rules. Data were collected in
terms of "pedagogical moves" and patterns of moves that could
be interpreted as "strategies" in the game of teaching. Thus, while
no prediction or verification was involved, the game metaphor
provided what Dewey called the "intellectual instrumentalities" by
which the research was conceptualized.[28] It is obvious, here, that
there is no separation between theory and the experience from which
the data are drawn. Data and theory are both symbolic con-
structs.[29]

Finally, it cannot be emphasized too strongly that curriculum
theory is fundamentally concerned with values, and any comparison between curriculum theory and theory in the natural sciences
may seriously underestimate that crucial fact. A brief examination
of political theory may serve not only to underscore the essential
value component, but help to expose what may be the most important function that curriculum theory serves. Metaphor, of course,
is no less important in political theory than in curriculum theory.
When we enter the domain of political theory, as Margaret Macdonald has observed, "One meets . . . a 'contract' which one is

carefully warned was never contracted; an 'organism' unknown to biology; a superior 'person' or higher 'self' with whom one can never converse; an 'association' or 'corporation' whose objects are obscure and which is not listed in any of the recognized directories."[30] The images that these metaphors conjure up are not for the purpose of picturing empirically verifiable relationships, but to bring vividly to the fore such value questions as: Why should one obey laws? Or: Why should one accept the authority of the state? In the case of the metaphor of a social contract, for example, we are being urged to accept the view that we ought to obey laws that we have actually consented to in the same way that we consent to enter voluntarily into a contract. What the social contract theory is doing here is not proposing or expressing empirical laws or generalizations, but exposing a criterion that *ought* to govern certain relationships. As Macdonald put it:

> The common sense of Locke and the eloquence of Rousseau reinforced and guided the revolt against dogmatic authority by vividly isolating and underlining with the contract metaphor the fact that no one is obliged to obey laws concerning none of which he has had a chance to express consent or dissent.[31]

Similarly, when we ask ourselves what we should teach or why we ought to teach one thing rather than another, there are hidden criteria which may be exposed by a curriculum theory, and this is perhaps its most salient function. When Dewey outlined his curriculum theory in *The Child and the Curriculum*, for example, he called attention to the criterion of the experience of the child which ought to be accorded at least equal status with the experience of the human race (as expressed in the organized disciplines of knowledge) when we consider the question of what we should teach. Social contract theory as expressed by Rousseau and Locke and curriculum theory in the form of Dewey's progressive organization of subject matter may of course be subjected to analytic scrutiny, and in some broad sense they may be deemed to be workable or unworkable, morally defensible or indefensible, but it would be hard to imagine such theories being subjected to a convincing experimental test. Although Dewey saw his Laboratory School as an effort at empirical verification of his theory in a broad sense, he certainly did not intend to test the theory in the sense, let us say, of subjecting data to tests of statistical significance.

Another case in point is the theory of curriculum as expressed by such persons as Pierre Bourdieu and Michael Apple, commonly

214 / Essays in Curriculum Theory

known as cultural reproduction. The most central feature of cultural reproduction is the metaphor of culture as a form of capital. The theory of cultural reproduction may stimulate certain kinds of empirical research and be enriched by such research, as is the case most notably with some of the work of Basil Bernstein, but it also serves the function of bringing into focus a dimension of curriculum thinking that might otherwise not be considered. For one thing, it focuses on the equal or unequal distribution of knowledge through the curriculum, and, if there is an unequal distribution of knowledge, it raises the question of whose interests are served by a maldistribution of cultural capital. Like social contract theory, the question of whether the theory of cultural reproduction points to a defensible criterion, or does so satisfactorily, is open to debate, but one should not misjudge how it functions metaphorically as a theory.

To sum up, then, models (whether iconic or analogue) and theories take root in the attempt to understand or explain, and without metaphor, there would be no models or theories. Models and theories in curriculum become more familiar and less rarified when seen as part and parcel of the universal attempt to transfer meaning from the familiar and comprehensible to the remote and perplexing. Metaphors that evolve into models or theories serve not only to direct research by creating a symbolic language that provides the framework for the collection and interpretation of data, but as a way of isolating a dimension of the question to be examined that is not visible without the aid of the metaphor. While distortions and misrepresentations are clearly possible through metaphors, especially when they begin to lose their "as if" quality, metaphor still represents our most potent instrument for seeing things beyond our world of everyday reality. In matters theoretical (to paraphrase a well-known dictum), the medium is the metaphor.

Notes

1. Ernest Nagel, "Philosophy of Science and Educational Theory," *Studies in Philosophy and Education* 7 (Fall 1969), p. 10.

2. Edward L. Thorndike, "Psychology in Secondary Schools," *School Review* 10 (February 1902), p. 119.

3. J. L. Austin, *Philosophical Papers* (Oxford: Clarendon Press, 1970), p. 201.

4. James M. Edie, "Expression and Metaphor," *Philosophy and Phenomenological Research* 23 (June 1963), p. 538.

5. Ibid., p. 548.

6. Ibid.

7. Max Black, *Models and Metaphors* (Ithaca, NY: Cornell University Press, 1962).

8. Anatol Rapoport, *Operational Philosophy* (San Francisco: International Society for General Semantics, 1969. Originally published by Harper and Row, 1953), p. 203.

9. As in John Dewey, *The Child and the Curriculum* (Chicago: University of Chicago Press, 1902), pp. 20–21.

10. E. H. Hutten, "The Roles of Models in Physics," *British Journal of Philosophy of Science* 4 (February 1954), p. 285.

11. Black, *Models and Metaphors*, p. 242.

12. Colin Murray Turbayne, *The Myth of Metaphor* (Columbia, S. C.: University of South Carolina Press, 1970), pp. 24–26.

13. Ibid., p. 27.

14. Gilbert Ryle, *The Concept of Mind* (New York: Barnes and Noble, 1949).

15. Israel Scheffler, *The Language of Education* (Springfield, Ill.: Charles C. Thomas, 1960), pp. 11–35.

16. Rapoport, *Operational Philosophy*, p. 205.

17. Mary B. Hesse, *Models and Analogies in Science* (Notre Dame: University of Notre Dame Press, 1966), p. 171.

18. Ibid., p. 173.

19. Ibid., p. 176.

20. William James, *Principles of Psychology*, Vol. 1 (New York: Henry Holt, 1890), pp. 666–7.

21. Harold Ordway Rugg, *The Experimental Determination of Mental Discipline in School Studies* (Baltimore: Warwick and York, 1916).

22. Samuel Bowles and Herbert Gintis, *Schooling in Capitalist America* (New York: Basic Books, 1976).

23. Ibid., p . 131.

24. Michael Olneck and David B. Bills, "What Makes Sammy Run? An Empirical Assessment of the Bowles and Gintis Correspondence Theory," *American Journal of Education* 89 (November 1980), p. 53.

25. Ibid., p. 54.

26. Richard H. Brown, *A Poetic for Sociology* (Cambridge: Cambridge University Press, 1977), p. 102.

27. Arno A. Bellack, Herbert M. Kliebard, Ronald T. Hyman and Frank L. Smith, Jr., *The Language of the Classroom* (New York: Teacher College Press, 1966).

28. John Dewey, *The Sources of a Science of Education* (New York: Liveright, 1929), p. 28.

29. Brown, *A Poetic for Sociology*, p. 104.

30. Margaret Macdonald, "The Language of Political Theory," in *Essays on Logic and Language*, ed. Antony Flew (New York: Philosophical Library, 1951), p. 167.

31. Ibid., p. 186.

Index

